中国高校英语课堂心理环境特征研究

毕雪飞◎著

Unraveling Psychosocial Characteristics of Learning Environments in EFL Classrooms at Tertiary Level in China

·广州·

图书在版编目（CIP）数据

中国高校英语课堂心理环境特征研究 = Unraveling Psychosocial Characteristics of Learning Environments in EFL Classrooms at Tertiary Level in China：英文 / 毕雪飞著. —广州：中山大学出版社，2023.8
ISBN 978-7-306-07882-7

Ⅰ. ①中… Ⅱ. ①毕… Ⅲ. ①英语—课堂教学—教学心理学—高等学校—中国—英文　Ⅳ. ①G441

中国国家版本馆 CIP 数据核字（2023）第 150563 号

出 版 人：	王天琪
策划编辑：	熊锡源
责任编辑：	熊锡源
封面设计：	林绵华
责任校对：	李昭莹
责任技编：	靳晓虹
出版发行：	中山大学出版社
电　　话：	编辑部 020-84111996，84111997
	发行部 020-84111998，84111981，84111160
地　　址：	广州市新港西路 135 号
邮　　编：	510275　　传　真：020-84036565
网　　址：	http://www.zsup.com.cn　　E-mail：zdcbs@mail.sysu.edu.cn
印 刷 者：	佛山家联印刷有限公司
规　　格：	880mm×1230mm　1/32　8.5 印张　298 千字
版次印次：	2023 年 8 月第 1 版　2023 年 8 月第 1 次印刷
定　　价：	35.00 元

如发现本书因印装质量影响阅读，请与出版社发行部联系调换

前　言

课堂心理环境是教育界的热门研究领域之一，课堂心理环境的质量是影响教育的重要因素。自 20 世纪六七十年代，Walberg 和 Anderson 开展的哈佛物理学课程改革项目（Harvard Project Physics）和 Moos 组织的斯坦福大学社会生态学研究对教育心理环境进行了开创性研究以来，在西方国家，各层级教育背景环境下的课堂学习环境的心理社会特征得到了广泛和深入的研究。近年来，课堂心理环境研究也逐渐引起亚洲国家教育研究者们的浓厚兴趣。本书通过实证调查研究，分析和探讨了中国高校英语专业师生对英语课堂心理环境的感知状况，揭示了在中国高等教育背景环境下英语作为外语的大学英语课堂心理环境的特征和本质。

本书共分为九章。

第一章是引言，介绍了本书的研究背景、研究目的、研究意义以及本书各章节的安排。本书的研究聚焦于以下四个研究目标：检验修改后的课堂心理环境经典量表在中国高校英语课堂心理环境特征调查研究中的信度和效度；揭示中国高校英语课堂心理环境感知的概况及特征；研究师生角色差异和学生性别差异对英语课堂心理环境感知的影响；探讨大学生英语课堂心理环境感知和英语学习动机的内在关联。

第二章是文献综述，从课堂心理环境研究和英语学习动机研究两个方面论述了研究的理论依据，以及梳理了国内外相关的实证研究成果。

第三章介绍了本书的研究设计，包括研究问题、研究对象、研究工具、数据采集和分析步骤、预试验阶段等。本书的研究对象是中山大学国际翻译学院英语专业一年级、二年级的本科生和综合英语任课教师，共计945名本科生和17位教师参与了本书的研究。作者选取了Aldridge等学者设计的课堂心理环境经典量表"这个班级发生了什么？"（What Is Happening In this Class，简称WIHIC）和高一虹等学者编制的中国大学本科生英语学习动机类型量表作为研究工具，并对两份量表的内容和语言措辞进行了修改和调整。为了使课堂心理环境量表"这个班级发生了什么？"适用于中国高校英语语言课堂环境，作者对该表进行了三次预测调整和修改。作者将量表收集的数据录入电脑后，采用SPSS 19.0数据分析软件对数据进行处理和分析，主要的统计方法涉及单因素重复测量多元方差分析、Bonferroni事后检验分析、典型相关分析等。

第四章检验了调整和修改后的课堂心理环境量表和中国大学本科生英语学习动机类型量表的信度和效度。主成分分析、信度系数 α 和方差分析等数据分析结果显示，调整后的量表具有较好的结构效度和内部一致性信度，量表维度具有良好的区分能力。

第五章对课堂心理环境量表数据进行了描述性统计分析。数据分析结果显示，总体上，教师和学生对现实和理想的英语课堂心理环境感知良好，然而，教师和学生对现实课堂环境六个心理维度的感知水平和理想期盼值分别存在着不同程度的差异。

第六章和第七章采用了探索性统计分析方法，分别从两个层面分析了课堂心理环境感知的师生差异和学生课堂心理环境感知的性别差异。两个分析层面包括六个心理因素感知维度层面和构成每个心理因素感知维度中的细微因素层面。第六章的研究发现，师生对现实和理想课堂心理环境的感知状况主要呈现出两种感知模式：师生分别希望能够体验比目前更积极的英语课堂心理环境；教师对课堂心理环境的现实感知水平以及对理想课堂心理环境的期盼值均高于学生对课堂心理环境的现实感知水平和理想期盼值。第七章的研究显示，学生对英语课堂心理环境的现实感知水平和理想期盼值分别存在显著的性别差异：女性学生对课堂心理环境的现实感知水平和对理想期盼值均分别显著高于男性学生对课堂心理环境的现实感知水平和理想期盼值。

第八章探讨了课堂心理环境因素和英语学习动机之间的内在关联。典型相关分析结果显示，课堂心理环境和英语学习动机间主要通过两组典型相关变量相互作用。第一组典型相关变量显示，积极参与课堂活动并完成学习任务的学生具有较强的内在兴趣型学习动机和个人发展型学习动机，即学生学习英语主要为了鉴赏英语语言和文化，满足社会期望，以及为了在未来的发展中增强个人能力和提升个人社会地位。第二组典型相关变量表明，教师对学生的学习帮助和情感关注有利于激发学生的工具型学习动机。例如，学生把学习英语视为获取信息或者在考试中获得满意结果的途径和手段。此外，典型相关分析路径模型中的相关性特质也揭示出学生的英语课堂心理环境感知水平和英语学习动机强度在递归和持续的互动中不断相互影响和增强。

最后一章是结论部分，总结了本书的主要研究结果，提出了研究的教学启示以及研究中存在的不足之处。

总之，本书通过对大学英语教师和学生对英语课堂心理环境的感知状况的调查和分析，深入地揭示了中国高校英语课堂学习环境的心理社会特征，阐述了英语课堂心理环境因素与学生英语学习动机的内在关联。作者希望本书的研究结果能在一定程度上指导中国高校的英语专业教育教学实践。在高校英语专业教学实践中，英语教师应该考虑这些由师生角色差异和学生性别差异引起的课堂心理环境的感知差异和需求差异，从而能更有效地营造良好积极的课堂心理环境，激发学生的英语学习动机，提高英语课堂的教学效果。

笔者希望借此机会向为本书做出重要贡献的人表达由衷的感谢。

本书是基于我的博士学位论文修改而成的，因此首先要感谢的人是我的博士生导师黄国文教授。他在学术上治学严谨、一丝不苟，在生活上和蔼可亲、平易近人，他的真知灼见和谆谆教导，使我一生受益。在我攻读博士学位的学习过程中，他给予我的信任、理解、鼓励和支持凝聚成了一股巨大的力量和信念，支持着我度过五年的艰辛时光，顺利完成博士学业。我还要感谢中山大学国际翻译学院的常晨光教授、王斌教授、林裕音教授、曾蕾教授，中山大学心理学系的潘俊豪副教授，澳大利亚科廷大学的 Barry Fraser 教授，他们对我的博士学位论文提出了宝贵的指导意见。我要感谢家人一直以来坚定的支持、默默的关爱和无私的付出。感谢中山大学国际翻译学院对我博士研究生阶段学习的支持和对本书出版的慷慨资助，为我提供了学术成长和实现梦想的宝贵机会。本书能够顺利出版，还要感谢中山大学出版社副编审熊锡源博士的辛勤工作。

笔者的水平和学识有限，书中肯定有疏漏和错误之处，敬请学界前辈和同仁以及广大读者批评指正。

毕雪飞
2022 年 10 月

Contents

List of Figures ·· I
List of Tables ·· V
List of Abbreviations ·· IX

Chapter 1 Introduction ·· 1
  1.1 Background of the study ·· 1
  1.2 Research aim and objectives ·· 3
  1.3 Significance of the study ··· 5
  1.4 Organization of the book ··· 6

Chapter 2 Literature Review ··· 8
  2.1 Introduction ··· 8
  2.2 Field of classroom psychosocial environment research
     ·· 8
    2.2.1 Theoretical basis of classroom psychosocial
         environment research ································· 9
    2.2.2 Approaches to measuring classroom
         psychosocial environments ························ 16
    2.2.3 Research involving classroom environment
         instruments ··· 22
    2.2.4 Research of classroom psychosocial environments
         in China ·· 27
  2.3 Field of research on motivation in L2 learning ······ 30
    2.3.1 Theoretical models of L2 motivation ··········· 30
    2.3.2 Research on L2 motivation ···························· 38
  2.4 Summary ·· 42

Chapter 3   Research Design and Methodology 43
3.1   Introduction 43
3.2   Research questions 43
3.3   Research design 44
3.4   Subjects 45
3.5   Instruments 47
    3.5.1   The modified WIHIC 47
    3.5.2   The modified MTCCU 49
3.6   Data collection procedures 51
3.7   Data analysis procedures 52
    3.7.1   Procedures for the validation of research instruments 52
    3.7.2   Procedures for the revelation of CE classroom psychosocial environments 53
3.8   The pilot phase 57
3.9   Summary 58

Chapter 4   Validity and Reliability of the Research Instruments 59
4.1   Introduction 59
4.2   Validity and reliability of the modified WIHIC 59
    4.2.1   Construct validity of the modified WIHIC 59
    4.2.2   Reliability of the modified WIHIC 64
4.3   Validity and reliability of the modified MTCCU 68
    4.3.1   Construct validity of the modified MTCCU 68
    4.3.2   Reliability of the modified MTCCU 70
4.4   Summary 71

Chapter 5   The Status Quo of CE Classroom Psychosocial Environments 72
5.1   Introduction 72

5.2 CE classroom psychosocial environments perceived by students ⋯ 73
    5.2.1 Actual CE classroom psychosocial environments perceived by students ⋯ 73
    5.2.2 Preferred CE classroom psychosocial environments perceived by students ⋯ 77
5.3 CE classroom psychosocial environments perceived by instructors ⋯ 82
    5.3.1 Actual CE classroom psychosocial environments perceived by instructors ⋯ 82
    5.3.2 Preferred CE classroom psychosocial environments perceived by instructors ⋯ 86
5.4 Summary ⋯ 90

Chapter 6 Discrepancies in Classroom Psychosocial Environment Perceptions ⋯ 91

6.1 Introduction ⋯ 91
6.2 General patterns of differences in perceptions between students and instructors ⋯ 91
6.3 Differences between actual and preferred perceptions of students ⋯ 99
    6.3.1 Differences between students' actual and preferred perceptions of SC ⋯ 101
    6.3.2 Differences between students' actual and preferred perceptions of TS ⋯ 103
    6.3.3 Differences between students' actual and preferred perceptions of IN ⋯ 105
    6.3.4 Differences between students' actual and preferred perceptions of TO ⋯ 106
    6.3.5 Differences between students' actual and preferred perceptions of CO ⋯ 108
    6.3.6 Differences between students' actual and preferred perceptions of EQ ⋯ 110
6.4 Differences between instructors' actual and preferred perceptions ⋯ 112

- 6.4.1 Differences between instructors' actual and preferred perceptions of SC ················ 114
- 6.4.2 Differences between instructors' actual and preferred perceptions of TS ················ 116
- 6.4.3 Differences between instructors' actual and preferred perceptions of IN ················ 118
- 6.4.4 Differences between instructors' actual and preferred perceptions of TO ················ 119
- 6.4.5 Differences between instructors' actual and preferred perceptions of CO ················ 121
- 6.4.6 Differences between instructors' actual and preferred perceptions of EQ ················ 123
- 6.5 Differences in actual perceptions between students and instructors ················ 125
  - 6.5.1 Differences in actual perceptions of TS between students and instructors ············ 127
  - 6.5.2 Differences in actual perceptions of IN between students and instructors ············ 129
  - 6.5.3 Differences in actual perceptions of TO between students and instructors ············ 131
- 6.6 Differences in preferred perceptions between students and instructors ················ 133
  - 6.6.1 Differences in preferred perceptions of SC between students and instructors ············ 134
  - 6.6.2 Differences in preferred perceptions of TS between students and instructors ············ 136
  - 6.6.3 Differences in preferred perceptions of IN between students and instructors ············ 138
  - 6.6.4 Differences in preferred perceptions of TO between students and instructors ············ 140
  - 6.6.5 Differences in preferred perceptions of CO between students and instructors ············ 141
  - 6.6.6 Differences in preferred perceptions of EQ between students and instructors ············ 144
- 6.7 Summary ················ 146

Chapter 7 Gender Differences in CE Classroom Psychosocial Environment Perceptions ········· 148
7.1 Introduction ················ 148
7.2 Data analysis of gender differences in classroom environment perceptions ············ 148
7.3 Gender differences in actual classroom environment perceptions ············ 152
    7.3.1 General pattern of gender differences in actual perceptions ············ 152
    7.3.2 Gender differences in students' actual perceptions of SC ············ 153
    7.3.3 Gender differences in students' actual perceptions of TS ············ 155
    7.3.4 Gender differences in students' actual perceptions of TO ············ 157
    7.3.5 Gender differences in students' actual perceptions of CO ············ 159
7.4 Gender differences in preferred classroom environment perceptions ············ 161
    7.4.1 Overall pattern of gender differences in preferred perceptions ············ 161
    7.4.2 Gender differences in students' preferred perceptions of SC ············ 163
    7.4.3 Gender differences in students' preferred perceptions of IN ············ 164
    7.4.4 Gender differences in students' preferred perceptions of TO ············ 165
    7.4.5 Gender differences in students' preferred perceptions of CO ············ 167
    7.4.6 Gender differences in students' preferred perceptions of EQ ············ 168
7.5 Summary ············ 170

Chapter 8 Associations Between Classroom Environment Perceptions and English Learning Motivation 172
  8.1 Introduction 172
  8.2 Overall status of motivation types of English majors 172
    8.2.1 Conceptualization of motivation types of English majors 172
    8.2.2 Motivation types of English majors in SIS, SYSU 175
  8.3 Associations between classroom environment perceptions and motivation types 178
  8.4 Summary 183

Chapter 9 Conclusions and Implications 185
  9.1 Summary of major research findings 185
    9.1.1 Validation of research instruments 186
    9.1.2 The status quo of CE classroom psychosocial environments 187
    9.1.3 Discrepancies in perceptions between students and instructors 189
    9.1.4 Gender differences in perceptions among students 191
    9.1.5 Associations between classroom environment perceptions and English learning motivation 193
  9.2 Pedagogical implications 194
  9.3 Limitations and suggestions for future research 196

References 198

Appendices 221
  Appendix A What Is Happening in This Class? (A Modified Form) Student Actual Form 221

Appendix B	What Is Happening In this Class? (A Modified Form) Student Preferred Form	226
Appendix C	Motivation Types of Chinese College Undergraduates (A modified form)	231
Appendix D	WIHIC (A Modified Version) Instructor Actual Form	234
Appendix E	WIHIC (A Modified Version) Instructor Preferred Form	239

List of Figures

Figure 2.1　The class group as a social system (P. 12)
Figure 2.2　The conceptual scheme of classroom climate (P. 14)
Figure 2.3　A model of the relationship between environmental and personal variables and student stability and change (P. 15)
Figure 2.4　The Socio-educational Model with indicator variables in the AMTB (P. 32)
Figure 2.5　A taxonomy of human motivation (P. 35)
Figure 5.1　Students' perceptions of the actual CE classroom environments (P. 74)
Figure 5.2　Students' perceptions of the preferred CE classroom environments (P. 78)
Figure 5.3　Frequency of students' responses to TS in the preferred CE classroom environment (P. 81)
Figure 5.4　Frequency of students' responses to SC in the preferred CE classroom environment (P. 81)
Figure 5.5　Instructors' perceptions of the actual CE classroom environments (P. 83)
Figure 5.6　Instructors' perceptions of the preferred CE classroom environments (P. 87)
Figure 6.1　Differences in perceptions among student actual, student preferred, instructor actual, and instructor preferred forms (P. 97)
Figure 6.2　Differences in perceptions between students' actual and preferred forms (P. 99)
Figure 6.3　Differences between students' actual and preferred perceptions of SC (P. 102)

I

Figure 6. 4	Differences between students' actual and preferred perceptions of TS (P. 105)
Figure 6. 5	Differences between students' actual and preferred perceptions of IN (P. 106)
Figure 6. 6	Differences between students' actual and preferred perceptions of TO (P. 107)
Figure 6. 7	Differences between students' actual and preferred perceptions of CO (P. 109)
Figure 6. 8	Differences between students' actual and preferred perceptions of EQ (P. 112)
Figure 6. 9	Differences in perceptions between instructors' actual and preferred forms (P. 113)
Figure 6. 10	Differences between instructors' actual and preferred perceptions of SC (P. 116)
Figure 6. 11	Differences between instructors' actual and preferred perceptions of TS (P. 117)
Figure 6. 12	Differences between instructors' actual and preferred perceptions of IN (P. 119)
Figure 6. 13	Differences between instructors' actual and preferred perceptions of TO (P. 120)
Figure 6. 14	Differences between instructors' actual and preferred perceptions of CO (P. 122)
Figure 6. 15	Differences between instructors' actual and preferred perceptions of EQ (P. 125)
Figure 6. 16	Differences in perceptions between student actual and instructor actual forms (P. 126)
Figure 6. 17	Differences in actual perceptions of TS between students and instructors (P. 128)
Figure 6. 18	Differences in actual perceptions of IN between students and instructors (P. 130)
Figure 6. 19	Differences in actual perceptions of TO between students and instructors (P. 132)

Figure 6. 20	Differences in perceptions between students' preferred and instructor preferred forms (P. 134)
Figure 6. 21	Differences in preferred perceptions of SC between students and instructors (P. 136)
Figure 6. 22	Differences in preferred perceptions of TS between students and instructors (P. 138)
Figure 6. 23	Differences in preferred perceptions of IN between students and instructors (P. 139)
Figure 6. 24	Differences in preferred perceptions of TO between students and instructors (P. 141)
Figure 6. 25	Differences in preferred perceptions of CO between students and instructors (P. 143)
Figure 6. 26	Differences in preferred perceptions of EQ between students and instructors (P. 145)
Figure 7. 1	Gender differences in actual CE classroom environment perceptions (P. 151)
Figure 7. 2	Gender differences in students' actual perceptions of SC (P. 154)
Figure 7. 3	Gender differences in students' actual perceptions of TS (P. 156)
Figure 7. 4	Gender differences in students' actual perceptions of TO (P. 158)
Figure 7. 5	Gender differences in students' actual perceptions of CO (P. 160)
Figure 7. 6	Gender differences in preferred CE classroom environment perceptions (P. 162)
Figure 7. 7	Gender differences in students' preferred perceptions of SC (P. 163)
Figure 7. 8	Gender differences in students' preferred perceptions of IN (P. 165)
Figure 7. 9	Gender differences in students' preferred perceptions of TO (P. 166)
Figure 7. 10	Gender differences in students' preferred perceptions of CO (P. 168)
Figure 7. 11	Gender differences in students' preferred perceptions of EQ (P. 170)
Figure 8. 1	Conceptual classification of motivation types (P. 173)

Figure 8. 2   Distributions of students English learning motivation types (P. 176)

Figure 8. 3   The canonical correlation path model for actual perceptions and motivation types (P. 181)

List of Tables

Table 2.1 Dörnyei's three-level framework of L2 motivation (p. 37)

Table 3.1 General information of student subjects in the survey study (p. 45)

Table 3.2 General information of instructor subjects in the survey study (p. 46)

Table 3.3 Descriptive information for the modified WIHIC (p. 48)

Table 3.4 Sample items in the four forms of the modified WIHIC (p. 49)

Table 3.5 Descriptive information for the modified MTCCU (p. 50)

Table 4.1 Factor loadings for student actual and preferred forms of the modified WIHIC (p. 60-62)

Table 4.2 Internal consistency reliability (Cronbach's alpha coefficient) and ability to differentiate between classes (ANOVA results) for the student actual form of the modified WIHIC (p. 66)

Table 4.3 Factor loadings for seven factors of the modified MTCCU (p. 69)

Table 4.4 Internal consistency reliability (Cronbach's alpha coefficient) for the modified MTCCU (p. 71)

Table 5.1 Descriptive statistics for actual perceptions of students (p. 73)

Table 5.2 Tests of within-subjects effects for actual perceptions of students (p. 75)

Table 5.3 Post-hoc tests of students' actual perceptions of the six

	WIHIC scales (p. 76)
Table 5.4	Descriptive statistics for preferred perceptions of students (p. 77)
Table 5.5	Tests of within-subjects effects for preferred perceptions of students (p. 79)
Table 5.6	Post-hoc tests of students' preferred perceptions of the six WIHIC scales (p. 79)
Table 5.7	Descriptive statistics for actual perceptions of instructors (p. 83)
Table 5.8	Tests of within-subjects effects for actual perceptions of instructors (p. 84)
Table 5.9	Post-hoc tests of instructors' actual perceptions of the six WIHIC scales (p. 85)
Table 5.10	Descriptive statistics for preferred perceptions of instructors (p. 86)
Table 5.11	Tests of within-subjects effects for preferred perceptions of instructors (p. 87)
Table 5.12	Post-hoc tests of instructors' preferred perceptions of the six WIHIC scales (p. 88)
Table 6.1	Descriptive statistics for actual and preferred perceptions of students and instructors (p. 92)
Table 6.2	Mauchly's Test of Sphericity of the six WIHIC scales (p. 93)
Table 6.3	Univariate ANOVA tests of the six WIHIC scales (p. 94)
Table 6.4	Post-hoc tests of the six WIHIC scales among four forms (p. 95)
Table 6.5	Differences between students' actual and preferred perceptions of SC (p. 102)
Table 6.6	Differences between students' actual and preferred perceptions of TS (p. 104)
Table 6.7	Differences between students' actual and preferred per-

	ceptions of IN (p. 105)
Table 6.8	Differences between students' actual and preferred perceptions of TO (p. 107)
Table 6.9	Differences between students' actual and preferred perceptions of CO (p. 108)
Table 6.10	Differences between students' actual and preferred perceptions of EQ (p. 111)
Table 6.11	Differences between instructors' actual and preferred perceptions of SC (p. 115)
Table 6.12	Differences between instructors' actual and preferred perceptions of TS (p. 116)
Table 6.13	Differences between instructors' actual and preferred perceptions of IN (p. 118)
Table 6.14	Differences between instructors' actual and preferred perceptions of TO (p. 119)
Table 6.15	Differences between instructors' actual and preferred perceptions of CO (p. 121)
Table 6.16	Differences between instructors' actual and preferred perceptions of EQ (p. 123)
Table 6.17	Differences in actual perceptions of TS between students and instructors (p. 127)
Table 6.18	Differences in actual perceptions of IN between students and instructors (p. 130)
Table 6.19	Differences in actual perceptions of TO between students and instructors (p. 131)
Table 6.20	Differences in preferred perceptions of SC between students and instructors (p. 135)
Table 6.21	Differences in preferred perceptions of TS between students and instructors (p. 137)
Table 6.22	Differences in preferred perceptions of IN between students and instructors (p. 139)
Table 6.23	Differences in preferred perceptions of TO between

	students and instructors (p. 140)
Table 6. 24	Differences in preferred perceptions of CO between students and instructors (p. 142)
Table 6. 25	Differences in preferred perceptions of EQ between students and instructors (p. 144)
Table 7. 1	Means and SDs for actual and preferred perception scores of male and female students (p. 149)
Table 7. 2	Post-hoc tests of perceptions of the twelve WIHIC scales between male and female students (p. 150)
Table 7. 3	Gender differences in students' actual perceptions of SC (p. 154)
Table 7. 4	Gender differences in students' actual perceptions of TS (p. 155)
Table 7. 5	Gender differences in students' actual perceptions of TO (p. 158)
Table 7. 6	Gender differences in students' actual perceptions of CO (p. 159)
Table 7. 7	Gender differences in students' preferred perceptions of SC (p. 163)
Table 7. 8	Gender differences in students' preferred perceptions of IN (p. 164)
Table 7. 9	Gender differences in students' preferred perceptions of TO (p. 165)
Table 7. 10	Gender differences in students' preferred perceptions of CO (p. 167)
Table 7. 11	Gender differences in students' preferred perceptions of EQ (p. 169)
Table 8. 1	Descriptive statistics for motivation types (p. 175)
Table 8. 2	Canonical correlation statistics for actual perceptions and motivation types (p. 179)

List of Abbreviations

ANOVA	Analysis of Variance
AMTB	Attitude Motivation Test Battery
CE	Comprehensive English
CCUFLCEI	Chinese College and University Foreign Language Classroom Environment Inventory
CCA	Canonical Correlation Analysis
CLCEI	Chinese Language Classroom Environment Inventory
CO	Cooperation
COCD	Classroom Observation Code Digest
CES	Classroom Environment Scale
CCQ	Classroom Climate Questionnaire
CLES	Constructivist Learning Environment Survey
CUCEI	College and University Classroom Environment Inventory
EFL	English as a foreign language
ECEI	English Classroom Environment Inventory
EQ	Equity
FA	Female actual
FP	Female preferred
GA	Going abroad
HKCES	Hong Kong Classroom Environment Scale
IN	Involvement
IA	Immediate achievement
IA	Instructor actual
II	Intrinsic interest
ID	Individual development
IM	Information medium
IP	Instructor preferred

ICEQ	Individualized Classroom Environment Questionnaire
KMO	Kaiser-Meyer-Olkin
L2	second/foreign language
LS	Learning situation
LEI	Learning Environment Inventory
MANOVA	multivariate analysis of variance
MA	Male actual
MTCCU	Motivation Types of Chinese College Undergraduates
MP	Male preferred
MCI	My Class Inventory
OSAR	Observation Schedule and Record
QTI	Questionnaire on Teacher Interaction
SIS	School of International Studies
SYSU	Sun Yat-sen University
SA	Student actual
SP	Student preferred
SC	Student cohesiveness
SDT	Self-determination theory
SR	Social responsibility
SD	standard deviation
SLEI	Science Laboratory Environment Inventory
TS	Teacher support
TO	Task orientation
WIHIC	What Is Happening In this Class?

Chapter 1
Introduction

1.1 Background of the study

　　Classroom learning environment has been established as a flourishing field of study and has attracted growing attention of worldwide researchers in these decades. As remarked by Wubbles (2006), the quality of classroom environments has already been accepted as a crucial factor in education. A learning environment is defined by Wilson (1996: 5) from a constructivist view as "a place where learners may work together and support each other as they use a variety of tools and information resources in their guided pursuit of learning goals and problem-solving activities". However, so far, there is no universal acceptance of the term used to refer to the learning environment of classrooms among researchers due to the different focuses or nature of their studies. Thus, classroom learning environment is also referred to as classroom psychosocial environment by Fraser and Fisher (1982), psychological milieu by Fisher and Fraser (1983a), classroom climate by Walberg and Anderson (1968a), or in the terms of classroom atmosphere, ambience, and ecology as reviewed by Adelman and Taylor (2005). The present study adopts the term used in Fraser and Fisher (1982) which focuses on the psychological, social, and academic nature of classroom learning environments.

　　In the past four decades since the pioneering study of psychosocial environments in educational context initiated in "Harvard Project Physics" carried out by Walberg and Anderson (1968a, 1968b) and the studies on social-ecology conducted by Moos (1979) at Stanford University in the sixties and seventies of the 20th century in the United States, the psychosocial characteristics of classroom learning environments in various educational contexts have been extensively studied in the West, particularly in Australia (e. g. Fraser, 1981, 1982; Fraser & Fisher, 1982; Fraser & O'Brien, 1985; Fraser & Treagust, 1986), and the United States (e. g. De Young, 1977; Sinclair & Fraser, 2002; Wubbles & Levy, 1991, 1993; Vahala & Winston, 1994). In recent years, researchers in other regions in the world also show increasing interests in the exploration of classroom psychosocial environments, such as in Singapore (e. g. Chionh & Fraser, 2009; Chua, Wong & Chen, 2006, 2009, 2011; Goh & Fraser, 1998, 2000; Quek, Wong & Fraser, 2005; Wong & Fraser, 1996), China (e. g. Aldridge & Fraser, 2000; Aldridge, Fraser & Huang, 1999; Fan & Dong, 2005; Sun, 2007; Wei, den Brok & Zhou, 2009; Wong, 1993), Korea (e. g. Fraser & Lee, 2009; Kim, Fisher & Fraser, 1999; Lee & Fraser, 2001), the United Arab Emirates (e. g. MacLeod & Fraser, 2010), Turkey (e. g. Telli, den Brok & Cakiroglu, 2007), Thailand (e. g. Santiboon, et al., 2012), Indonesia (e. g. Margianti, Fraser & Aldridge, 2001; Fraser, Aldrige & Soerjaningsih, 2010), the Philippines (e. g. Rivera & Ganaden, 2001), India (e. g. Koul & Fisher, 2005), Brunei Darussalam (e. g. Majeed, Fraser & Aldridge, 2002), Uganda (e. g. Opolot-Okurut, 2010), and South Africa (e. g. Aldridge, et al., 2006).

Researchers approach classroom psychosocial environments mainly by assessing students' and teachers' perceptions of the psychosocial characteristics of classroom environments, and further investigating the relationships of the perceptions of students to their cognitive and affective learning outcomes. Statistically significant relationships have been discovered and established in previous studies as reviewed by Fraser (1998a) and Freiberg (1999) between the nature of classroom psychosocial environments and a variety of educational outcomes, including student engagement, behavior, self-efficacy, achievement, social and emotional development, principal leadership style, stages of educational reform, and overall quality of school life.

In China, traditional values of education also attach great

importance to the role of educational environments. The historical anecdote is well known to most Chinese that the mother of the great philosopher, Mencius, moved three times in order to locate an environment conducive to young Mencius' intellectual development. Recognizing the importance of environments to learning, Chinese educators and researchers have been devoted to the investigation and improvement of both the physical and psychological classroom environments so as to provide good conditions for teaching and learning in elementary and secondary schools. However, relatively less attention has been paid to the psychosocial classroom environments in higher education by Chinese researchers and educators. Therefore, it is timely for the present study to explore the psychosocial characteristics of English classroom environments in higher education in China in order to bridge the gap and provide a better understanding of English classroom environments and offer some guidance for the improvement of classroom environments to make it more conducive for teaching and learning in the Chinese context of English as a Foreign Language (EFL).

1.2 Research aim and objectives

The research in this book is based on the case study of the Comprehensive English classrooms in the School of International Studies (SIS) at Sun Yat-sen University (SYSU), one of the top universities located in South China. Founded in 2005, the SIS aims to prepare the society with bilingual talents with liberal knowledge, critical thinking, global visions, applied skills, and foreign languages proficiency. Closely linked with the current social needs, the SIS established three departments of English: Department of Translation and Interpreting, Department of Business Communication, and Department of Chinese as a Foreign Language. The Comprehensive English (CE) is one of the key and compulsory curriculums for first-year and second-year English majors in Chinese colleges and universities to enhance their English language proficiency through comprehensive training of basic English language skills including listening, speaking, reading, and writing, and hence to improve the

English communicative competence of students.

In general, the aim of the present study is to investigate the nature of English classroom psychosocial environments by measuring and analyzing students' and instructors' perceptions of their classroom psychosocial environments and by exploring the associations between students' perceptions of their English classroom psychosocial environments and their English learning motivation. Students' and instructors' perceptions of English classroom psychosocial environments are assessed by the modified questionnaire "What Is Happening In this Class?" (WIHIC) initially developed by Fraser, Fisher and McRobbie (1996) and further revised by Aldridge, Fraser and Huang (1999). The WIHIC has been widely applied and validated in various educational contexts in many countries in the world, yet little has been done for the validation and employment of the WIHIC in the studies of English classroom psychosocial environments at the tertiary level in China. Therefore, the present study will take the initiative to validate and employ the WIHIC in the EFL classrooms in higher education in China.

In particular, the present study primarily focuses on the research objectives as

(1) to validate the student and instructor actual and preferred forms of the adapted "What Is Happening In this Class?" (WIHIC) used in English classrooms in the Chinese EFL context at tertiary level;

(2) to exhibit the status quo of English classroom psychosocial environments as perceived by students and instructors;

(3) to examine some determinants of English classroom psychosocial environment perceptions, particularly the discrepancies in perceptions and preferences between students and instructors as well as male and female students;

and (4) to determine whether the psychosocial nature of English classroom environments affects the English learning motivation of students.

1.3 Significance of the study

The present research is one of the few classroom psychosocial environment studies undertaken in the Chinese EFL context in higher education. Revealing the psychosocial nature of English classroom environments, the present study is significant in both its academic and pedagogical contributions in the field of classroom environment research and English language teaching and learning in China.

Firstly, the present study presents an initial effort to adapt the actual and preferred forms of the WIHIC to the Chinese EFL context and to provide validity evidence for the modified forms of the WIHIC. The attempt of validation in this study will not only broaden the applicability of the WIHIC questionnaire, but also provide an effective instrument for Chinese EFL researchers and educators to measure and explore the nature of classroom psychosocial environments.

Secondly, the present study will provide a full and in-depth understanding of English classroom environments for tertiary educators. With this knowledge, educators are in a better position to effectively improve English classroom environments through eliminating the gaps between the actual and ideal English classrooms as perceived and preferred by both students and instructors and through bridging the gaps in perceptions and expectations of the English classroom environments between male and female students. Therefore, the research findings of the present study will be of great value for facilitating and creating supportive classroom psychosocial environments conducive for English teaching and learning process. As pointed out by Fraser and Treagust (1986), it may be viewed as "both means to valuable ends and as worthy ends in their own rights" to foster a positive and constructive classroom environment.

Thirdly, the current study is also an initial attempt in China to examine the influence of the psychosocial nature of English classroom environments on English learning motivation of English majors in colleges and universities. The associations established in this book between the psychosocial factors of classroom environments and motivation will offer insights for researchers and educators into the effectiveness of classroom psychosocial environments on affective learning outcomes of students. The results will also provide a new angle to understand the complex construct of learning motivation of Chinese students in colleges and universities.

In addition, the present study is also significant in terms of methodology in that multiple statistical analyses are integrated in this study to guarantee a thorough and comprehensive examination on the psychosocial characteristics of classroom environments, including *t*-tests for paired samples, analysis of variance (ANOVA), one-way ANOVA for repeated measures, one-way multivariate analysis of variance (MANOVA) for repeated measures, and Canonical's Correlation Analysis.

1.4 Organization of the book

The book consists of nine chapters.

Chapter 1 serves as the opening chapter to introduce the background of the study, the research aim and objectives, as well as the significance of the study.

Chapter 2 provides a comprehensive review of the literature on the theoretical foundations and empirical studies of classroom psychosocial environments and second/foreign language learning motivation.

Chapter 3 introduces the methodology of the research including research questions, research design, research instruments, participants, and data collection and analysis procedures.

Chapter 4 examines the validity and reliability of the two research instruments employed in the present study.

Chapter 5 presents the status quo of CE classroom psychosocial environments as actually and ideally perceived by students and instructors in the SIS at SYSU.

The psychosocial characteristics of CE classroom environments are revealed through the analyses and comparisons of students' and instructors' actual and preferred perceptions of the classroom psychosocial environments in Chapter 6 and through the examination and comparisons of male and female students' actual and preferred perceptions of the classroom psychosocial environments in Chapter 7.

Chapter 8 explores the impacts of the psychosocial nature of CE classroom environments on English learning motivation of students by investigating the associations between students' actual CE classroom psychosocial environment perceptions and their English learning motivation types. In addition, the status quo of English learning motivation types for English majors in their first two years in the SIS at SYSU is also presented in this chapter.

Chapter 9 is the closing chapter of the book to summarize the major research findings and to discuss the pedagogical implications of the present study. Limitations of the study are discussed and suggestions for possible future studies are provided in this chapter.

Chapter 2
Literature Review

2.1 Introduction

Except for the introduction and the summary, this chapter consists of two parts. The first part of the review outlines the theoretical foundations of classroom psychosocial environment research and discusses the research domains of studies in this field both at home and abroad. The second part of the review elaborates the theories on motivation in second/foreign language (L2) learning and introduces the major research domains of international and domestic empirical studies on motivation, particularly its relation to other learning factors. The review of the literature in this part also aims to clear the ground for the current examination of associations between the psychosocial aspects of English classroom environments and motivation of English learning, and hence to establish the link between the research of classroom psychosocial environments and the research of motivation in an English as foreign language (EFL) setting.

2.2 Field of classroom psychosocial environment research

This section begins by reviewing the theoretical grounds of research on the conceptualization of classroom psychosocial environments, followed by the introduction of some historically important instruments of assessing classroom psychosocial environments and the outline of research domains of studies involving the application of classroom environment instruments. The end of this section presents an overview of the current status of research on classroom psychosocial environments in China.

2.2.1 Theoretical basis of classroom psychosocial environment research

The study of psychosocial environments originates in social psychology. The notion of psychological environment can be traced back to the study of Lewin (1936) who believed that the individual behavior was determined by the interactions between the characteristics of the individual and the environment. He argued that the investigation of needs, action, or emotions of a person could not be undertaken without considering the characteristics of the person, his momentary state, and his psychological environment. Lewin (1935: 241; 1936: 12) proposed a mathematical formula $B = \mathfrak{f}(PE)$ to present that the individual behavior (B) is a function of the person (P) and his environment (E). According to Lewin(1936: 15–16), the psychological life space, or psychological field, including both the person and the environment, is to be regarded as a totality of possibilities accounts for the behavior of the person within the situation and the possible changes of the person or of the situation itself. The psychological life space is the unification of three groups of quasi-physical, quasi-social, and quasi-conceptual facts, referring to the physical, social, and conceptual facts that affect the individual in his momentary state. Lewin (1936) has endeavored to investigate and represent the properties of psychological life space and to reveal the tensions between individuals and their environments by means of mathematical and typological concepts in his typological psychology.

To explore human personality, Murray (1938) also emphasized the tensions between individual needs and environmental press in his needs-press model. A need is defined by Murray (1938) as follows:

> A need is a construct (a convenient fiction or hypothetical concept) that stands for a force (the physic-chemical nature of which is unknown) in the brain region, a force which organizes perception, apperception, intellection,

conation, and action in such a way to transform in a certain direction an existing, unsatisfying situation. A need is sometimes provoked directly by internal process of a certain kind (viscerogenic, endocrinogenic, thalamicogenic) arising in the course of vital sequences, but more frequently (when in a state of readiness) by the occurrence of one of a few commonly effective press (or by anticipatory images of such press). Thus, it manifests itself by leading the organism to search for or to avoid encountering or, when encountered, to attend and respond to certain kinds of press.

(Murray, 1938: 124)

Press is defined by Murray (1938: 118) as an indicator of "a directional tendency in an object or situation". According to Murray (1938: 119), " [e]verything that can supposedly harm or benefit the well-being of an organism may be considered *pressive*" and the perception of the pressive situations by the subject will probably bring about some sort of adaptive behavior. In particular, " [t]he press of an object is what it can do *to the subject* or *for the subject* — the power that it has to affect the well-being of the subject in one way or another" (Murray, 1938: 121). An environment can be analyzed from the point of view of what press it applies or offers to the individuals that live within or belong to it (Muarry, 1938: 120). Press is classified by Murray (1938: 120-122) into three categories: positive press which is usually enjoyable and beneficial versus negative press which is commonly distasteful and harmful; mobile press is the moving forces which may affect the subject harmfully or beneficially if the subject remains passive versus immobile press that has no effect unless the subject approaches, manipulates, or influences them in some way; and alpha press or physical environment which refers to the environmental forces that are discernible and actually exist versus beta press or psychological environment which is the interpretations of the phenomena the subject perceives. It can be drawn from the specification that the environmental press provides an external counterpart that fulfills or inhibits internal personal needs. Murray

(1938: 141) contended that human personality was the resultant of the interactions among the internal needs of the person, external press, conscious intentions, accepted standards, and customary modes of behavior.

In line with the rationale of Murray's needs-press model, Stern (1970) refined the concepts of needs and press by simplifying and classifying the two terms. According to Stern (1970: 6–7), psychological needs refer to the "organizational tendencies which appear to give unity and direction to a person's behavior" and can be identified as "a taxonomic classification of the characteristic spontaneous behaviors manifested by individuals in their life transactions" while environmental press refers to "the phenomenological world of the individual, the unique and inevitably private view each person has of the events in which he takes part" and can be identified as "a taxonomic classification of characteristic behaviors manifested by aggregates of individuals in their mutual interpersonal transactions".

Stern (1970) pointed out that the relationship between psychological needs and environmental press was associated with congruence-dissonance. The congruence refers to the similarity or match of personal needs and environmental press and the dissonance, on the other hand, is the unstable needs and press combination which leads to a modification of the press in a more congruent direction or to a withdrawal of the participants. According to Stern (1970: 8), "a congruent relationship would be one producing a sense of satisfaction or fulfillment for the participant. Discomfort and stress are the concomitants of dissonance". Stern (1970) also made a further distinction of environmental press that was relevant to the participant's behavioral outcomes of particular psychological significance. The anabolic press provides "stimuli which are potentially conducive to self-enhancing growth" and the catabolic press, on the contrary, generates "stimuli that are antithetical to personal development or are likely to produce countervailing responses" (Stern, 1970: 8). In other words, the environment either facilitates or inhibits the expression of certain needs. To measure the individual needs and environmental press, indexes were developed based on the rationale that needs and press are reflected in behavioral perceptions which may be inferred from the self-reported interest of individuals in specific activities. Thus, the environment is defined as it is perceived and experienced.

Since the interactions between environmental characteristics and individual needs are of importance in understanding and predicting human behavior, the conception of person-environment interaction has been incorporated in educational field to research the school achievement and learning behavior of individual students in educational institutions. The environmental variable that arouses the interest of research is broadly referred to as the social climate of classrooms.

Inquiring into the social interactions within the school settings, Getzels and Thelen (1960) stated that the school class could be conceived as a social system with a particular structure and function in the matrix of society. As reviewed by Chávez (1988), the socio-psychological theory of Getzels and Thelen (1960) regarding the class as a social system was specifically tailored to groups within classroom structures. It was pointed out by Getzels and Thelen (1960) that the class group behavior could be predicted and affected by the social interactions between individual personalities and need-dispositions at the personal dimension as well as institutional roles and expectations at the normative dimension in the social system of classroom. Getzels and Thelen (1960) revealed the nature of the relationships of these elements represented in the following framework in Figure 2.1.

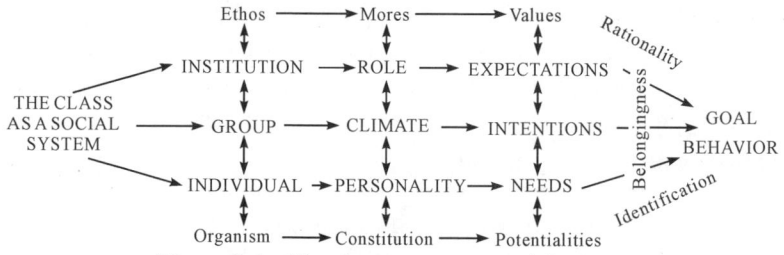

Figure 2.1 The class group as a social system

Source: Getzels & Thelen, 1960: 80.

As illustrated in the framework, the class group mediates and works out the balance between the institutional requirements and individual dispositions by supporting or imposing either the institutional role-expectations or the personality-dispositions. An ideal classroom as a social system was characterized by Getzels and Thelen (1960) as follows:

> (a) Each individual identifies with the goals of the system so that they become part of his own needs. (b) Each individual believes that the expectations held for him are rational if the goals are to be achieved. (c) He feels that he *belongs* to a group with similar emotional identifications and rational beliefs.
>
> (Getzels & Thelen, 1960: 80)

Drawing on Getzels and Thelen's (1960) theoretical scheme of the class as a social system, Walberg (1968a) pointed out the distinction between structural dimension and affective dimension of classroom climate associated respectively with the institutional expectations and individual personality dispositions in the framework of Getzels and Thelen (1960). The structural dimension refers to "the structure or organization of the classroom, for example, democratic, stratified, or heterogeneous" and it "applies to the shared, group-sanctioned behavior", while the affective dimension indicates the "idiosyncratic personal dispositions to act in a given way to satisfy individual personality needs" such as satisfaction, intimacy, and friction in the class (Walberg, 1968a: 3). Walberg (1968a) identified ten structural variables (i.e. goal diversity, democratic, subservient, strict control, disorganized, stratification, egalitarian, formality, and speech constraint) and seven affective variables (i.e. internal friction, classroom intimacy, interest heterogeneity, group status, satisfaction, alienation, and personal intimacy) to measure class climate. His study concluded that the variables in the affective domain were significantly related to variables in the structural domain and the two sets of variables were mutually predictable. Based on a series of studies, Walberg proposed and established the conceptual scheme of classroom climate. As shown in Figure 2. 2 below, the structural and affective dimensions of classroom climate are predictable from teacher personality (Walberg, 1968b) and from the mental abilities and personalities of students (Walberg & Anderson, 1968b). Furthermore, the structural and affective dimensions of classroom climate can affect and predict the individual student cognitive, behavioral, and affective learning outcomes (Walberg & Anderson, 1968a).

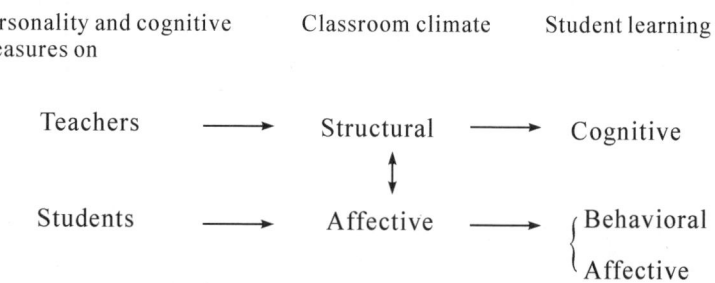

Figure 2. 2   The conceptual scheme of classroom climate

Source: Adapted from Walberg & Anderson, 1968a: 3.

In an attempt to understand how an environment functions and to work out the environmental impacts on human behavior, Rudolph Moos started with the research of social environments in psychiatric treatment settings, and extended his research to the social climate in other settings, such as correctional and community environments and educational environments. Moos (1979) posed that educational environments could exert potent influences on the stability and change in student behavior and attitudes. He presented a social-ecological conceptual framework, shown in Figure 2. 3 on the next page, to illustrate the person-environment interactions in educational settings. Moos (1979) emphasized that the social-ecological framework considered both the social-environment and physical-environment variables.

As noted in Figure 2. 3 below, the model displays the process of how environmental system and personal system affect the stability and change in student behavior and attitudes. To start with the process, the environmental system and personal system interact through the mediating processes of cognitive appraisal and activation. The next step moves to the efforts made by students to adapt to the environment by using a set of coping skills which are in part affected by the environmental system and personal system and in turn change the two systems. At last, efforts at adaption and coping result in the outcome indexes as personal interests and values, aspiration level, mood and health of the students. As indicated in Figure 2.3, there are mutual influences between these outcome indexes and the personal and environmental systems.

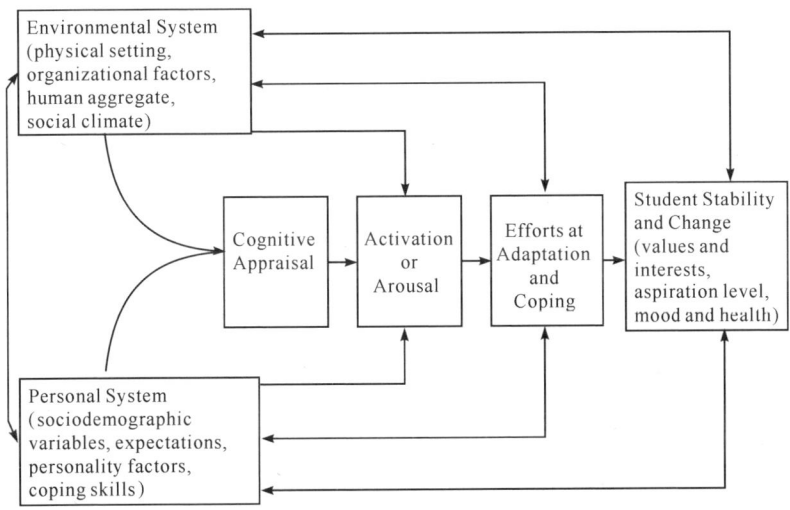

Figure 2.3 A model of the relationship between environmental and personal variables and student stability and change

Source: Moos, 1979: 5.

Based on the extensive research conducted by Moos and his associates on ten types of social settings including educational settings (student living groups and high school classes), primary settings in which most people function (families, work settings, and social and task-oriented groups), treatment-oriented settings (hospital-based and community-based psychiatric treatment programs and sheltered-care settings), and total institutions (correctional institutions and military basic training companies), Moos (1979) presented an integrative conceptualization of the three domains of social-environmental dimensions: relationship dimensions, personal growth or goal orientation dimensions, and system maintenance and change dimensions. Moos (1979) specified the three domains of social climate dimensions as follows:

> [...] relationship dimensions assess the extent to which people are involved in the setting, the extent to which they support and help one another, and the extent to which they express themselves freely and openly [...] Personal growth, or goal orientation, dimensions measure the basic goals of the setting, that is, the areas in which personal development and self-enhancement tend to occur [...] System maintenance and change dimensions measure the extent to which the environment is orderly and clear in its expectations, maintains control, and responds to change.
> (Moos, 1979: 14-16)

The three social environmental domains which were stated by Moos (1979: 19) to be "of general utility" in various social environments provide the theoretical grounds for the conceptualization and assessment of psychosocial environments in educational settings.

2.2.2 *Approaches to measuring classroom psychosocial environments*

The approach to measuring psychosocial environments in educational settings has undergone remarkable development. According to Chávez's (1984) review of the literature on classroom environment research from the late twenties to the eighties of the 20th century, the use of low-inference measures to study classroom environments was well established in the early sixties, while the studies of classroom environments with high-inference measures were not prevalent until the mid-sixties. Inference is defined by Rosenshine (1970: 500) as "the process intervening between the objective data seen or heard and the judgment concerning a higher-order construct of cognitive or social interaction". In classroom environment research, explained by Rosenshine (1970), low-inference measures require the observer to classify teaching behaviors according to relatively objective categories, such as words per minute, movements per minute, and the behaviors in relatively objective category system, whereas high-inference measures require considerable inference from what is seen or heard in the classroom to the labeling of the behavior, such as ratings of the teacher on such scales as "partial-fair", "autocratic-democratic", or "dull-stimulating".

Chávez (1984) provided an overall review of the studies that employed low-inference measures of one type or another to study classroom environments or to influence the classroom environment research, involving the system of seven categories developed by Withall (1949), the "Classroom Observation Code Digest" (COCD) by Cornell, Lindvall, and Saupe (1952), the "Observation Schedule and Record" (OSAR) by Medley and Mizel (1958), and the "Interaction Analysis System" by Flanders (Amidon & Flanders, 1963). Among these low-inference measures, as reviewed by Chávez (1984), the "Interaction Analysis System" developed by Flanders is the most sophisticated system and has been extensively applied to record and observe classroom interactions in terms of the verbal interactions of the teacher with students in the sixties and seventies of the last century. The "Interaction Analysis System" classifies behavior into seven categories for teacher talk: accepts feelings, praises, accepts ideas, questions, lectures, gives direction, and criticizes; two categories for student talk: student talk-responding and student talk-initiation; and another category notes silence or confusion referring to the periods of silence and confusion in which communications cannot be understood by the observer. In the reviews of the development in classroom observation systems by Amidon and Simon (1965) and Meux (1967), the existing systems were grouped into three divisions according to the different focuses: cognitive classroom observation systems that are primarily concerned with the intellectual activity in the classroom, affective classroom observation systems that focus on the social-emotional behavior in the classroom, and multidimensional or multi-aspect classroom observation systems that include both the cognitive and affective attributes. In this sense, the "Interaction Analysis System" can be sorted into the category of affective classroom observation systems.

Despite the prevalence of the observation systems, the application of the systems still has some methodological problems of validity, conceptual interrelations of systems, context, and empirical relations among one-score-per-classroom variables, as pointed out by Meux (1967). Musella (1970) also discussed the limitations of direct classroom observation that researchers probably faced with: (1) insufficient observation time upon which to base judgment, (2) inadequacy of recorded observations as valid and reliable samples of the total teaching experiences of the teacher, and (3) uncertainty of the validity and reliability of the observers-assessors, evaluators, judges, and raters. It was also pointed out by Fraser (1986) that the observational approach relied on the observation of outsiders who might miss some important data perceived by the actual participants in the classroom and additionally, the observation of outsiders might not present the long-standing attributes of classroom environments since teachers are inconsistent in their day-to-day behavior.

In the late fifties and early sixties of the 20th century, high inference measures were developed to study classroom environments by capturing students' perceptions of the psychosocial environments within classrooms. Indexes and scales for the assessment of classroom environments were developed based on "the various aspects of environment in high schools, colleges, and evening colleges which help to give them their unique cultural atmospheres" (Stern, 1970: 14). However, the advocacy of these indexes and scales were questioned that whether students' responses to these environment instruments could be regarded as the realistic and reliable revelation of the environments. Randhawa and Fu (1973: 318) responded that "finances and expediency are additional factors in selecting a certain approach for collecting data on the classroom learning environment" and the approach of inventory was economical and fast for the purpose of data collection in comparison with the shortcomings of the observational approach.

The milestones in the historical development of the evaluation and assessment of classroom psychosocial environments are associated with the research programs of "Harvard Project Physics" and the perceptual measures of human environments initiated by Herbert Walberg and Rudolf Moos respectively. Their studies contributed two classic instruments to assess the characteristics of psychosocial environments within classrooms: "Learning Environment Inventory" (LEI) and "Classroom Environment Scale" (CES). The LEI is the improved version of the "Classroom Climate Questionnaire" (CCQ) devised by Walberg (1966) to measure the nature of interpersonal relationships and the structural characteristics of classroom environments. After several revisions, the final version of the LEI contains 105 statements grouped into 15 scales to measure the affective and structural dimensions of classroom environments: "Cohesiveness", "Diversity", "Formality", "Speed", "Material environment", "Friction", "Goal direction", "Favoritism", "Difficulty", "Apathy", "Democracy", "Cliqueness", "Satisfaction", "Disorganization", and "Competitiveness". Another instrument, the "My Class Inventory" (MCI) with five scales of the original LEI and simplified wording of statements, is the reduced form of the LEI developed for students in elementary schools or students with reading difficulties with the LEI. Fraser, Anderson, and Walberg (1982) provided detailed introduction and description of the LEI and the MCI. The CES was developed by Trickett and Moos (1973) to assess the social environments of junior high and high school classrooms. Moo's conceptual scheme of environments underlies the development of the nine dimensions of assessment in this 90-item perceived environment scale. "Involvement", "Affiliation", and "Teacher Support" pertain to the relationship dimensions. "Task orientation" and "Competition" are the measures of personal development dimensions. "Order and organization", "Rule clarity", "Teacher control", and "Innovation" are based on the system maintenance and change dimensions.

Since then, numerous instruments aiming to measure various learning contexts have been developed and validated, such as the "Constructivist Learning Environment Survey" (CLES) (Taylor, Fraser & Fisher, 1997), "Science Laboratory Environment Inventory" (SLEI) (Fraser, Giddings & McRobbie, 1995; Fraser & McRobbie, 1995), "Individualized Classroom Environment Questionnaire" (ICEQ) (Fraser, 1990), "College and University Classroom Environment Inventory" (CUCEI) (Fraser & Treagust, 1986), "Questionnaire on Teacher Interaction" (QTI) (Wubbles, Créton & Hooymayers, 1985; Wubbles & Levy, 1991; Wubbels & Levy, 1993) and "What Is Happening In this Class?" (WIHIC) (Fraser *et al.*, 1996). As reviewed by Fraser (1998, 2007), the two striking features of the field of classroom environment research over the past few decades are the availability of numerous economical, validated and widely used questionnaires in the English language, and their translation, cross-validation and use in a range of other languages.

Among these emerging classroom environment instruments, the QTI and WIHIC are the two widely applied scales in recent years. The QTI was initially a Dutch instrument with 77 items named the "Questionnaire for Interactional Teacher-behavior" constructed by Wubbles, Créton, and Hooymayers (1985) to plot teacher behavior and teacher-student interaction in classrooms. A reduced 64-item English version of the QTI was validated in the study of Wubbles and Levy (1991) in the United States. Later, an English version of the QTI with 48 items was developed and validated by Fisher, Henderson, and Fraser (1995) in Australia. The theoretical basis underlying the QTI is the model proposed by Wubbles, Creton, and Hooymayers (1985) based on the interpersonal theory of Leary (1957) to map teacher behavior through the use of a "Proximity dimension" (Cooperation-Opposition) and an "Influence dimension" (Dominance-Submission). These dimensions can be represented in a coordinate system divided into eight equal sections to describe the eight different aspects of interpersonal teacher behavior: Leadership, Helpful/Friendly, Understanding, Student Responsibility/Freedom, Uncertain, Dissatisfied, Admonishing and Strict. The eight scales of the QTI correspond to the eight behavior aspects in this model.

The original WIHIC questionnaire developed by Fraser *et al.* (1996) has been refined and field tested by subsequent studies. The latest version of the WIHIC contains 56 items in seven scales and has been validated in the study of Aldridge *et al.* (1999). The seven scales are designed in accordance with the three dimensions in Moos' conceptual scheme of human environments. The scales of "Student cohesiveness", "Teacher support", and "Involvement" belong to relationship dimension, and the scales of "Investigation", "Task orientation", and "Cooperation" belong to personal development dimension, while the scale of "Equity" belongs to system maintenance and change dimension. Fraser (2002) once remarked that the WIHIC questionnaire combined the most salient scales from previous measuring instruments with additional scales of contemporary educational concerns to bring parsimony to the field of learning environments.

The WIHIC has been proved to be a valid and reliable instrument for measuring classroom psychosocial environments by numerous studies. The construct validity of the WIHIC was tested by Dorman (2003) through confirmatory factor analysis and structural equation modeling in his cross-national study of 3,980 students from Australia, Canada, and the United Kingdom. The factorial invariance of model parameters across three countries, three grade levels, and gender in this research has proved that the WIHIC is an internationally applicable instrument of classroom environments. Dorman (2008) employed the multitrait-multimethod modeling approach to further validate the construct validity of the WIHIC. His study provided strong evidence of the sound psychometric properties of the WIHIC which was claimed by Dorman (2008: 181) to have achieved "almost bandwagon status in the assessment of classroom environments". Moreover, the WIHIC has been widely applied and validated in a wide range of classrooms at various levels of education in studies around the world. The international applicability and sound validity of the WIHIC were considered as part of the reasons to choose this instrument in the present study to explore the psychosocial characteristics of college classroom environments in the Chinese EFL context.

Furthermore, numerous studies have applied the WIHIC in natural science classrooms at primary and secondary schools: geography and mathematics classes in Singaporean middle schools (e.g. Chionh & Fraser, 2009); science classes in Californian middle schools (e.g. Den Brok et al., 2006), in Korean high schools (e.g. Lee & Fraser, 2001), and in Indian high schools (e.g. Koul & Fisher, 2005), to name just a few. Given the fact that the WIHIC has been employed in college classrooms in Arabic speaking countries (e.g. Macleod & Fraser, 2010), in university computing classrooms in Indonesia (e.g. Margianti et al., 2001) and in Chinese language classrooms in secondary schools in Singapore (e.g. Chua et al., 2006), there has been few attempts in the application of the WIHIC in the EFL classrooms in China's higher education, even though English is regarded as a subject of paramount importance in China according to Jin and Cortazzi (2003). Therefore, the present study will broaden the applicability of the WIHIC questionnaire.

2.2.3 Research involving classroom environment instruments

Research domains of studies involving classroom environment instruments as reviewed by Fraser (1994, 1998a, 2002, 2007) mainly cover the following focuses: associations between student learning outcomes and environmental variables, discrepancies in perceptions of the psychosocial characteristics of the same classroom between students and instructors, comparisons of the perceptions and preferences of students for classroom psychosocial environments, determinants of classroom psychosocial environment perceptions, cross-national studies of the psychosocial nature of classroom learning environments, evaluation of educational innovations, transition from primary to secondary schools, and the facilitation of environmental changes in classrooms. Following these research traditions, the present study is primarily concerned with the first four domains of classroom environment research in view of the purposes of the current investigation. An outline of the four established research domains is provided respectively below.

Walberg (1969) admitted that the assessment of classroom psychosocial environments might make it possible to improve the accuracy of predicting learning and to manipulate the environment to bring about optimal conditions of learning. In fact, considerable studies have shown that student perceptions of the psychosocial characteristics of classroom environments account for appreciable amounts of variance in student cognitive and affective learning outcomes beyond that attributable to student characteristics such as general ability (Haertel, Walberg & Haertel, 1981). Studies on environment-outcome associations have been extensively conducted involving a wide range of classrooms, environment instruments, and samples from different school levels and numerous countries. These studies have revealed the associations between classroom psychosocial environments and student cognitive class achievements (e.g. Anderson, 1970; Anderson & Walberg, 1968; Chionh & Fraser, 2009; Fraser & Fisher, 1982; Fraser & Treagust, 1986; Goh & Fraser, 1998, 2000; Rita & Martin-Dunlop, 2011; Teh & Fraser, 1995; Vahala & Winston, 1994; Walberg, 1969; Walberg & Anderson, 1968a; Wei et al., 2009), affective learning outcomes such as student attitudes (e.g. Chionh & Fraser, 2009; Dorman & Fraser, 2009; Fisher, Henderson & Fraser, 1995; Fraser, Aldridge & Soerjaningsih, 2010; Goh & Fraser, 1998, 2000; McRobbie & Fraser, 1993; Teh & Fraser, 1995; Wong & Fraser, 1996), student self-esteem (e.g. Chionh & Fraser, 2009), student academic efficacy (e.g. Doorman, 2003), student classroom involvement and attendance (e.g. DeYoung, 1977), and student satisfaction (e.g. Aldridge & Fraser, 2000; Aldridge et al., 1999; Khoo & Fraser, 2008; Majeed, Fraser & Aldridge, 2002; Wong & Fraser, 2005; Walberg, 1969). Being aware of the importance of classroom psychosocial environments as a potential predictor of learning, researchers have been devoted to the investigation of the effects of classroom environmental variables on student behaviors in order to optimize the cognitive and affective learning outcomes of students.

Therefore, as asserted by Fraser (2007), the investigation of environment-outcome associations has so far become the strongest tradition in classroom environment research, and hence studies in this line are so extensive that it is hardly to be reviewed exhaustively.

Moreover, in recent years, researchers tend to show growing interests in the exploration of the effects of classroom psychosocial environments on the affective learning outcomes of student motivation (e.g. Chua *et al.*, 2009; Lapointe, Legault & Batiste, 2005; Opolot-Okurut, 2010). Chua *et al.* (2006) employed the "Chinese Language Classroom Environment Inventory" (CLCEI), the modified version of the WIHIC, to assess 1,460 secondary students' perceptions of their Chinese language classrooms in Singapore. Simple correlation and multiple regression analyses were used to examine the relationship between students' perceptions of the classroom psychosocial environments and their motivation to learn the Chinese language. The research results indicated that the "Task Orientation" dimension, among the six dimensions of the classroom psychosocial environments assessed in the CLCEI, was the strongest predictor of students' motivation to learn the Chinese language. Opolot-Okurut (2010) also found out the similar result in his study of the secondary mathematics classrooms in Uganda with a modified WIHIC. In the study of Lapointe, Legault, and Batiste (2005), they examined the links between students' perceptions of teacher interpersonal behavior measured by the QTI and three motivational variables (self-efficacy beliefs, intrinsic value, and test anxiety) for adolescents enrolled in three distinct schooling tracks (learning disabled, average and talented students). The results of their study showed that self-efficacy and intrinsic value of the average and talented students were positively linked to the teacher behaviors of leadership, helping/friendly, understanding, while student responsibility/freedom was negatively linked to teacher behaviors which were dissatisfied and admonishing. These studies have inspired and laid the ground for the present research which attempts to explore the influence of the nature of English language classroom psychosocial environments on the motivation of college students in the Chinese EFL context.

The investigation of discrepancies in the perceptions and preferences of classroom psychosocial environments between students and teachers has been favored by researchers in order to reveal the nature of classroom psychosocial environments in preschools, elementary and secondary schools, and colleges and universities (e. g. Chionh & Fraser, 2009; Chua, Wong & Chen, 2011; Fisher & Fraser, 1983a; Fisher, Fraser & Bassett, 1995; Fraser, 1982, 1984; Fraser & O'Brien, 1985; Fraser & Treagust, 1986; Hofstein & Lazarowitz, 1986; Lee, Lee & Wong, 2003; Margianti et al., 2001; Wong, 1995). The characteristics of classroom psychosocial environments have been exhibited in these studies that teachers perceive more positive classroom psychosocial environments than do their students in the same classroom and both students and teachers prefer a more positive classroom psychosocial environment than the one that is presently perceived. Some researchers have furthered the research locus to the examination of associations between the actual-preferred congruence of environment perceptions (or person-environment fit) and student cognitive and affective learning outcomes (e. g. De Young, 1977; Fraser & Fisher, 1983a, 1983b; Fraser & Rentoul, 1980; Nielsen & Moos, 1978; Rich & Bush, 1978; Wong & Watkins, 1996). Research findings have revealed that the interactions between actual and preferred classroom psychosocial environments account for a substantial and statistically significant amount of variance in student cognitive and affective achievements. It has been found that in the classes where students had a higher preference for the classroom psychosocial environment, the relationship between achievement and the actual environment perceptions was more positive than that in the classes where students had a lower preference. Furthermore, students achieved better in the classrooms where the actual classroom psychosocial environment was more congruent with the preferred one. Moreover, improved student satisfaction and class attendance were also found in classes when there was a reduction in the discrepancy between actual and preferred classroom psychosocial environments, as reported by De Young (1977).

Along the tradition in classroom psychosocial environment research, the determinants of classroom psychosocial environments have been examined to show how classroom psychosocial environments vary with variables at the student level such as student gender (e.g. Chua, Wong & Chen, 2011; Den Brok et al., 2006; Dowdell, Tomson & Davies, 2011; Goh & Fraser, 1998; Khoo & Fraser, 2008; Majeed, Fraser & Aldridge, 2002; Sinclair & Fraser, 2002), student age (e.g. Khoo & Fraser, 2008), student gift (e.g. Rita & Martin-Dunlop, 2011), and student ethnic background (e.g. Den Brok et al., 2003; Koul & Fisher, 2005); at the class level such as teacher cultural background (e.g. Khine & Fisher, 2001), class subject (e.g. Chionh & Fraser, 2009; Fraser & Lee, 2009; Waxman & Huang, 1998), express and normal streams of classes (e.g. Wong & Fraser, 1994), and grade level (e.g. Chandra & Fisher, 2009; Kim, Fisher & Fraser, 1999; Waxman & Huang, 1998); and at the school level such as socioeconomic status (e.g. Den Brok et al., 2006), adequacy of resources, parental involvement and collegiality (e.g. Aldridge, Fraser & Laugksch, 2011), affiliation, professional interest and achievement orientation (e.g. Fraser & Rentoul, 1982). Among these variables, student gender has received more attention than the others from researchers as the determinant of classroom psychosocial environments. It has been found that student gender consistently affects students' perceptions of the psychosocial environments in natural science classrooms, in particular. In general, it has been revealed that female students perceive the classroom psychosocial environments more positively than male students in the same classroom.

Enlightened by these studies, the current investigation follows the research tradition in this field to explore the nature of EFL classroom psychosocial environments by examining the discrepancies in perceptions and preferences of classroom psychosocial environments between students and teachers, gender differences in classroom psychosocial environment perceptions, and effects of the psychosocial aspects of classroom environments on student motivation of English learning.

2.2.4 Research of classroom psychosocial environments in China

Most of the studies on classroom psychosocial environments in China mainly focus on the introduction and review of the historical development of classroom psychosocial environment research and studies carried out in the western countries (e. g. Fan & Dong, 2005; Lu & Yang, 2008; Qu, 2002; Sun, 2010; Tian, 1992, 1995; Zhang, 1989; Zeng, 2005). There are limited empirical studies conducted to reveal the characteristics of psychosocial environments in the Chinese educational context.

In the cross-border studies of the classroom psychosocial environments of junior high school science classes in Australia and Taiwan Province of China carried out by Aldridge *et al.* (1999) and Aldridge and Fraser (2000), 1,879 students from 50 classes in Taiwan were involved in their studies and a Mandarin version of the WIHIC was validated in Taiwan with the support of data analyses of reliability and factorial validity. Multiple research methods (observations, interviews, and narrative stories) were employed in the two studies to gain deeper insights of the classroom psychosocial environments in the two places. Results of their studies reported that students in Taiwan viewed their classroom psychosocial environments less favorably than Australian students, but the Taiwanese students held a more positive attitude towards science than their Australian counterparts. In Hong Kong, Lee, Lee, and Wong (2003) developed and validated the "Hong Kong Classroom Environment Scale" (HKCES) to assess upper primary and junior secondary school students' perceptions of classroom psychosocial environments. The psychosocial properties of actual and ideal classroom psychosocial environments were also explored in their study through the examination of discrepancies in perceptions in terms of gender and school type. Thomas and Mee (2005) conducted a 2-month intervention study in the classrooms of Primary Year 3 General Studies in Hong Kong to investigate the impact of classroom psychosocial environment changes on students' metacognition. Though the statistical analysis suggested no significant enhancement in students' metacognition resulted from the changes in classroom psychosocial environments, student interviews and classroom observations provided supportive data for some changes which were conducive to the development of students' metacognition.

More domestic studies on classroom psychosocial environments have been carried out in other regions of China. Xin, Lin, and Yu (2000) translated the QTI into Chinese and validated the Chinese version of the QTI with a sample of 347 teachers from elementary and secondary schools in Shandong province and Beijing. Their study found that Chinese teacher behavior could be divided into two types: cooperation-dominance and opposition-submission. Wei et al. (2009) also translated the QTI into Chinese and investigated the relationships between teachers' interpersonal behavior and students' fluency in English in secondary schools in Southwest China. The research indicated that teacher uncertainty was negatively correlated with student achievement, and teacher cooperation with students was a significant predictor for student achievement. Another study on classroom psychosocial environments in secondary schools was carried out by Liu and Liu (2010). The "English Classroom Environment Inventory" (ECEI) was developed and validated in their study with a sample of 1,235 secondary students in Northeast China. The nature of English classroom psychosocial environments in secondary schools was investigated and the results of the study indicated that students' perceptions of the classroom psychosocial environments differed in terms of school locality, student gender, and grade level, but in general, students had a positive perception of their existing English language classroom psychosocial environments.

The empirical studies of Sun and Lin (2008) and Sun (2007, 2009, 2010) have extended the scope of classroom psychosocial environment research to the English language classrooms in China's higher education. In light of the four classic environment instruments including "Classroom Environment Scale" (Moos &

Trickett, 1987), "Questionnaire on Teacher Interaction" (Wubbles & Levy, 1993), "What Is Happening In this Class?" (Fraser et al., 1996), and "College and University Classroom Environment Inventory" (Fraser & Treagust, 1989), Sun (2007) designed the "Chinese College and University Foreign Language Classroom Environment Inventory" (CCUFLCEI) to investigate the English language classroom psychosocial environments for non-English majors in Chinese universities. A large-scale survey was administered with a sample of 2,200 students and 60 teachers from 10 different key universities in China. Their studies involved Oral English classrooms, English Reading classrooms and Comprehensive English classrooms for non-English majors. Results indicated that the existing English classroom psychosocial environments (including Oral English, English Reading, and Comprehensive English classrooms) were perceived differently by teachers and students, male and female students, and students with different levels of English proficiency. Research findings also suggested that there were certain correlations between students' academic achievement and some psychosocial environmental dimensions measured in the CCUFLCEI. Their studies contributed to the classroom psychosocial environment research in China by revealing some of the psychosocial characteristics of English classrooms at the tertiary level in Chinese EFL context. However, there are still some limitations and inadequacies in their studies. First of all, their studies confined to the English language classrooms for non-English majors; second, their studies did not examine the preferences of students and teachers for an ideal classroom psychosocial environment; and moreover, their studies primarily focused on the investigation of the relationships between classroom psychosocial environment factors and student cognitive learning outcomes, while the impact of environmental dimensions on student affective learning outcomes was not touched upon, as argued by Huang (2006: 480) that "cognitive measures alone cannot give a comprehensive picture of academic learning processes and outcomes". In view of these, the present study can serve as a complement to the series of studies conducted by Sun and her colleagues to present a comprehensive and in-depth picture of the psychosocial characteristics of English language classrooms in Chinese colleges and universities.

2.3 Field of research on motivation in L2 learning

This section initially reviews some influential theories of L2 motivation from social psychological, cognitive, and situated approaches. The review of these theoretical models mainly focuses on the conceptualization of motivation and the categorization of motivational types as well as the contextualization of L2 motivation in learning situations. The following section examines the research literature on L2 motivation centering on the empirical studies of relationships between motivation and other learner factors in L2 learning both at home and abroad.

2.3.1 *Theoretical models of L2 motivation*

The complex and multi-faceted nature of human motivation has been fascinating motivational psychologists for centuries. The view of motivation in psychology has changed dramatically over the last half of the 20th century, as stated by Eccles, Wigfield, and Schiefele (1998: 1074), "from a biologically based drive perspective to a behavioural-mechanistic perspective, and then to a cognitive-mediational/constructivist perspective". They foresaw that the central theme of motivation in psychology in the 21st century would be the role of affect, less conscious processes, and the contextual influences. Among these diverse motivational theories in psychology, Dörnyei (2001, 2005) divided the contemporary leading motivation theories into two streams: motivational psychology that links human behavior to motives stemming from human mental processes (i.e. Expectancy-value theories, Self-efficacy theory, Attribution theory, Goal theories, and Self-determination theory) and social psychology that views human behavior in the light of social and interpersonal context (the theory of reasoned action and the theory of planned behavior). These psychological theories on motivation have provided theoretical frameworks for and exerted influences on the investigation of motivation to learn a L2.

2.3.1.1 A social psychological approach: Gardner's motivation theory

In the L2 field, the most influential motivation theory over the past few decades was proposed by Gardner, Lambert, and their associates in Canada from the social psychological approach. In line with the view held by social psychology that individual's attitudes towards a target exert influence on their behavior in responses to the target, Gardner (1985: 6) asserted that "students' attitudes toward the specific language group are bound to influence how successful they will be in incorporating aspects of that language". In Gardner's model, motivation colligates effort, want, and affect, and hence it has cognitive, affective and conative characteristics. Motivation to learn a L2 is defined by Gardner (1985: 10) as "the extent to which the individual works or strives to learn the language because of a desire to do so and the satisfaction experienced in this activity". Distinct from motivation, orientation, another important concept in Gardner's theory, refers to the "collection of reasons that reflect common or conceptual similar goals" (Gardner, 2005: 4). Two types of orientations are identified among L2 learners: integrative orientation and instrumental orientation. Integratively oriented L2 learners learn the language to involve communication or social-emotional contact with the other community, while instrumentally oriented L2 learners learn the language for pragmatic aims such as obtaining a better job or a higher salary. The central theme in Gardner's motivation theory is the construct of the integrative motive defined as a "motivation to learn a second language because of positive feelings toward the community that speaks that language" (Gardner, 1985: 82–83). Gardner (1985) pointed out that the integrative motive facilitated second language acquisition, and such generalization has been supported by considerable studies. The core component of the integrative motive is the integrativeness which reflects " an individual's openness to taking on characteristics of another cultural/linguistic group" (Gardner, 2005: 7). The integrativeness is found to be the most powerful component of students' affective disposition in determining students' language choice and the amount of effort they intend to expend in learning the language, as reported by the studies of Dörnyei and Clément (2001) and Csizér and Dörnyei (2005) based on the analysis of data collected in a large-scale nationwide attitude/motivation survey carried out in Hungary.

The role of motivation in second language acquisition is shown in Gardner's (1985) socio-educational model in which motivation serves as the cornerstone. This model of learning has been revised over years and expanded by Tremblay and Gardner (1995) by incorporating some constructs of motivation (i. e. Goal salience and Self-efficacy) derived from Goal theories and Expectancy-value theories in psychology. The main constructs in the socio-educational model can be measured by the "Attitude Motivation Test Battery" (AMTB) provided by Gardner (1985). Figure 2.4 presents the revised version of socio-educational model proposed by Gardner (2005) with measures in the AMTB.

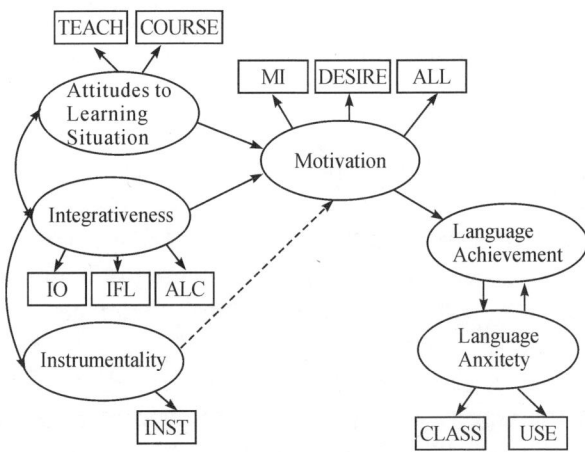

Figure 2.4 The Socio-educational Model with indicator variables in the AMTB
Source: Gardner, 2005: 12.

As presented in the model, motivation is one of the major variables that account for individual differences in language achievement. The levels of individual's motivation to learn a L2 are mainly influenced by the individual's attitudes toward the learning situation and integrativeness, as well as instrumentality under some circumstances. Attitudes toward the learning situation refer to individual's affective reactions to any aspect of the class such as class atmosphere, materials quality, the curriculum, and the teacher, etc. These attitudes are assessed by the scales of "Language teacher-evaluation" (TEACH) and "Language course-evaluation" (COURSE) in the AMTB. Integrativeness which reflects an individual's openness to other cultures can be measured by the scales of "Integrative orientation" (IO), "Interest in foreign languages" (IFL), and "Attitudes toward the language community" (ALC) in the AMTB. Instrumentality or the instrument orientation is measured by the scale of "Instrumental orientation" (INST) in the AMTB. Motivation is examined by three measures of "Motivational intensity" (MT), "Desire to learn the language" (DESIRE) and "Attitudes toward learning the language" (ALL) in the AMTB. Language anxiety which plays a complex role in second language learning is assessed by the scales of "Language class anxiety" (CLASS) and "Language use anxiety" (USE) that measure the individual's anxiety in two broad situations, namely, the language class and the contexts outside of the classroom situation where the language might be used.

2.3.1.2 A cognitive approach: Self-determination theory and L2 motivation

The Self-determination theory (SDT) advocated by Deci and Ryan (1985) is an influential motivational theory in psychology that focuses on the type or orientation rather than the amount or level of motivation as stated by Deci and Ryan (2008) that the type or quality of an individual's motivation would be more important than the total amount of motivation for predicting many important outcomes such as psychological health and well-being, effective performance, creative problem solving, and deep or conceptual learning. SDT differentiates types of motivation based on different goals that bring about the action, and the most basic distinction is between intrinsic motivation and extrinsic motivation. Amotivation is another category of motivation distinguished from intrinsic and extrinsic motivation referring to "a lack of intention and motivation" (Deci & Ryan, 2008: 182).

Intrinsic motivation is defined by Ryan and Deci (2000a: 55-56) as "the doing of an activity for its inherent satisfactions", while extrinsic motivation, in contrast, refers to "doing something because it leads to a separable outcome". It is proposed by Ryan and Deci (2000a: 56) that intrinsic motivation is an important construct which reflects the natural motivational tendency of human being to "take interest in novelty, to actively assimilate, and to creatively apply our skills" and this feature of human nature affects performance, persistence, and well-being across life's epochs. It is also pointed out by Ryan and Deci (2000a) that extrinsic motivation is an equally important construct since most of the activities people do are not intrinsically motivated. Rather than being unitary, extrinsic motivation is argued by SDT to vary considerably depending on the degree of autonomy or self-determination. Four subtypes of extrinsic motivation including external regulation, introjected regulation, identification, and integrated regulation are identified in SDT depending on the degree of internalization and integration of the values and behavioral regulations. Internalization refers to an active process that takes in an outer regulation, while integration is the process to fully transform it into an inner one so that it will emerge from their sense of self (Deci & Ryan, 1985; Ryan & Deci, 2000a). SDT has also been concerned with the social and environmental factors that facilitate and undermine both types of motivation and has proposed the postulate that intrinsic motivation is enhanced and the internalization and integration of extrinsic motivation are facilitated when the basic human psychological needs for autonomy, competence, and relatedness are satisfied (Deci & Ryan, 1985; Ryan & Deci, 2000a, 2000b).

Figure 2.5 presents the taxonomy of different types of human motivation and the continuum along which amotivation, extrinsic motivation, and intrinsic motivation are placed depending on the degree of self-determination. As indicated in Figure 2.5, the four subtypes of extrinsic motivation vary in their degrees of determination, ranging from external regulation which is the least autonomous form to integration which is the most autonomous one.

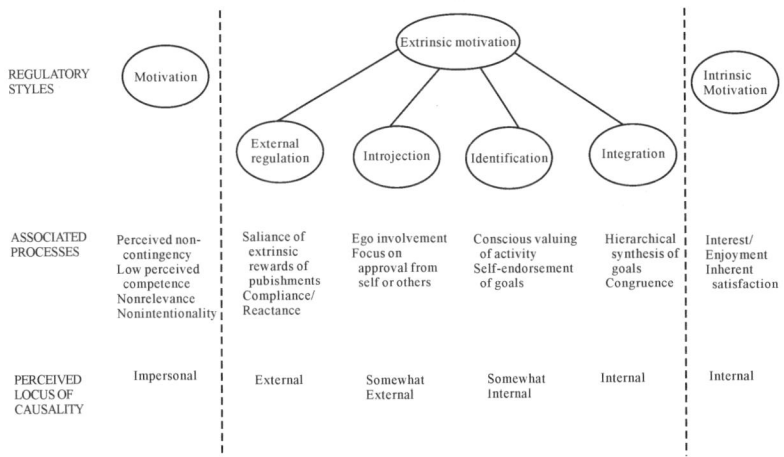

Figure 2.5 A taxonomy of human motivation

Source: Ryan & Deci, 2000a: 61.

Noels and her colleagues have been devoted to applying the constructs of intrinsic and extrinsic motivation in self-determination theory to the study of L2 motivation. Noels, Clément, and Pelletier (1999) examined the associations of intrinsic and extrinsic motivation with various language learning outcomes, including effort, anxiety, and language competence. Research findings indicated that stronger feelings of intrinsic motivation were related to positive language learning outcomes, including greater motivational intensity, greater self-evaluations of competence, and a reduction in anxiety. Noels et al. (2003) employed a valid and reliable instrument to assess the different subtypes of intrinsic and extrinsic motivation in second language learning. Their study investigated the relationships between these subtypes of intrinsic and extrinsic motivation and the orientations to language learning identified by Clément and Kruidenier (1983) including travel, friendship, knowledge, and instrumental orientations. Research results showed that external regulation and the instrumental orientation were strongly correlated, and identified regulation and intrinsic motivation were highly correlated with the travel, friendship, and knowledge orientations. Links between intrinsic and extrinsic motivation and the integrative orientation proposed by Gardner (1985) were also examined in their study and the results showed that the integrative orientation correlated more strongly with the more self-determined forms of motivation such as identified regulation and intrinsic orientation (Noels, 2001b; Noels, Clément & Pelletier, 2001).

In light of the assumption of SDT that the satisfaction of needs for autonomy, competence, and relatedness facilitates and promotes human motivation, Noels (2001b; Noels et al., 1999) explored the relations between L2 learners' intrinsic and extrinsic motivation and their generalized feelings of autonomy and competence measured in terms of students' perceptions of teachers' communication style in classrooms. Research results showed that students' perceptions of teachers' communication styles were associated with their intrinsic motivation. The more controlling the teacher was perceived to be, the less autonomous and competent the students felt, and the lower was students' intrinsic motivation.

Noels (2001a) put forward an integrated theoretical model of motivational processes to systematically present the various motivation orientations and to indicate the psychological mechanism by which motivation may be promoted or diminished in different contexts. Noels' model explains how orientations are affected by significant factors including L2 community, teacher, and family members and how orientations may be differentially related to L2 variables involving ethno-linguistic identity, proficiency, and personal identity.

2.3.1.3 A situated approach: Dörnyei's three-level model of L2 motivation

In order to further understand L2 motivation in the learning situation from an educational perspective, Dörnyei (1994) conceptualized a three-level comprehensive framework of L2 motivation synthesizing a number of relevant motivational components. The constituents of Dörnyei's model of L2 classroom motivation are listed in Table 2.1 below.

Table 2.1 **Dörnyei's three-level framework of L2 motivation**

LANGUAGE LEVEL	Integrative Motivational Subsystem
	Instrumental Motivational Subsystem
LEARNER LEVEL	Need for Achievement
	Self-Confidence
	* Language Use Anxiety
	* Perceived L2 Competence
	* Causal Attributions
	* Self-Efficacy
LEARNING SITUATION LEVEL	
Course-Specific Motivational Components	Interest
	Relevance
	Expectancy
	Satisfaction
Teacher-Specific Motivational Components	Affilliative Drive
	Authority Type
	Direct Socialization of Motivation
	* Modelling
	* Task Presentation
	* Feedback
Group-Specific Motivational Components	Goal-Orientedness
	Norm & Reward System
	Group Cohesion
	Classroom Goal Structure

Source: Dörnyei, 1994: 280.

The model comprises the language level, the learner level, and the learning situation level. The three levels of L2 motivation are consistent with the three basic components of learning process, i.e.

the L2, the L2 learner, and the L2 learning environment, and also reflect the three aspects of language, i. e. the educational subject matter dimension, the personal dimension, and the social dimension.

The language level focuses on L2 orientations and motives which are grouped in accordance with Gardner's categorization into integrative motivational subsystem and instrumental motivational subsystem. The learner level integrates the constructs of motivation viewed as stable personality traits proposed in different approaches and classifies them into two categories: need for achievement and self-confidence. Self-confidence includes the L2 learner's language use anxiety, perceived L2 competence, causal attributions, and self-efficacy. The learning situation level summarizes the motivational components specific to learning situations into three sets: (1) course-specific motivational components related to the syllabus, the teaching materials, the teaching method, and the learning tasks; (2) teacher-specific motivational components encompassing the teacher's personality, teaching style, feedback, and relationship with the students; and (3) group-specific motivational components concerning the dynamics of the learning group.

2.3.2 *Research on L2 motivation*

2.3.2.1 Instruments of measuring L2 motivation

As indicated by Dörnyei (2001, 2005) in his review of motivation research methodology, due to the strong social psychological influence on L2 motivation research, the use of scales and questionnaires to collect motivational data is an established practice in the L2 field. The AMTB provided in the Gardneran approach to measure the major conceptual variables in the socio-educational model is a classic standardized test of L2 motivation in the motivational literature. Gardner (2010) introduced the latest form of the battery, "International AMTB for English as a Foreign Language", and a short form of the battery, the mini-AMTB.

Though the AMTB is originated in the Canadian context for the investigation of English-speaking students learning French as a second language, its sound psychometric properties attested in past studies (e. g. Gardner & MacIntyre, 1993; Gardner, 2010; Gardner & Smythe, 1981; Lalonde & Gardner, 1985) permit the adaption of some or all the scales in the battery in studies of L2 motivation in different learning contexts where English is learned as a second or foreign language (e. g. Dörnyei & Clément, 2001; Gardner et al., 2004; Gardner, Tremblay& Masgoret, 1997; Harris & Murtagh, 1999; Kraemer, 1993; Masgoret & Gardner, 2003; Murtagh, 2007; Yashima, 2002). Besides this classic battery, there are some other motivational questionnaires developed and used by some influential researchers in the L2 field, such as the questionnaire developed by Noels et al. (2003) to study student motivation of learning English as a second language in Canadian colleges, the questionnaires to investigate the student motivation of learning English as a foreign language in Hungary developed by Clément, Dörnyei, and Noels (1994) and Dörnyei (1990a, 1990b), and student motivation of learning English as a foreign language in Egypt developed by Schmidt, Boraie, and Kassabgy (1996).

In China, learners' motivation to learn English as a foreign language has also been assessed and studied (e. g. Hua, 1998; Liu & Huang, 2011; Qin, 2007; Qin & Wen, 2002; Shi, 2000; Wang & Liu, 2002; Warden & Lin, 2000; Wen & Wang, 1996; Wen, 2001; Wen & Johnson, 1997; Zhang, 1998). In line with the view of Dörnyei (1990a, 1990b) that instrumental motivation might be more important than integrative motivation for foreign language learners, the studies of Hua (1998) and Shi (2000) found out supportive results that there was a lack of integrative motivation proposed in Gardner's classic model among Chinese learners of English and the dominant L2 motivation type was certification motivation, which is instrumental motivation in nature since students learn English with the purpose to pass the exams to obtain English certificates or diploma. In order to better understand students' English learning motivation in the Chinese EFL context, Gao et al. (2004) adopted an inductive approach to conduct a bottom-up classification of Chinese university students' English learning motivation. Their study contributed a questionnaire to assess L2 motivation types of Chinese university undergraduates, which is referred to in the present study as the "Motivation Types of Chinese College Undergraduates" (MTCCU). The MTCCU was validated with a large stratified sample of 2,278 undergraduates from 30 Chinese universities in 29 provinces, autonomous regions and municipalities across China. This instrument has been widely applied in studies on motivation of Chinese college EFL students including undergraduates of both non-English majors and English majors, and graduates of non-English majors (e.g. Li, Gao & Qian, 2003a, 2003b; Gao et al., 2008; Gao et al., 2003; Gao et al., 2003, 2004, 2007; Liu & Gao, 2008, 2010; Xu & Gao, 2011; Zhou, Gao & Zang, 2011).

2.3.2.2 Empirical studies on L2 motivation

The role of motivation in L2 learning has been extensively studied. Dörnyei (2001, 2005) classified the existing L2 studies into four main domains, namely, survey studies, factor analytical studies, correlational studies and studies using structural equation modeling. The review in this part is primarily concerned with the empirical studies under the category of correlational studies considering the research objective of the present study.

In the West, most of the empirical studies in the L2 field focus on revealing the relationships of motivation to second language achievement (e.g. Clément et al., 1994; Dörnyei, 1990b; Gardner, 1988, 1991; Gardener & Lambert, 1972; Oxford et al., 1993) and to other learner factors, such as language attitude, language aptitude, language anxiety, learning strategies, and learning styles (e.g. Gardner, Day & MacIntyre, 1992; Gardner & Lambert, 1959; Gardner, Tremblay & Masgoret, 1997).

In China, researchers also show great interests in the impact of L2 motivation on Chinese college learners' English achievement (e.g. Guo, 2009; Hao & Hao, 2001; Ma, 2005; Shi, 2000; Wen & Johnson, 1997; Wen & Wang, 1996; Wu, Liu & Jeffrey, 1993; Yang & Ding, 2004; Yuan, 2003). These studies suggest that motivation is a critical affective factor influencing English language learning and motivation can be regarded as a predictor of English language achievement. Chinese researchers are also concerned with the relationships of learners' motivation towards English as a foreign language to other learner factors. Qin (2002) reported that variation in causal attribution and its conceptions accounted much for the individual differences in motivational behavior in EFL learning. Li and Wu (2007) found that EFL learners' task motivation during in-class learning would be effectively enhanced by the three task features, namely, topic familiarity, task type, and contextual supporting material. The research of Zhang (1998) indicated that there were significant positive correlations between EFL learners' motivation potency and the frequency of strategy use in secondary schools. Wen (2001) studied the relations among motivation, beliefs, and strategies based on longitudinal questionnaire data and the research results indicated that the relations among the three variables were stable and motivation affected beliefs and strategies. Liu and Cha (2010) examined the impact of motivation on EFL learners' choice of learning strategies in context of web-based autonomous learning. In the recent studies initiated by Gao and her associates (e.g. Li, Gao & Qian, 2003b; Liu & Gao, 2008, 2010; Gao et al., 2007; Xu & Gao, 2011; Zhou & Gao, 2009; Zhou, Gao & Zang, 2011), English learning motivation types and self-identity change were found to be positively correlated among graduates and undergraduates in Chinese colleges and universities.

  The review of the empirical studies conducted domestically shows that little attention has been paid by researchers to the investigation of relationships between students' motivation of learning English and the psychosocial aspects of classroom environments. Therefore, the present study is carried out to inspect the associations between college students' English learning motivation and their classroom environment perceptions in the Chinese EFL context.

2.4 Summary

The review of literature in this chapter has provided the research background as well as the theoretical and methodological bases for the current investigation of CE classroom psychosocial environments at the tertiary level in China. In the first part of the review on classroom psychosocial environment research, theoretical foundations of research and conceptualization of psychosocial environments were discussed, and approaches to measuring classroom environments and some historically important instruments of assessing classroom environments were introduced. Research domains of classroom environment research in traditions were reviewed followed by the summarization of empirical studies of classroom environments both at home and abroad. In the second part of the review on research of second and foreign language motivation, L2 motivation was conceptualized and categorized during the introduction of some influential theories of L2 motivation in social psychological, cognitive, and situated approaches. Domestic and international studies on L2 motivation, particularly studies on its relation to other learning factors and students' academic achievement, were presented and discussed.

Research gaps in previous studies emerged during the extensive review on the literature in this chapter, and hence the present study is conducted to bridge some of the research gaps and provide a better understanding of the psychosocial environments in the EFL classrooms in China.

Chapter 3
Research Design and Methodology

3.1 Introduction

This chapter introduces the design and methodology employed in the present study to examine the psychosocial characteristics of English classroom psychosocial environments in Chinese colleges and universities. The research questions are raised and the research design of the current study is outlined, followed by the introduction of research subjects, instruments, and procedures of data collection and analysis. At the end of this chapter, results of the pilot study are reported and discussed.

3.2 Research questions

The present study is designed to explore the nature of psychosocial environments of English as a foreign language (EFL) classrooms in Chinese colleges and universities, and based on the research objectives stated in Chapter 1, the present study centers upon the following specific research questions:

(1) What are the construct validity and internal reliability of the modified "What Is Happening In this class?" (WIHIC) to assess the psychosocial environments of English classrooms in Chinese colleges and universities?

(2) What are the characteristics of English classroom psychosocial environments at the tertiary level in the Chinese EFL context?

(3) What associations exist between students' perceptions

of the psychosocial aspects of English classroom environments and their motivation of learning the English language?

The second research question is further elaborated as:

(1) What is the status quo of the comprehensive English (CE) classroom psychosocial environments as perceived by students and instructors?
(2) To what extent do students and instructors differ in their perceptions and preferences of CE classroom psychosocial environments?
(3) What are the gender differences among students in their perceptions and preferences of CE classroom psychosocial environments?

The third research question is further stated as:

(1) What is the overall status of English learning motivation of English majors in Chinese colleges and universities?
(2) To what extent are students' perceptions of CE classroom psychosocial environments related to their English learning motivation?

3.3 Research design

To find out answers for the research questions raised above, the current research was mainly divided into two parts:

(1) The first sub-study was devoted to measuring and investigating Chinese college students' and instructors' perceptions of their CE classroom psychosocial environments. It described the validation of the modified WIHIC to assess the perceptions of the classroom psychosocial environments in the Chinese EFL context. Results of the survey were reported and analyzed to reveal students' and instructors' perceptions of the psychosocial characteristics of CE classroom environments.

Chapter 3 Research Design and Methodology

(2) The second sub-study examined the characteristics of English majors' motivation of learning English and explored the associations between students' perceptions of CE classroom psychosocial environments and their motivation to learn English. Students' English learning motivation types were assessed by the adapted Motivation types of Chinese college undergraduates (MTCCU). Results of the survey were reported and analyzed to explore the associations between students' perceptions of the psychosocial aspects of the classroom environments and their English learning motivation types.

3.4 Subjects

The present survey study involved a total of 945 students, who were the first-year English majors from 20 intact classes and second-year English majors from 20 intact classes in the School of International Studies (SIS) at Sun Yat-sen Univtrsity (SYSU). These student subjects were of similar age, educational background, and years of learning English. The general information of the student subjects including age, gender, college year, and years of English learning is provided in Table 3.1 below.

Table 3.1 General information of student subjects in the survey study

	Age			Gender		College Year		Years of Teaching English			
	16–17	18–20	21–23	Male	Female	1st	2nd	5–6	7–10	11–14	15–19
No.	12	800	106	160	726	504	441	21	622	242	30
Perc. /%	1.3	87.1	11.6	18.1	81.9	53.3	46.7	2.3	68.0	26.4	3.3
Mean	19			—		—		9.9			

Note: The numbers of missing values were age, 27; sex, 59; and years of English learning, 30.

As shown in Table 3.1 above, 87.1% of the student subjects aged from 18 to 20 years old and the average age of all student subjects was 19 years old. Among these subjects, 18.1% were male students and 81.9% were female students. The disproportionate ratio of male students to female students exhibits a common phenomenon that female students constitute the major part in English majors in schools of foreign languages in Chinese colleges and universities. These students have learned English for years ranging from 5 to 19 years and on average they have learned English for almost 10 years.

Another group of subjects who participated in the survey included all the 17 instructors who taught the course of Comprehensive English to the 40 classes of first-year and second-year English majors in the SIS at SYSU. Table 3.2 presents the general information of these instructor subjects.

Table 3.2 General information of instructor subjects in the survey study

	Age			Gender		College Year		Years of Teaching English		
	24-26	27-29	30-32	Male	Female	1st	2nd	0.5-1	3-5	6-8
No.	4	6	4	4	13	9	8	3	9	5
Perc. /%	28.6	42.8	28.6	23.5	76.5	52.9	47.1	17.6	52.9	29.5
Mean	28			—		—		3.8		

Note: There were 3 missing values of age.

As shown in Table 3.2 above, the age of instructors ranged from 24 to 32 years old with an average age of 28 years old. Among the 17 instructors surveyed in the study, 23.5% were male instructors and 76.5% were female instructors, with a gender ratio of approximately 1 : 3 between male and female instructors. The low proportion of male instructors also reflects a common phenomenon that female instructors constitute a major part of the faculty staff in schools of foreign languages in Chinese colleges and universities. The instructors in the present study had the experience of teaching English as a college instructor for years varied from 0.5 to 8 years with an average of 3.8 years. In addition, five international instructors from English speaking countries in the SIS at SYSU were interviewed in the pilot study to provide feedback on the modification of the WIHIC used in the current study.

3.5 Instruments

Two survey instruments were employed in the present study. The modified WIHIC was used to measure students' and instructors' perceptions and preferences of the CE classroom psychosocial environments. The modified MTCCU were adopted to assess students' motivation types of English learning.

3.5.1 *The modified WIHIC*

The modified WIHIC used in the present study was customized from the WIHIC questionnaire provided by Aldridge *et al.* (1999) by omitting the "Investigation" scale which was designed to measure the skills and processes of inquiry and their use in problem solving and investigation. There were three reasons for the omission of the "Investigation" scale. In the first place, the "Investigation" scale in the original WIHIC was more suitable for the assessment of students' perceptions in natural science classes rather than in language classes. In the second place, Chua *et al.* (2006) have validated the Chinese Language Classroom Environment Inventory (CLCEI) questionnaire used in their study on the Chinese language classroom environments in secondary schools in Singapore, which was customized and modified from the original WIHIC by removing the "Investigation" scale. The validation results in their study showed that the factorial validity of the CLCEI was comparable to that of the original WIHIC. In addition, Fraser *et al.* (1996) stated that the WIHIC would allow the exclusion of irrelevant scale(s) to suit any classroom environment under study without affecting its reliability and validity. Finally, the omission of "Investigation" scale would make it more convenient to compare the research results obtained in this study in China with those in the study of Chua *et al.* (2006) in Singapore in order to further understand the psychosocial characteristics of EFL classroom environments in the Chinese context.

The modified version of the WIHIC used in this study consists of six scales to examine six different psychosocial aspects of the CE classroom environments. The current 48 items in the six scales have been examined and modified through field testing three times to suit the Chinese EFL context. Each item in the modified WIHIC is scored on a five-point Likert scale with alternatives of "Almost never", "Seldom", "Sometimes", "Often", and "Almost always" to indicate the degree of agreement with each statement. Items from the six scales were arranged in a cyclic order to reduce the puzzlement of the respondents about the similarity of the items in the same scale. Table 3.3 below provides an overview of the modified WIHIC, including the classification of each scale under the scheme of Moos, the scale description, and a sample item in the scale.

Table 3.3 Descriptive information for the modified WIHIC

Six Dimensions	Moos Category	Scale Description	Sample Item
Student cohesiveness (SC)	R	Extent to which students know, help, and are supportive of one another.	*I work well with other class members.*
Teacher support (TS)	R	Extent to which the teacher helps, befriends, trusts, and shows interest in students.	*The teacher considers my feelings.*
Involvement (IN)	R	Extent to which students have attentive interest, participate in discussions, perform additional work, and enjoy the class.	*I give my opinions during class discussions.*
Task orientation (TO)	P	Extent to which it is important to complete activities planned and to stay on the subject matter.	*I know what I am trying to accomplish in this class.*
Cooperation (CO)	P	Extent to which students cooperate rather than compete with one another on learning tasks.	*When I work in groups in this class, there is teamwork.*
Equity (EQ)	S	Extent to which students are treated equally by the teacher.	*I get the same opportunity to answer questions as other students.*

Note: R: Relationship dimension; P: Personal development dimension; S: System maintenance and system change dimension.

In accordance with the original WIHIC, there are also four forms of the modified WIHIC, namely, the student actual form, the student preferred form, the instructor actual form, and the instructor preferred form. The student actual form and the instructor actual form are used to investigate students' and instructors' perceptions of the actual CE classroom psychosocial environments, and the student preferred form and the instructor preferred form are used to examine students' and instructors' perceptions of the preferred CE classroom psychosocial environments. A sample item in each of the four forms of the modified WIHIC is provided in Table 3.4.

Table 3.4 Sample items in the four forms of the modified WIHIC

Form	Sample Item
Student actual	*I am treated the same as other students in this class.*
Student preferred	*I would be treated the same as other students in this class.*
Instructor actual	*All students are treated the same in this class.*
Instructor preferred	*All students would be treated the same in this class.*

3.5.2 *The modified MTCCU*

The MTCCU questionnaire was designed by Gao *et al.* (2003) to investigate college students' English learning motivation types in the Chinese EFL context. Table 3.5 presents an overview of the modified MTCCU including the scale name, scale description, and sample item in each scale.

In the present study, the MTCCU was adapted by removing Item 12 ("The direct object of my English learning is to obtain high scores in examinations concerning going abroad or career development in China.") from the English version of the questionnaire provided in the study of Gao *et al.* (2007) in that it was found in the factor analysis conducted by Gao *et al.* (2003) that Item 12 had factor loadings above 0.3 and below 0.4 on three factors (i.e. "Immediate achievement", "Going abroad", and

Table 3.5 Descriptive information for the modified MTCCU

Scale Name	Scale Description	Sample Item
Intrinsic interest (II)	Appreciation or fondness of the target language and certain aspects of its culture.	*I fell in love with English at the first sight, without particular reasons.*
Immediate achievement (IA)	Learning the target language to obtain satisfactory results in exams, e.g., for university entrance or graduation.	*An important purpose for my English learning is to obtain a university degree.*
Learning situation (LS)	Learning English because of aspects of the learning environment such as the quality of teaching, teaching materials, teachers, and affiliation with the learning group.	*After entering university, my effort of English learning has depended to a large extent on the quality of English textbooks.*
Going abroad (GA)	Learning English to go abroad for various purposes, such as "finding better education or job opportunities", "experiencing English-speaking cultures", and "immigration".	*I learn English in order to find better education and job opportunities abroad.*
Social responsibility (SR)	Learning the target language to combine "harmonizing the family" and "putting the country in order", emphasizing individuals' responsibility to fulfill social expectations.	*I learn English in order to let the world know more about China.*
Individual development (ID)	Learning English to increase one's own ability and social status in future development, which could be as specific as "finding a good job" and as general as acquiring "a sense of achievement".	*Acquiring good English skills is a stepping-stone to one's success in life.*
Information medium (IM)	Learning English to obtain information and learn other academic subjects.	*I learn English in order to facilitate the learning of other academic subjects.*

"Individual development"). Therefore, Item 12 was not grouped into any of the factors in the questionnaire in their study and in some other studies carried out by Gao and her associates (e.g. Gao et al., 2004; Gao et al. 2007) to explore the English learning motivation types of Chinese college students. The remaining 29 items in the modified MTCCU are categorized into seven scales to represent seven types of motivation: "Intrinsic interest" (II), "Immediate achievement" (IA), "Learning situation" (LS), "Going abroad" (GA), "Social responsibility" (SR), "Individual development" (ID), and "Information medium" (IM).

3.6 Data collection procedures

A large-scale survey was carried out in the SIS at SYSU at the end of the second term of the school year in June, 2011 to collect the data for analysis in the present study. All the first-year and second-year English majors in the SIS at SYSU were asked to respond to the questionnaire booklet consisting of three parts (i.e. the student actual form and the student preferred form of the modified WIHIC and the modified MTCCU) in class time. Appointments after class were made with the 17 instructors who were teaching the course of Comprehensive English. Each of the instructors was asked to answer the questionnaire containing the instructor actual form and the instructor preferred form of the modified WIHIC. Both the students and the instructors were informed of the general research purpose before they completed the questionnaire. It was explained to the students that their responses were not related to their course scores or the evaluation of their teachers and their responses would be kept confidential only for the academic research of this study. Both the students and instructors were told to be free not to participate. The survey was administered in the absence of the CE instructors in order to ensure that the responses of students would not be influenced by the presence of their teachers. The researcher was present in the time and location while the survey was carried out to solve the questions and puzzles of respondents concerning the questionnaire.

A total of 976 copies were returned among the 1,000 copies of questionnaire issued to students with a high return rate of 97.6%. Among the returned questionnaire, 31 copies of questionnaire were eliminated as invalid responses since they were incompletely answered or completed without following the instructions. Therefore, the survey obtained 945 copies of valid questionnaire with a valid response rate of 96.8%. As for the 40 copies of questionnaire administered to instructors, both the return rate and valid response rate were 100%.

3.7 Data analysis procedures

The data collected in the study were processed and analyzed by SPSS 19.0. All the following statistical methods of analysis and the unit of analysis chosen in this study were consistent with the previous studies of classroom psychosocial environments in the research tradition, and this would allow the comparisons between the results obtained in the present study with those in previous research.

3.7.1 Procedures for the validation of research instruments

In the first sub-study, the survey data were analyzed statistically to test initially the validity and reliability of the two research instruments, the modified WIHIC and the modified MTCCU.

The modified WIHIC was validated with the samples in the present study by performing statistical analyses to estimate the construct validity and internal consistency reliability of the questionnaire as well as the ability of each WIHIC scale to differentiate between students' perceptions of classroom psychosocial environments in different classes. These statistical analyses mainly involved the following procedures:

(1) The principal components factor analysis with varimax rotation using the individual student mean as the unit of analysis was undertaken to estimate the construct validity of both the student actual form and the student preferred form.

(2) The Cronbach's alpha coefficient (α) was calculated with three sets of means as the unit of analysis (i.e. the individual student mean, the class mean, and the individual instructor mean) and used as an index to estimate the internal consistency reliability of the modified WIHIC as a whole for its four forms (i.e. the

student actual form, the student preferred form, the instructor actual form, and the instructor preferred form) and the internal consistency reliability of each scale in the four forms.

(3) One-way analysis of variance (ANOVA) was performed using the class membership as the independent variable and each WIHIC scale as the dependent variable to explore the capability of each scale in the student actual form to differentiate the perceptions of students in different classes. The results of this analysis were reported in terms of the eta^2 statistic, which is the ratio of "between" to "total" sums of squares, to show the proportion of variance in scale scores explained by class membership.

The modified MTCCU was validated with samples in the present study by conducting statistical analyses to estimate the construct validity and the internal consistency reliability of the questionnaire, involving the following statistical procedures:

(1) The principal components factor analysis with oblimin rotation was performed to test the construct validity of the questionnaire.

(2) The Cronbach's alpha coefficient (α) was calculated and used as the index to estimate the internal consistency of each scale as well as the questionnaire as a whole.

3.7.2 Procedures for the revelation of CE classroom psychosocial environments

Four sets of data generated from students' and instructors' responses to the four forms of the modified WIHIC were analyzed through the following statistical procedures to reveal the psychosocial nature of CE classroom environments.

3.7.2.1 The status quo of CE classroom psychosocial environments

(1) To reveal the overall patterns of students' and instructors' perceptions and preferences of the six psychosocial environmental dimensions assessed in the modified WIHIC in their CE classroom environments, descriptive statistics were performed respectively on

the four sets of data collected by the four forms of the WIHIC, using the individual student mean and the individual instructor mean as the unit of analysis respectively, including average mean score, standard deviation, minimum, and maximum for each scale in the four forms. Considering the different numbers of items in each scale, the study calculated the average mean score of a scale by dividing the total score of a scale by the number of items in that scale.

(2) One-way repeated measures ANOVA was run on the data collected from each of the four WIHIC forms to examine the differences in perceptions of students as well as instructors towards the six environmental scales in their actual and preferred CE classroom psychosocial environments. When the results of repeated measures ANOVA showed that there was significant difference in perceptions of the six environmental scales, the Bonferroni post-hoc tests were run to further examine the specific differences in perceiving the six environmental scales among students as well as instructors.

3.7.2.2 Discrepancies in perceptions between students and instructors

The class mean of students and the mean of individual instructors were calculated and used as the unit of analysis in order to have an equal number of cases (4 sets of data with 40 mean scores for each set) in the statistical procedures for comparisons. The comparisons of perceptions were made between four paired groups, namely, student actual perceptions versus student preferred perceptions, instructor actual perceptions versus instructor preferred perceptions, student actual perceptions versus instructor actual perceptions, and student preferred perceptions versus instructor preferred perceptions.

The discrepancies in perceptions and preferences of classroom psychosocial environments between students and instructors were investigated at two levels: at the level of WIHIC environmental scale and at the level of the aspects within each scale.

(1) In order to reduce the Type I error rate associated with the

performance of multiple t-tests, the one-way multivariate analysis of variance (MANOVA) for repeated measures was employed to analyze the discrepancies between students' and instructors' actual and preferred perceptions of classroom psychosocial environments at the level of WIHIC scales. The one-way MANOVA for repeated measures was performed using the set of six WIHIC scales as the dependent variables and the form of the instrument as a four-level repeated measures factor. The magnitude of Wilks' lambda criterion was examined.

(2) When the MANOVA yielded a statistically significant result ($p<0.05$) in terms of Wilks' lambda criterion, post-hoc tests using the Bonferroni correction were run to compare perceptions in different forms of the same scale (i.e. student actual perceptions versus student preferred perceptions, instructor actual perceptions versus instructor preferred perceptions), and to compare perceptions between students and instructors on the same scale (i.e. student actual perceptions versus instructor actual perceptions, student preferred perceptions versus instructor preferred perceptions).

(3) As for the scales that were found to be perceived differently with statistical significance, t-tests for paired samples were performed on all the items within the scales to reveal more specific differences in perceptions and preferences of the environmental aspects within the scales between students and instructors.

3.7.2.3 Gender differences in student perceptions

To avoid the unequal number of male and female students in each class, within-class gender subgroup mean was used as the unit of analysis, which consists of 40 paired mean scores, including 40 male subgroup means and the corresponding 40 female subgroup means for each WIHIC scale. The comparisons of perceptions were made between two paired groups, namely, male student actual perceptions versus female student actual perceptions, and male student preferred perceptions versus female student preferred perceptions. Gender differences in perceptions of classroom psychosocial environments were also explored at two levels: at the level of WIHIC environmental scale and at the level of the aspects within each scale.

(1) The one-way MANOVA for repeated measures using the set of twelve WIHIC scales (six actual and six preferred) as the dependent variables and gender (male and female) as a two-level repeated measures factor was performed to examine the magnitude of Wilks' lambda criterion.

(2) When the MANOVA yielded a statistically significant result ($p<0.05$) in terms of Wilks' lambda criterion, Bonferroni post-hoc test was conducted for each WIHIC scale to compare the different perceptions between male and female students of the same scale (i.e. male student actual perceptions versus female student actual perceptions, and male student preferred perceptions versus female students preferred perceptions).

(3) For the scales that were found to be perceived differently with statistical significance, t-tests for paired samples were carried out on all the items within the scales to reveal more specific differences in perceptions and preferences of the aspects within the scales between male and female students.

3.7.2.4 Associations between classroom environment perceptions and motivation

(1) Descriptive statistics were performed on the data collected by the modified MTCCU including average mean score, standard deviation, minimum, and maximum for each type of motivation to examine the overall status of English learning motivation types of students in the study.

(2) The Canonical Correlation Analysis (CCA) was carried out to examine the associations between predictive variables of students' actual perceptions of the six psychosocial aspects of CE classroom environments and the criterion variables of seven motivation types, with the student individual mean as the unit of analysis. The CCA was chosen in the study in that it can provide a parsimonious picture of relationships between a set of correlated environment dimensions and a set of correlated motivation types by

limiting the probability of committing Type I error.

3.8 The pilot phase

The two instruments (i.e. the modified WIHIC and the modified MTCCU) used in this study have been field tested through three pilot studies. The first two pilot studies were small-scale informal interviews with six students in each study. Students with different English proficiency levels according to their final examination scores of the Comprehensive English course were chosen to complete the questionnaires and the subjects were interviewed afterwards to point out what was needed to be clarified or improved concerning the two questionnaires. After the first two pilot studies, the modified MTCCU remained unchanged, but the modified WIHIC was adapted further to suit the Chinese EFL context. The wording of Item 8 in "Teacher support" scale was revised in that some students in the first pilot study had difficulty in understanding the phrase "go out of one's way" in this item. Therefore, the wording of Item 8 was revised from "the teacher goes out of his/her way to help me" to "the teacher makes an extra effort to help me". Five foreign instructors from English speaking countries in the SIS were asked to identify the extent of similarity in meaning between the revised and the original sentences by choosing a number out of seven numbers ranging from "1" to "7" in a scale, in which "1" indicates being identical in meaning while "7" means being totally different in meaning. Among the five foreign instructors, one instructor chose number "1" and four instructors chose number "2" to indicate the extent of similarity in meaning between the two sentences. The survey results suggested that the modified Item 8 could replace the original one without affecting its original meaning.

After the revision, the two instruments were subjected to a larger scale formal pilot study with a random sample of 67 English majors from two first-year classes and one second-year class in the SIS. The Cronbach's alpha coefficients of the student actual form ($\alpha = 0.95$) and preferred form ($\alpha = 0.96$) calculated using the individual student as the unit of analysis and the Cronbach's alpha coefficient of the modified MTCCU ($\alpha=0.70$) showed that the two questionnaires had satisfactory internal consistency reliability. The construct validity of the two questionnaires was not analyzed in that the number of subjects was not large enough to conduct factor analysis which requires no less than 100 subjects involved according to Qin (2008).

3.9 Summary

This chapter has presented the research design and methodology of the study. The subjects involved in the study were 945 first-year English majors and second-year English majors enrolled in the course of Comprehensive English and 17 instructors of Comprehensive English in the SIS at SYSU. The instruments used in the survey included the modified WIHIC to assess students' and instructors' perceptions of their actual and preferred CE classroom psychosocial environments and the modified MTCCU to measure students' English learning motivation types. The two instruments were field tested in three pilot studies, and the results of the last pilot study have displayed the sound internal consistency reliability of the two revised questionnaires.

The data were collected in a large-scale survey carried out in class time for the student respondents and out of class time for the instructor respondents. Aiming to find out the answers to the research questions, the data were analyzed by SPSS 19.0 through major statistical procedures including factor analysis, reliability analysis, descriptive statistics, one-way repeated measures ANOVA, one-way repeated measures MANOVA, t-tests for paired samples, and CCA.

Chapter 4
Validity and Reliability of the Research Instruments

4.1 Introduction

As part of the main study, this chapter attests the validity and reliability of the two research instruments, i.e. the adapted "What Is Happening In this Class?" (WIHIC) and the modified Motivation Types of Chinese College Undergraduates (MTCCU), with the samples collected in the present study. The validation results of the two instruments are reported, discussed, and compared with those provided in previous studies respectively in Section 4.2 and Section 4.3 of this chapter.

4.2 Validity and reliability of the modified WIHIC

The student actual form and the student preferred form of the modified WIHIC were validated through statistical analyses on the construct validity, the internal consistency reliability, and the ability of each scale to differentiate the perceptions of students in different classes. The results of these statistical analyses were compared with those provided for the WIHIC by Aldridge et al. (1999) and the Chinese Language Classroom Environment Inventory (CLCEI) by Chua et al. (2006), which was adapted from the original WIHIC to the Singaporean context.

4.2.1 Construct validity of the modified WIHIC

The sampling adequacy and necessity for a factor analysis of both the actual form and the preferred form of the modified WIHIC were tested respectively by performing the tests of Kaiser-Meyer-Olkin (KMO) and Barlett's test of sphericity. Test results for the actual form (KMO =0.96; Approx. Chi-Square =21855.359, $p<0.001$) and for the preferred form (KMO =0.98; Approx. Chi-Square =34570.249, $p<0.001$) showed that the sample data in both forms were adequate for a factor analysis.

The principal components factor analysis with varimax rotation was performed for the sample data using individual student mean as the unit of analysis in the student actual form and the student preferred form respectively. Six factors were extracted from the factor analysis in each form. Most of the items in the student actual form and the student preferred form were loaded into the six *a priori* scales "student cohesiveness" (SC), "teacher support" (TS), "involvement" (IN), "task orientation" (TO), "cooperation" (CO), and "equity" (EQ). The six factors extracted in total accounted for 52.97% of the variance in the student actual form and 65.68% of the variance in the student preferred form. Table 4.1 lists the variance explained by each factor and the eigenvalue of each factor in the student actual form and the student preferred form. Table 4.1 also displays the factor loading of each scale in the student actual form and the student preferred form, in which factor loadings of less than 0.40 were disregarded.

Table 4.1 Factor loadings for student actual and preferred forms of the modified WIHIC

	SC		TS		IN		TO		CO		EQ	
	Act.	Prf.	Act.	Prf.	Act.	Prf.	Act.	Prf.	Act.	Prf.	Act.	Prf.
Q1	0.63	0.67										
Q7	0.59	0.68										
Q13	0.67	0.60										
Q19	0.63	0.65										
Q25	0.46	0.43										
Q37	0.52	0.48										
Q2			0.66	0.69								

Chapter 4 Validity and Reliability of the Research Instruments

Continued

	SC		TS		IN		TO		CO		EQ	
	Act.	Prf.	Act.	Prf.	Act.	Prf.	Act.	Prf.	Act.	Prf.	Act.	Prf.
Q8			0.68	0.74								
Q15			0.41	0.67								
Q21			0.42	0.57								
Q26			0.66	0.75								
Q27			0.59	0.65								
Q32			0.62	0.65								
Q38			0.67	0.75								
Q44			0.48	0.41								
Q45			0.57	0.64								
Q3					0.63	0.59						
Q9					0.64	0.55						
Q33					0.41	0.47						
Q4							0.56	0.57				
Q10							0.53	0.54				
Q16							0.62	0.70				
Q22							0.43	0.58				
Q28							0.72	0.71				
Q34							0.60	0.65				
Q40							0.51	0.58				
Q46							0.62	0.64				
Q5									0.54	0.58		
Q11									0.56	0.43		
Q17									0.44	0.55		
Q23									0.59	0.69		
Q29							0.43	0.49	0.49	0.51		

Continued

	SC		TS		IN		TO		CO		EQ	
	Act.	Prf.	Act.	Prf.	Act.	Prf.	Act.	Prf.	Act.	Prf.	Act.	Prf.
Q31									0.46	0.45		
Q35									0.65	0.70		
Q39			0.45	0.49					0.60	0.52		
Q41									0.64	0.67		
Q43									0.62	0.50		
Q47									0.66	0.64		
Q6											0.55	0.51
Q12											0.61	0.52
Q14			0.40	0.43							0.61	0.55
Q18											0.53	0.50
Q20			0.41	0.41							0.55	0.46
Q24											0.64	0.61
Q30											0.60	0.60
Q36											0.53	0.57
Q42											0.41	0.56
Q48											0.62	0.65
Variance /%	6.47	8.47	10.97	15.20	5.67	5.43	8.70	12.70	11.31	12.98	9.83	10.90
Eigen-value	3.11	4.06	5.27	7.30	2.72	2.61	4.18	6.10	5.43	6.23	4.72	5.23

Note: $N=945$.

Results of principal components factor analysis with varimax rotation listed in Table 4.1 above showed that 8 out of the 48 items in the actual form and the corresponding 8 items in the preferred form loaded into different scales from their *a priori* scales. Item 14 ("The teacher considers my feelings.") which was originally grouped into the scale of "teacher support" (TS) by Aldridge *et al.* (1999) loaded into the scale of "equity" (EQ) with factor loadings of 0.61 and 0.55 for the actual and preferred forms respectively. Item 15 ("The teacher asks me questions."), Item 21 ("My ideas and suggestions are used during classroom discussions."), Item 27 ("I ask the teacher questions.") and Item 45 ("I am asked to explain how I solve problems.") which were formerly clustered into the scale of "involvement" (IN) by Aldridge *et al.* (1999) loaded into the scale of "teacher support" (TS) with factor loadings of 0.41, 0.42, 0.59, 0.62, and 0.57 for the actual form and 0.67, 0.57, 0.65, and 0.64 for the preferred form respectively. Both Item 31 ("I help other class members who are having trouble with their work.") and Item 43 ("In this class, I get help from other students.") which were classified into the scale of "student cohesiveness" (SC) by Aldridge *et al.* (1999) currently loaded into the scale of "cooperation" (CO) with factor loadings of 0.46 and 0.62 for the actual form and 0.45 and 0.50 for the preferred form respectively. Item 39 ("Students discuss with me how to go about solving problems.") which was sorted into the scale of "involvement" (IN) by Aldridge *et al.* (1999) loaded into the scale of "cooperation" (CO) with factor loadings of 0.60 and 0.52 for the student actual form and the student preferred form respectively.

As shown in Table 4.1, most of the items in both the student actual form and the student preferred form had factor loadings greater than 0.40 on their factors and less than 0.40 on the other scales, with exceptions for four items in the student actual form and their corresponding items in the student preferred form. Item 29 ("I learn from other students in this class.") in "cooperation" (CO) scale also loaded in the scale of "task orientation" (TO) with factor loadings of 0.43 and 0.49 for the student actual form and the student preferred form respectively. Item 39 ("Students discuss with me how to go about solving problems.") in the scale of "cooperation" (CO) also loaded in the scale of "teacher support" (TS) with factor loadings of 0.45 and 0.49 for the student actual form and the student preferred form respectively. Item 14 ("The teacher considers my feelings.") in "equity" (EQ) scale also loaded in "teacher support" (TS) scale with factor loadings of 0.40 and 0.43 for the student actual form and the student preferred form respectively. Item 20 ("The teacher helps me when I have trouble with the work.") in "equity" (EQ) scale also loaded in the scale of "teacher support" (TS) with factor loadings of 0.41 and 0.41 for the student actual form and the student preferred form respectively.

In summary, in spite of the redistribution of eight items among some scales and the double-loading pattern of four items, the modified six-scale version of WIHIC was found to exhibit satisfactory factorial validity to assess the perceptions of English majors towards their actual and preferred English language classroom environments in the Chinese EFL context.

4.2.2 Reliability of the modified WIHIC

The Cronbach's alpha coefficient was used as the index of scale internal consistency reliability for the student forms with two units of analysis, the individual student mean and the class mean, and for the instructor forms with the individual instructor mean as the unit of analysis. The Cronbach's alpha coefficient of the student actual form was 0.96 with the individual student mean as the unit of analysis, and 0.97 with the class mean as the unit of analysis. The Cronbach's alpha coefficients of the student preferred form were both 0.98 with the individual student mean and the class mean as the unit of analysis. The Cronbach's alpha coefficients reached 0.94 for both the instructor actual form and the instructor preferred form with the individual instructor mean as the unit of analysis. These Cronbach's alpha coefficients suggested the sound internal consistency of the four modified WIHIC forms.

Table 4.2 presents the summary of the alpha reliability of each scale in the four forms of the modified WIHIC. The ability of each scale in the student actual form to differentiate the perceptions of students in different classes is also presented in Table 4.2. The values of the Cronbach's alpha reliability coefficients in Table 4.2 showed that each scale displayed satisfactory internal consistency, with either the individual student mean or the class mean as the unit of analysis.

For the student actual form, the Cronbach's alpha coefficients in Table 4.2 ranged from 0.79 to 0.88 when the individual student mean was used as the unit of analysis, and from 0.84 to 0.94 when the class mean was used as the unit of analysis. These statistics were similar in value to those reported previously for the WIHIC by Aldridge *et al.* (1999), which ranged from 0.81 to 0.93 in Australia and from 0.85 to 0.90 in Taiwan Province of China with the individual student mean as the unit of analysis, and ranged from 0.87 to 0.97 in Australia and from 0.90 to 0.96 in Taiwan Province with the class mean as the unit of analysis. Moreover, the Cronbach's alpha coefficients obtained were also similar to the statistics reported for the CLCEI in the Singaporean context by Chua *et al.*(2006), which ranged from 0.82 to 0.91 when the individual student mean was used as the unit of analysis, and ranged from 0.87 to 0.96 when the class mean was used as the unit of analysis.

For the student preferred form, the Cronbach's alpha coefficients in Table 4.2 ranged from 0.85 to 0.93 when the individual student mean was used as the unit of analysis, and from 0.87 to 0.95 when the class mean was used as the unit of analysis. The statistics of Cronbach's alpha coefficients obtained were also similar but a bit lower in value to those reported for the CLCEI in the Singaporean context by Chua *et al.* (2006), which ranged from 0.90 to 0.93 when the individual student mean was used as the unit of analysis, and ranged from 0.96 to 0.97 when the class mean was used as the unit of analysis.

For the instructor actual form and the instructor preferred form, the Cronbach's alpha coefficients in Table 4.2 ranged from 0.66 to 0.92 for the instructor actual form, and ranged from 0.54 to 0.90 for the instructor preferred form, when the individual instructor mean was used as the unit of analysis.

Table 4.2 Internal consistency reliability (Cronbach's alpha coefficient) and ability to differentiate between classes (ANOVA results) for the student actual form of the modified WIHIC

Environment Scale	Scale Items	Scale Description	Unit of Analysis	Alpha Reliability		ANOVA Results (Student actual)
				Actual	Preferred	Eta^2
Student cohesiveness (SC)	Q1, Q7, Q13, Q19, Q25, Q37	Extent to which students are familiar and friendly to each other.	Individual student	0.80	0.89	0.06^*
			Student class mean	0.84	0.92	
			Individual instructor	0.78	0.77	
Teacher support (TS)	Q2, Q8, Q15, Q21, Q26, Q27, Q32, Q38, Q44, Q45	Extent to which the teacher helps, befriends, trusts, interacts and show interest in students.	Individual student	0.88	0.92	0.18^{***}
			Student class mean	0.94	0.94	
			Individual instructor	0.75	0.71	
Involvement (IN)	Q3, Q9, Q33	Extent to which students participate and engage in class discussions.	Individual student	0.79	0.85	0.11^{***}
			Student class mean	0.92	0.87	
			Individual instructor	0.76	0.67	
Task orientation (TO)	Q4, Q10, Q16, Q22, Q28, Q34, Q40, Q46	Extent to which it is important to complete activities planned and to stay on the subject matter.	Individual student	0.81	0.91	0.09^{***}
			Student class mean	0.87	0.93	
			Individual instructor	0.66	0.54	

Continued

Environment Scale	Scale Items	Scale Description	Unit of Analysis	Alpha Reliability		ANOVA Results (Student actual)
				Actual	Preferred	Eta^2
Cooperation (CO)	Q5, Q11, Q17, Q23, Q29, Q31, Q35, Q39, Q41, Q43, Q47	Extent to which students cooperate and help rather than compete with one another on learning tasks.	Individual student	0.88	0.93	0.09***
			Student class mean	0.93	0.95	
			Individual instructor	0.92	0.90	
Equity (EQ)	Q6, Q12, Q14, Q18, Q20, Q24, Q30, Q36, Q42, Q48	Extent to which students are treated equally by the teacher.	Individual student	0.88	0.93	0.13***
			Student class mean	0.94	0.94	
			Individual instructor	0.88	0.86	

Note: $N=945$; * $p<0.05$; ** $p<0.01$; *** $p<0.001$.

The results of one-way ANOVA listed in the last column of Table 4.2 showed that each scale in the student actual form was able to differentiate significantly ($p<0.05$) the perceptions of students in different classes. The eta^2 statistic in Table 4.2 showed that the amount of variance explained by class membership ranged from 0.06 to 0.18 for the student actual form. The values of eta^2 statistic obtained for the present study were close to those reported by Aldridge *et al.* (1999) ranging from 0.07 to 0.15 in Australia and from 0.07 to 0.36 in Taiwan Province of China, and those provided by Chua *et al.* (2006) for the CLCEI ranging from 0.08 to 0.13. Furthermore, the low eta^2 values in Table 4.2 indicated the similarity of classroom learning environments among the 40 different classes in the present study. In summary, students within the same class perceived the classroom psychosocial environments similarly, while students from different classes varied significantly ($p < 0.05$) in their perceptions of the classroom psychosocial environments.

4.3 Validity and reliability of the modified MTCCU

In line with the research tradition in this field, the modified MTCCU was also validated through statistical analyses on the construct validity and the internal consistency reliability. The results of these statistical analyses were compared with those reported for the original MTCCU by Gao *et al.* (2003).

4.3.1 Construct validity of the modified MTCCU

The results of sampling adequacy (KMO =0.86) and Bartlett's test of sphericity (Approx. Chi-Square = 8549.007, $p < 0.001$) indicated that the sample data could be processed through a factor analysis. The principal components factor analysis with direct oblimin rotation was undertaken and seven factors were extracted which explained 57.85% of the total variance. The factor loadings with direct oblimin rotation for the seven factors extracted are presented in Table 4.3, in which factor loadings with values less

Chapter 4 Validity and Reliability of the Research Instruments

than 0.40 were suppressed. The variance accounted by each factor and the eigenvalue of each factor are also listed at the end of Table 4.3.

Table 4.3 Factor loadings for seven factors of the modified MTCCU

	II	IA	LS	GA	SR	ID	IM
Q1	0.71						
Q17	0.56						
Q18	0.81						
Q19	0.67						
Q20	0.72						
Q22	0.54						
Q2		0.62					
Q3		0.77					
Q4		0.64					
Q6		0.47					
Q11		0.54					
Q5			−0.66				
Q7			−0.79				
Q8			−0.78				
Q9			−0.71				
Q10			−0.70				
Q25				−0.80			
Q26				−0.76			−0.42
Q27				−0.76			
Q21					0.80		
Q23					0.87		
Q24					0.54		
Q12						0.75	

Continued

	II	IA	LS	GA	SR	ID	IM
Q13						0.57	
Q15						0.73	
Q28						0.74	
Q29						-0.62	
Q14							-0.60
Q16							-0.66
Variance / %	19.99	3.66	11.83	5.25	4.73	7.99	4.41
Eigenvalue	5.80	1.06	3.43	1.52	1.37	2.32	1.28

Note: N=945.

With reference to the results of factor analysis on MTCCU reported by Gao et al. (2003), it could be observed in Table 4.3 that the factor structure of seven scales replicated the modified MTCCU. Besides, it was shown in Table 4.3 that Item 26 ("I learn English so that I can go abroad to experience English-speaking cultures.") was loaded in the "Going abroad" (GA) and "Information medium" (IM) scales with factor loadings of -0.76 and -0.42 respectively. In spite of the double-loading pattern of Item 26 on two different scales, it was grouped into its *a priori* scale since its factor loading on its *a priori* scales was greater than that on the other scale. On the whole, the results listed in Table 4.3 provided support for the construct validity of the modified MTCCU.

4.3.2 *Reliability of the modified MTCCU*

The value of the Cronbach's alpha coefficient of the modified MTCCU as a whole was found to be 0.81, which is even greater than that of 0.77 for the original MTCCU reported by Gao et al. (2003). The Cronbach's alpha coefficient of each scale in the modified MTCCU is shown in Table 4.4.

Table 4.4 showed that the values of the Cronbach's alpha

coefficients obtained for the seven scales ranged from 0.58 for "Information medium" to 0.79 for "Learning situation". These results suggested that each scale had adequate internal consistency in the modified MTCCU.

Table 4.4 Internal consistency reliability (Cronbach's alpha coefficient) for the modified MTCCU

Scale name	Scale items	Alpha coefficient
Intrinsic interest (II)	Q1, Q17, Q18, Q19, Q20, Q22	0.78
Immediate achievement (IA)	Q2, Q3, Q4, Q6, Q11	0.63
Learning situation (LS)	Q5, Q7, Q8, Q9, Q10	0.79
Going abroad (GA)	Q25, Q26, Q27	0.72
Social responsibility (SR)	Q21, Q23, Q24	0.66
Individual development (ID)	Q12, Q13, Q15, Q28, Q29	0.74
Information medium (IM)	Q14, Q16	0.58

Note: $N=945$.

4.4 Summary

This chapter has reported the validation of the two research instruments used in the present study. In Section 4.2, the WIHIC, in its modified form, was validated for use with the samples in terms of the construct validity, the internal consistency reliability, and the ability to differentiate the perceptions of students in different classrooms. The results of the validation of the modified WIHIC used in college English language classrooms in mainland China were similar to those reported in previous research in science classes in both Australia and Taiwan Province of China by Aldridge et al.(1999) and in the Chinese language classes in Singapore by Chua et al.(2006). These results have shown the sound psychometric feature of the modified WIHIC. In addition, the slightly modified version of MTCCU, which was validated in Section 4.3, has also demonstrated satisfactory internal consistency and strong factorial validity.

Chapter 5
The Status Quo of CE Classroom Psychosocial Environments

5.1 Introduction

This chapter aims to describe the typical Comprehensive English (CE) classroom psychosocial environments in terms of the six environmental dimensions assessed in the modified "What Is Happening In this Class?" (WIHIC). The CE classroom psychosocial environments as perceived and preferred by students and instructors are profiled using the descriptive statistics of data generated from students' and instructors' responses to the four forms of the modified WIHIC, followed by the further characterization by examining the specific differences in perceptions of the six environmental dimensions among students as well as instructors. Section 5.2 presents the actual and preferred CE classroom psychosocial environments as perceived by students and Section 5.3 describes the CE classroom psychosocial environments as perceived and preferred by instructors.

In Section 5.2 and Section 5.3, the classroom psychosocial environment perceptions of students and instructors are featured with reference to the categories marked by Oxford and Burry-Stock (1995) in a five Likert scale (summative rating scale) of frequency-of-strategy-use, with responses for each strategy ranging from "never or almost never true of me", "generally not true of me", "somewhat true of me", "generally true of me", to "always or almost always true of me". In the present study, scale averages of 3.50–5.00 are considered as high level of perception indicating favorable perceptions of the environment; scale averages of 2.50–3.49 are regarded as medium level of perception suggesting positive but moderate perceptions of the environment; and scale averages of 1.00 – 2.49 are designated as low level of perception exhibiting negative perceptions of the environment.

5.2 CE classroom psychosocial environments perceived by students

This section depicted the CE classroom psychosocial environments as perceived and preferred by students. The overall patterns of students' perceptions of the actual and preferred CE classroom psychosocial environments were revealed and graphically presented, followed by the examination of differences in their perceptions of the six WIHIC environmental scales in the existing and ideal classroom psychosocial environments respectively.

5.2.1 *Actual CE classroom psychosocial environments perceived by students*

Descriptive statistics were performed on the data collected by the student actual form of the modified WIHIC, using the individual student mean as the unit of analysis, including average mean score, standard deviation (SD), minimum (Min.), and maximum (Max.) for each WIHIC scale displayed in Table 5.1.

Table 5.1 Descriptive statistics for actual perceptions of students

Scale	No. of items	Mean	SD	Min.	Max.
SC	6	4.20	0.56	1.83	5.00
TS	10	3.19	0.67	1.00	5.00
IN	3	3.42	0.74	1.00	5.00
TO	8	3.73	0.59	1.50	5.00
CO	11	3.64	0.60	1.27	5.00
EQ	10	3.82	0.65	1.50	5.00

Note: N=945; "Almost never" =1; "Seldom" =2; "Sometimes" =3; "Often" =4; "Almost always" =5.

Figure 5.1 below provides a graphical representation of the status quo of students' actual perceptions of the six environmental scales based on the mean scores listed in Table 5.1. As shown in Figure 5.1, students' perceptions of "Student cohesiveness" (SC), "Equity" (EQ), "Task orientation" (TO), and "Cooperation" (CO) achieved the high level of perception since the mean scores of these scales fell within the range of 3.50–5.00. Students' perceptions of the other two scales, "Involvement" (IN) and "Teacher support" (TS), reached the medium level of perception as their mean scores fell within the range of 3.00–3.49. Therefore, the status quo of the actual CE classroom psychosocial environments perceived by students reflected in Figure 5.1 was featured in the way that students were favorably experiencing friendly and cooperative relationships among class members, and they received fair treatment by their instructors. They approved of their own performance of completing activities planned, working persistently, and staying on the subject matter in class. Students were also experiencing a positive but moderate degree of participation in class activities as well as support provided by instructors.

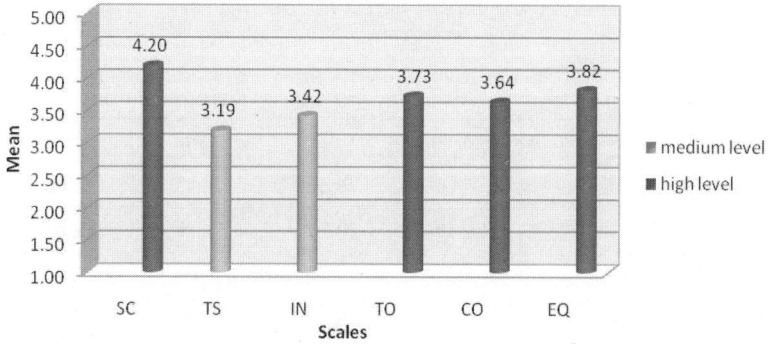

Figure 5.1 Students' perceptions of the actual CE classroom environments

In addition, the standard deviation (SD) for "Involvement" scale shown in Table 5.1 was relatively higher than the other scales, suggesting that there was a greater variance among students' perceptions of their involvement in class, while the SD for "Student cohesiveness" was relatively lower than the other scales, indicating that students were in greater agreement on the presence of a strong and favorable friendship among class members.

The specific differences in students' actual perceptions of the six environmental scales were examined by one-way repeated measures analysis of variance (ANOVA). The Mauchly's Test of Sphericity indicated that the assumption of sphericity was violated ($W = 0.678$, $p < 0.001$), therefore degrees of freedom were corrected using Greenhouse-Geisser estimates of sphericity. Results in Table 5.2 showed that there was a significant difference at $p < 0.001$ in students' perceptions of the six environmental dimensions.

Table 5.2 Tests of within-subjects effects for actual perceptions of students

Source		Type III Sum of Squares	df	Mean Square	F	Sig.
Perception	Sphericity Assumed	571.996	5	114.399	673.888	.000
	Greenhouse-Geisser	571.996	4.302	132.952	673.888	.000
	Huynh-Feldt	571.996	4.324	132.271	673.888	.000
	Lower-Bound	571.996	1.000	571.996	673.888	.000
Error (Perception)	Sphericity Assumed	801.267	4720	.170		
	Greenhouse-Geisser	801.267	4061.341	.197		
	Huynh-Feldt	801.267	4082.248	.196		
	Lower-Bound	801.267	944.000	.849		

The results of post-hoc comparisons with Bonferroni correction displayed in Table 5.3 below revealed the specific differences in perceptions of the six scales among students. The results indicated that students' perceptions of the six scales were significantly different from each other at $p < 0.001$. The mean scores listed in Table 5.3 suggested the rank of students' perceptions of the six scales in terms of favorability: from the most favorably perceived "Student cohesiveness" ($M = 4.20$, SD $= 0.56$), followed by "Equity" ($M = 3.82$, SD $= 0.65$), "Task orientation" ($M = 3.73$,

SD = 0.59), "Cooperation" (M = 3.64, SD = 0.60), "Involvement" (M = 3.42, SD = 0.74), to the least favorably perceived "Teacher support" (M = 3.19, SD = 0.67).

Table 5.3 Post-hoc tests of students' actual perceptions of the six WIHIC scales

(I) perception	(J) perception	Mean Difference (I-J)	Std. Error	Sig.	95% Confidence Interval for Difference	
					Lower Bound	Upper Bound
SC	TS	1.011***	.021	.000	.948	1.074
	IN	.789***	.022	.000	.724	.855
	TO	.476***	.018	.000	.422	.530
	CO	.565***	.016	.000	.518	.611
	EQ	.382***	.018	.000	.329	.436
TS	IN	-.222***	.019	.000	-.276	-.167
	TO	-.535***	.020	.000	-.594	-.477
	CO	-.446***	.018	.000	-.500	-.393
	EQ	-.629***	.016	.000	-.675	-.583
IN	TO	-.314***	.022	.000	-.379	-.249
	CO	-.225***	.020	.000	-.284	-.166
	EQ	-.407***	.020	.000	-.465	-.349
TO	CO	.089***	.017	.000	.039	.139
	EQ	-.093***	.018	.000	-.148	-.039
CO	EQ	-.182***	.018	.000	-.234	-.131

Note: N=945; *** p<0.001.

A noteworthy feature exhibited about the existing CE classroom psychosocial environments is that students had the most favorable experiences of peer relations, which was in distinctive contrast with the least favorable, though positive, experiences of student-teacher interactions. One of the possible reasons is that students had more time and opportunities to get familiar and to establish cohesive ties among themselves both in class and after class. It was observed by the researcher that in the CE classrooms, more time were available for students to discuss and communicate with their classmates than with their instructors. After class, the contact among students was prolonged as most of them lived on the same campus, however, their interactions with the instructors were nearly confined to the limited class hours. Therefore, it is more likely that students would build and experience more favorable interpersonal relations with their classmates than with their instructors.

5.2.2 Preferred CE classroom psychosocial environments perceived by students

To reveal the status quo of the CE classroom psychosocial environments preferred by students with respect to the six environmental scales, descriptive statistics were performed on the data collected by the student preferred form of the modified WIHIC, using individual student mean as the unit of analysis, including average mean score, standard deviation (SD), minimum (Min.), and maximum (Max.) for each scale listed in Table 5.4.

Table 5.4 Descriptive statistics for preferred perceptions of students

Scale	No. of items	Mean	SD	Min.	Max.
SC	6	4.51	0.57	1.83	5.00
TS	10	4.00	0.70	1.80	5.00
IN	3	4.19	0.72	1.00	5.00
TO	8	4.43	0.58	1.88	5.00
CO	11	4.31	0.61	2.00	5.00
EQ	10	4.37	0.60	1.80	5.00

Note: $N=945$; "Almost never" =1; "Seldom" =2; "Sometimes" =3; "Often" =4; "Almost always" =5.

Based on the mean scores listed in Table 5.4, Figure 5.2 graphically represents the preferences of students for the six environmental scales.

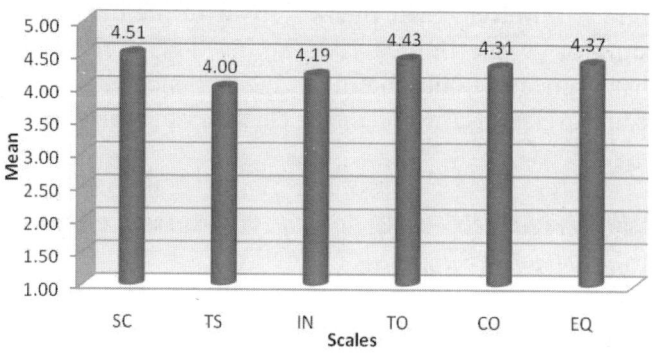

Figure 5.2　Students' perceptions of the preferred CE classroom environments

As shown in Figure 5.2, all the mean scores of the six scales reached the high level of perception (3.50 – 5.00), suggesting students' preferences for the high-frequency-occurrence of teaching and learning practices related to all the six environmental dimensions in an ideal CE classroom psychosocial environment. In addition, the SD for the "Involvement" scale was relatively higher than the other scales, indicating that students differed more in their expectations for the engagement in class discussions, while the SD for the "Student cohesiveness" scale was relatively lower than the other scales, suggesting that students were more consistent in their preferences for a harmonious interpersonal relationship with classmates.

One-way repeated measures ANOVA was also used to test the specific differences in students' preferences for the six environmental scales in the ideal CE classroom environments. The Mauchly's Test of Sphericity showed that the assumption of shpericity was violated ($M = 0.53$, $p < 0.001$), and degrees of freedom were corrected using Greenhouse-Geisser estimates of sphericity. The results in Table 5.5 showed that there was a significant difference $[F(3.869, 3652.657) = 294.995]$ at $p <$

0.001 in students' preferred perceptions of the six environmental dimensions.

Table 5.5 Tests of within-subjects effects for preferred perceptions of students

Source		Type III Sum of Squares	df	Mean Square	F	Sig.
Perception	Sphericity Assumed	160.628	5	32.126	294.995	.000
	Greenhouse-Geisser	160.628	3.869	41.513	294.995	.000
	Huynh-Feldt	160.628	3.887	41.322	294.995	.000
	Lower-Bound	160.628	1.000	160.628	294.995	.000
Error (Perception)	Sphericity Assumed	514.018	4720	.109		
	Greenhouse-Geisser	514.018	3652.657	.141		
	Huynh-Feldt	514.018	3669.567	.140		
	Lower-Bound	514.018	944.000	.545		

The differences in students' preferences for the six scales were further tested by post-hoc pair-wise comparisons with Bonferroni correction. Test results listed in Table 5.6 together with the descriptive statistics shown in Table 5.4 indicated that "Student cohesiveness" ($M = 4.51$, $SD = 0.57$) was most favored by students, followed by "Task orientation" ($M = 4.43$, $SD = 0.58$), "Equity" ($M = 4.37$, $SD = 0.60$), "Cooperation" ($M = 4.31$, $SD = 0.61$), "Involvement" ($M = 4.19$, $SD = 0.72$), and "Teacher support" ($M = 4.00$, $SD = 0.70$) which was relatively least emphasized by students in the ideal CE classrooms.

Table 5.6 Post-hoc tests of students' preferred perceptions of the six WIHIC scales

(I) Perception	(J) Perception	Mean Difference (I-J)	Std. Error	Sig.	95% Confidence Interval for Difference	
					Lower Bound	Upper Bound
SC	TS	.513***	.019	.000	.457	.570
	IN	.324***	.019	.000	.268	.379

Continued

(I) Perception	(J) Perception	Mean Difference (I-J)	Std. Error	Sig.	95% Confidence Interval for Difference	
					Lower Bound	Upper Bound
SC	TS	.083***	.013	.000	.046	.121
	CO	.206***	.013	.000	.168	.243
	EQ	.140***	.013	.000	.102	.177
TS	IN	-.190***	.016	.000	-.237	-.142
	TO	-.430***	.017	.000	-.480	-.380
	CO	-.308***	.015	.000	-.352	-.263
	EQ	-.374***	.015	.000	-.418	-.329
IN	TO	-.240***	.017	.000	-.290	-.190
	CO	-.118***	.015	.000	-.163	-.073
	EQ	-.184***	.016	.000	-.231	-.136
TO	CO	.122***	.013	.000	.084	.161
	EQ	.056***	.012	.000	.020	.092
CO	EQ	-.066***	.012	.000	-.101	-.031

Note: $N=945$; *** $p<0.001$.

It was noteworthy that students placed higher priority on establishing group cohesiveness than receiving the personal and academic support from their instructors. Moreover, as indicated by the SDs for the two scales, students were in greater agreement with each other on their expectations of "Student cohesiveness", while they held more divergent opinions on their preferences for "Teacher support". The frequencies of students' responses to "Student cohesiveness" and "Teacher support" scales were further inspected and the results were represented graphically in Figure 5.3 and Figure 5.4 respectively.

Chapter 5 The Status Quo of CE Classroom Psychosocial Environments

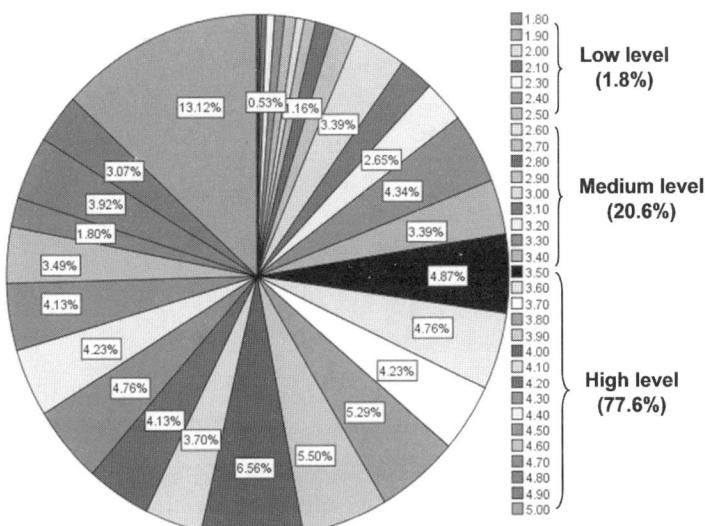

Figure 5.3 Frequency of students' responses to TS in the preferred CE classroom environment

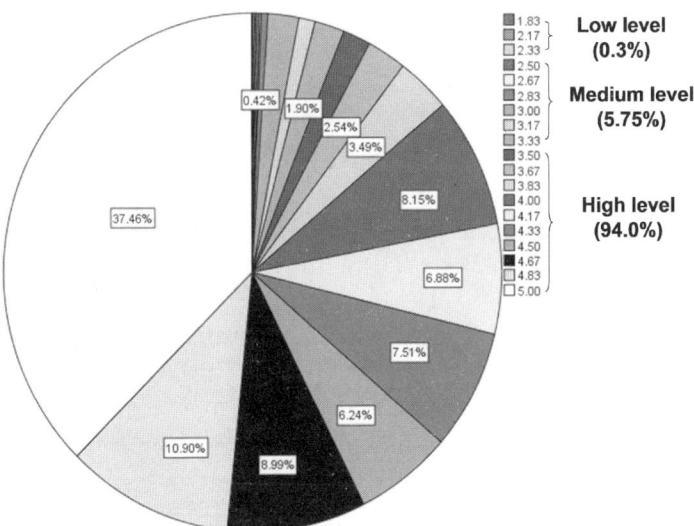

Figure 5.4 Frequency of students' responses to SC in the preferred CE classroom environment

As reflected in Figure 5.3 and Figure 5.4, 94.0% of the students held a high level of perception towards "Student cohesiveness" compared with 77.6% of the students towards "Teacher support". Furthermore, 37.5% of the students would expect the "almost always" occurrence of practices associated with "Student cohesiveness" as indicated by the choice of "5", in contrast with 13.1% of the students for "Teacher support". This reflects the more consistent needs of students for a harmonious and friendly peer relationship than the support of their instructors.

In addition, Figure 5.3 and Figure 5.4 also illustrate the greater variation existing among students' expectations of the student-instructor interactions than those of the peer friendships. Therefore, it is concluded that students have different needs for the concern, care, and support of their instructors, which should be considered by educators when they endeavor to create an enabling and supportive classroom psychosocial environment.

5.3 CE classroom psychosocial environments perceived by instructors

This section examines the features of CE classroom psychosocial environments as perceived and preferred by instructors. The profiles of instructors' actual perceptions and preferences of the CE classroom environments are presented and the characteristics of instructors' perceptions towards the six environmental dimensions measured in the modified WIHIC are analyzed and discussed.

5.3.1 Actual CE classroom psychosocial environments perceived by instructors

To study the characteristics of instructors' perceptions of the actual CE classroom psychosocial environments in terms of the six environmental dimensions, descriptive statistics were performed on the data collected by the instructor actual form of the modified WIIHIC, using the individual instructor mean as the unit of

Chapter 5 The Status Quo of CE Classroom Psychosocial Environments

analysis, including average mean score, standard deviation (SD), minimum (Min.), and maximum (Max.) for each scale listed in Table 5.7.

Table 5.7 Descriptive statistics for actual perceptions of instructors

Scale	No. of items	Mean	SD	Min.	Max.
SC	6	4.25	0.47	3.17	5.00
TS	10	4.22	0.41	3.20	5.00
IN	3	3.98	0.65	2.33	5.00
TO	8	3.98	0.35	3.13	4.50
CO	11	3.72	0.53	2.82	4.82
EQ	10	4.09	0.60	2.40	4.90

Note: $N=40$; "Almost never" =1; "Seldom" =2; "Sometimes" =3; "Often" =4; "Almost always" =5.

Instructors' perceptions of the six environmental scales in the actual CE classroom environments are represented in Figure 5.5 based on the descriptive statistics listed in Table 5.7.

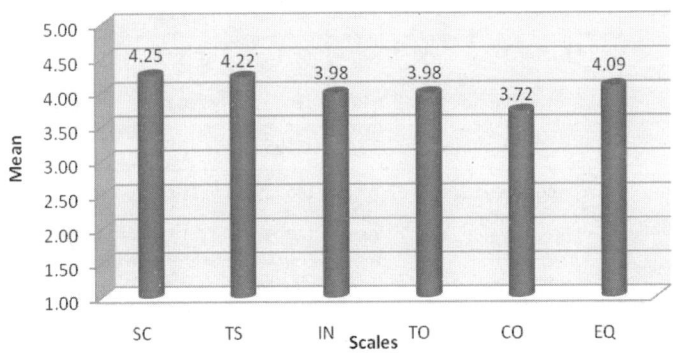

Figure 5.5 Instructors' perceptions of the actual CE classroom environments

As shown in Figure 5.5, the mean scores of the six scales fall within the range of 3.50 – 5.00, indicating a high level of perception for instructors towards all the six environmental dimensions. In other words, instructors were experiencing a favorable CE classroom psychosocial environment characterized with friendly and cooperative peer relationships among task-oriented students who were rather active in class participation, effective and supportive student-instructor interactions, and adequate opportunities for students to be equally treated by their instructors.

The differences in instructors' perceptions of the six environmental scales were further examined by the one-way repeated measures ANOVA test. The initially test of sphericity result showed that the assumption of sphericity was violated ($W = 0.386$, $p<0.01$), therefore degrees of freedom were corrected using Greenhouse-Geisser estimates of sphericity. The results in Table 5.8 show that there was a substantial difference [$F(3.725, 145.293) = 10.763$, $p < 0.001$] in perceptions of the six environmental dimensions among instructors.

Table 5.8　Tests of within-subjects effects for actual perceptions of instructors

Source		Type III Sum of Squares	df	Mean Square	F	Sig.
Perception	Sphericity Assumed	7.640	5	1.528	10.763	.000
	Greenhouse-Geisser	7.640	3.725	2.051	10.763	.000
	Huynh-Feldt	7.640	4.168	1.833	10.763	.000
	Lower-Bound	7.640	1.000	7.640	10.763	.002
Error (Perception)	Sphericity Assumed	27.684	195	.142		
	Greenhouse-Geisser	27.684	145.293	.191		
	Huynh-Feldt	27.684	162.546	.170		
	Lower-Bound	27.684	39.000	.710		

Results of post-hoc pair-wise comparisons with Bonferroni correction among the perceptions of the six scales are presented in Table 5.9. It is shown that there was no substantial difference among instructors' perceptions of "Student cohesiveness", "Teacher support", and "Equity", while "Student cohesiveness" was perceived more favorably than the other three environmental scales, namely, "Involvement", "Task Orientation", and

"Cooperation". "Teacher support" was perceived similarly with "Involvement", but more positively than the scales of "Task orientation", "Cooperation", and "Equity". "Involvement" was found to be perceived similarly with "Task orientation", "Cooperation", and "Equity". There was no significant difference in instructors' perceptions of "Task orientation" and "Equity", but "Task orientation" was perceived more favorably than "Cooperation" which was in turn perceived less favorably than "Equity".

Table 5.9 Post-hoc tests of instructors' actual perceptions of the six WIHIC scales

(I) perception	(J) perception	Mean Difference (I-J)	Std. Error	Sig.	95% Confidence Interval for Difference	
					Lower Bound	Upper Bound
SC	TS	.037	.074	1.000	-.194	.268
	IN	.279*	.079	.017	.031	.528
	TO	.276*	.075	.010	.042	.510
	CO	.536***	.075	.000	.302	.770
	EQ	.169	.093	1.000	-.121	.459
TS	IN	.242	.100	.299	-.070	.555
	TO	.239**	.057	.002	.062	.417
	CO	.499***	.063	.000	.304	.695
	EQ	.133	.086	1.000	-.137	.402
IN	TO	-.003	.107	1.000	-.338	.332
	CO	.257	.083	.057	-.004	.518
	EQ	-.110	.106	1.000	-.440	.220
TO	CO	.260*	.082	.043	.004	.515
	EQ	-.107	.085	1.000	-.373	.159
CO	EQ	-.367**	.083	.001	-.626	-.108

Note: $^*p<0.05$; $^{**}p<0.01$; $^{***}p<0.001$.

In summary, "student cohesiveness" was perceived similarly with "Teacher support" and "Equity" but more favorably in comparisons with the other three scales, while "Cooperation" was perceived relatively least favorably among all the six scales in the actual CE classroom psychosocial environments. Furthermore, "Student cohesiveness" was found to be consistently perceived by students and instructors as the most favorable psychosocial aspect in the actual CE classroom psychosocial environments.

In addition, an inspection on the values of SD listed in Table 5.7 revealed that in the actual CE classrooms, instructors agreed more on their perceptions of "Task orientation" than the other scales as suggested by the lowest value of SD, while they differed more in their perceptions of "Involvement" than the other scales as indicated by the highest value of SD.

5.3.2 Preferred CE classroom psychosocial environments perceived by instructors

To investigate the features of the classroom psychosocial environments as ideally perceived by instructors, descriptive statistics were performed on the data collected by the instructor preferred form of the modified WIHIC, using individual instructor mean as the unit of analysis, including average mean score, standard deviation (SD), minimum (Min.), and maximum (Max.) for each scale displayed in Table 5.10. Based on the statistics listed in Table 5.10, the profile of instructors' preferred perceptions of the six scales is depicted in Figure 5.6.

Table 5.10 Descriptive statistics for preferred perceptions of instructors

Scale	No. of items	Mean	SD	Min.	Max.
SC	6	4.83	0.25	4.00	5.00
TS	10	4.62	0.36	3.90	5.00
IN	3	4.83	0.30	4.00	5.00
TO	8	4.88	0.16	4.25	5.00
CO	11	4.73	0.35	4.00	5.00
EQ	10	4.58	0.43	3.70	5.00

Note: $N=40$; "almost never" =1; "seldom" =2; "sometimes" =3; "often" =4; "almost always" =5.

Chapter 5 The Status Quo of CE Classroom Psychosocial Environments

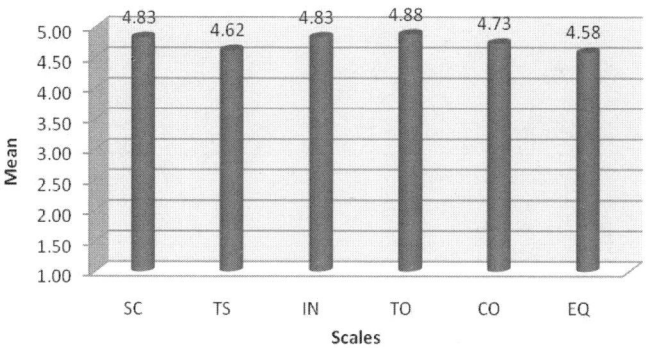

Figure 5.6 Instructors' perceptions of the preferred CE classroom environments

It is distinctively noticed in Figure 5.6 that all the mean scores of the six scales were quite high ranging from 4.58 to 4.88, and all of them naturally reached the high level of perception which reflected the high expectations of instructors for a frequent occurrence of the teaching and learning practices related to the six environmental scales in the CE classroom psychosocial environments.

One-way repeated measures ANOVA was run to test the differences in preferences of instructors for the six environmental scales. The result of Mauchly's Test of Sphericity showed that the assumption of shpericity was violated (M=0.055, p<0.001), and degrees of freedom were corrected using Greenhouse-Geisser estimates of sphericity. The results in Table 5.11 show that there was a significant difference [F (2.667, 104.006) =13.282] at p< 0.001 in instructors' preferences for the six environmental dimensions.

Table 5.11 Tests of within-subjects effects for preferred perceptions of instructors

	Source	Type III Sum of Squares	df	Mean Square	F	Sig.
Perception	Sphericity Assumed	3.141	5	.628	13.282	.000
	Greenhouse-Geisser	3.141	2.667	1.178	13.282	.000
	Huynh-Feldt	3.141	2.881	1.090	13.282	.000
	Lower-Bound	3.141	1.000	3.141	13.282	.001

Continued

Source		Type III Sum of Squares	df	Mean Square	F	Sig.
Error (Perception)	Sphericity Assumed	9.224	195	.047		
	Greenhouse-Geisser	9.224	104.006	.089		
	Huynh-Feldt	9.224	112.355	.082		
	Lower-Bound	9.224	39.000	.237		

Table 5.12 lists the results of post-hoc pair-wise comparisons with Bonferroni correction of instructors' preferred perceptions of the six environmental scales. Results in Table 5.12 show that there was no substantial difference in instructors' preferences for "Student cohesiveness" and those for "Involvement", "Task orientation", and "Cooperation" respectively, but "Student cohesiveness" was perceived more favorably than "Teacher support" and "Equity" respectively.

Table 5.12　Post-hoc tests of instructors' preferred perceptions of the six WIHIC scales

(I) perception	(J) perception	Mean Difference (I−J)	Std. Error	Sig.	95% Confidence Interval for Difference	
					Lower Bound	Upper Bound
SC	TS	.218**	.047	.001	.072	.365
	IN	.000	.028	1.000	−.088	.088
	TO	−.048	.023	.607	−.119	.023
	CO	.104	.041	.234	−.025	.232
	EQ	.253**	.066	.006	.048	.458
TS	IN	−.218**	.047	.001	−.366	−.071
	TO	−.266***	.048	.000	−.416	−.117
	CO	−.115*	.032	.012	−.213	−.016
	EQ	.035	.059	1.000	−.148	.218

Chapter 5   The Status Quo of CE Classroom Psychosocial Environments

Continued

(I) perception	(J) perception	Mean Difference (I-J)	Std. Error	Sig.	95% Confidence Interval for Difference	
					Lower Bound	Upper Bound
IN	TO	-.048	.040	1.000	-.174	.078
	CO	.104*	.033	.042	.002	.205
	EQ	.253*	.071	.015	.031	.476
TO	CO	.152*	.046	.028	.009	.294
	EQ	.301***	.059	.000	.117	.485
CO	EQ	.150	.061	.294	-.042	.342

Note: *$p<0.05$; **$p<0.01$; ***$p<0.001$.

"Teacher support" was perceived similarly with "Equity", but less favorably than "Involvement", "Task orientation", and "Cooperation" respectively. As for the scale of "Involvement", it was perceived similarly with "Task orientation", but more favorably than "Cooperation" and "Equity". "Task orientation" was perceived more favorably than "Cooperation" and "Equity" respectively. Between "Cooperation" and "Equity", "Cooperation" was perceived more favorably than "Equity".

In summary, the scales of "Student cohesiveness", "Involvement", and "Task orientation" were more emphasized by instructors than the other scales, while the scales of "Teacher support" and "Equity" were relatively less valued, though favored, than the other scales.

Instructors' preferred or ideal perceptions of the environmental scales reflected their expectations and emphasis on the teaching and learning practices associated with the corresponding scales. It is interesting to notice that instructors addressed more emphasis on cohesive relationships, class engagement and sense of task orientation of students than the support and equal treatment provided by the instructors themselves. Furthermore, the lowest SD value for "Task orientation" shown in Table 5.10 indicates that instructors were most consistent in their expectations of a highly task-oriented classroom environment, while the highest SD value for "Equity" suggests the greatest variation among instructors' stress on the equal treatment of students.

5.4 Summary

This chapter has examined and depicted the characteristics of the CE classroom psychosocial environments in terms of how the classroom environments were perceived and preferred by students and instructors. Section 5.2 has figured out the status quo of the CE classroom psychosocial environments experienced and expected by students based on the descriptive statistics performed on the data collected by both the student actual form and the student preferred form of the modified WIHIC. The results revealed that students generally experienced favorable "Student cohesiveness", "Task orientation", "Cooperation", and "Equity", as well as positive but moderate "Teacher support" and "Involvement". However, students would expect a high level of perception towards all the six psychosocial environmental dimensions. The CE classroom psychosocial environments were further characterized by the differences in students' perceptions as well as preferences among the six WIHIC environmental scales through one-way repeated measures ANOVA tests. Results showed that students perceived the six environmental aspects with substantial differences and they had different expectations for the six environmental aspects. Section 5.3 has reported the status quo and characteristics of the actual and preferred CE classroom psychosocial environments as perceived by instructors. Results showed that instructors experienced a favorable CE classroom psychosocial environment since their actual perceptions of all the six environmental scales have reached the high level of perception; furthermore, they would prefer a high level of perception towards all the six environmental scales in the ideal classroom environments. The differences in instructors' perceptions as well as preferences among the six WIHIC environmental scales were examined through one-way repeated measures ANOVA test. Results showed that instructors perceived the six environmental dimensions with substantial differences and they laid different stresses on the six environmental dimensions.

Chapter 6
Discrepancies in Classroom Psychosocial Environment Perceptions

6.1 Introduction

This chapter, consisting of seven sections, is devoted to the exhibition of the nature of Comprehensive English (CE) classroom psychosocial environments by examining the discrepancies in students' and instructors' actual and preferred perceptions of their CE classroom psychosocial environments. The general patterns of differences in the actual and preferred perceptions between students and instructors are examined initially in Section 6.2, followed by close inspection on the differences between students' actual and preferred perceptions in Section 6.3, differences between instructors' actual and preferred perceptions in Section 6.4, differences in the actual perceptions between students and instructors in Section 6.5, and differences in the preferred perceptions between students and instructors in Section 6.6. In an attempt to make an exhaustive analysis and to access an in-depth understanding, differences in perceptions are analyzed and interpreted in comparisons both at the level of "What Is Happening In this Class?" (WIHIC) scales and at the level of the items within each WIHIC scale.

6.2 General patterns of differences in perceptions between students and instructors

Four sets of environment perception scores generated from the data collected by the four forms of the modified WIHIC (i.e. the student actual form, the student preferred form, the instructor actual form, and the instructor preferred form) represented students' and instructors' actual and preferred perceptions of the CE classroom psychosocial environments. The class mean and the individual instructor mean were used as the unit of analysis in order to keep an equal number of cases in the statistical procedures for comparisons. The means of the four sets of environment perception scores were calculated across the 40 classes: the class mean of students' actual scores, the class mean of students' preferred scores, the mean of instructor's actual scores, and the mean of instructor's preferred scores. The four sets of means were used to describe and compare the different perceptions of students and instructors of the actual and preferred classroom psychosocial environments. Table 6.1 provides the descriptive statistics for the four sets of data, including mean and standard deviation (SD) for each scale.

Table 6.1 Descriptive statistics for actual and preferred perceptions of students and instructors

Environment Scale	No. of items	Student actual form		Student preferred form		Instructor actual form		Instructor preferred form	
		Class mean	SD	Class mean	SD	Item mean	SD	Item mean	SD
SC	6	4.20	0.15	4.51	0.15	4.25	0.47	4.83	0.25
TS	10	3.21	0.28	4.00	0.18	4.22	0.41	4.62	0.36
IN	3	3.43	0.25	4.19	0.17	3.98	0.65	4.83	0.30
TO	8	3.73	0.18	4.43	0.16	3.98	0.35	4.88	0.16
CO	11	3.65	0.18	4.30	0.15	3.72	0.53	4.73	0.35
EQ	10	3.83	0.23	4.37	0.14	4.09	0.60	4.60	0.43

Note: $N=40$; "Almost never" =1; "Seldom" =2; "Sometimes" =3; "Often" =4; "Almost always" =5.

It is observed in Table 6.1 that the mean scores of scales in both the student preferred form and the instructor preferred form were generally higher than the mean scores of their corresponding scales in the student actual form and the instructor actual form.

Chapter 6 Discrepancies in Classroom Psychosocial Environment Perceptions

This indicates that both students and instructors would prefer a more favorable CE classroom environment than what was being perceived. However, there is a need of further comparisons as to whether the differences between the actual and preferred perceptions of the WIHIC environmental scales held by students and instructors were statistically significant.

One-way multivariate analysis of variance (MANOVA) for repeated measures was run using the six WIHIC scales as dependent variables and the form of the modified WIHIC as a four-level repeated measures factor. The result of multivariate test (Wilks' lambda =0.014, $p<0.001$) yielded a significant difference among the four forms on the set of dependent variables as a whole. Univariate ANOVA tests were performed to examine whether there were significant differences among the four forms on each scale. The results of Mauchly's Test of Sphericity in Table 6.2 showed that the assumption of sphericity for all the six WIHIC scales was violated, therefore Greenhouse-Geisser estimates of sphericity were used to adjust the degrees of freedom.

Table 6.2 Mauchly's Test of Sphericity of the six WIHIC scales

Within Subjects Effect	Measure	Mauchly's W	Approx. Chi-Square	Sig.	Epsilon		
					Greenhouse-Geisser	Huynh-Feldt	Lower-Bound
Form	SC	.240	53.873	.000	.564	.587	.333
	TS	.487	27.143	.000	.664	.700	.333
	IN	.247	52.758	.000	.541	.562	.333
	TO	.389	35.619	.000	.610	.638	.333
	CO	.271	49.260	.000	.601	.628	.333
	EQ	.245	53.010	.000	.623	.653	.333

Note: $N=40$.

Results of ANOVA tests displayed in Table 6.3 indicated that there were significant differences among the four forms on each scale since the Greenhouse-Geisser estimates of sphericity of each scale was significant at $p<0.001$.

To further interpret the significant differences for the four-level form factor, post-hoc pair-wise comparisons with Bonferroni correction were performed between different forms of the modified WIHIC. Differences in students' and instructors' actual and preferred perceptions of the CE classroom psychosocial environments were revealed through four pairs of comparisons among the four different WIHIC forms in terms of the six WIHIC scales, namely, the student actual form versus the student preferred form, the student actual form versus the instructor actual form, the student preferred form versus the instructor preferred form, and the instructor actual form versus the instructor preferred form.

Table 6.3 Univariate ANOVA tests of the six WIHIC scales

Source		Measure	Type III Sum of Squares	df	F	Sig.
Form	SC	Sphericity Assumed	9.987	3	39.716	.000
		Greenhouse-Geisser	9.987	1.692	39.716	.000
		Huynh-Feldt	9.987	1.760	39.716	.000
		Lower-Bound	9.987	1.000	39.716	.000
	TS	Sphericity Assumed	42.273	3	180.567	.000
		Greenhouse-Geisser	42.273	1.992	180.567	.000
		Huynh-Feldt	42.273	2.099	180.567	.000
		Lower-Bound	42.273	1.000	180.567	.000
	IN	Sphericity Assumed	40.416	3	95.874	.000
		Greenhouse-Geisser	40.416	1.624	95.874	.000
		Huynh-Feldt	40.416	1.685	95.874	.000
		Lower-Bound	40.416	1.000	95.874	.000
	TO	Sphericity Assumed	30.890	3	202.440	.000
		Greenhouse-Geisser	30.890	1.830	202.440	.000
		Huynh-Feldt	30.890	1.915	202.440	.000
		Lower-Bound	30.890	1.000	202.440	.000
	CO	Sphericity Assumed	31.435	3	102.322	.000
		Greenhouse-Geisser	31.435	1.803	102.322	.000
		Huynh-Feldt	31.435	1.885	102.322	.000
		Lower-Bound	31.435	1.000	102.322	.000
	EQ	Sphericity Assumed	12.774	3	31.774	.000
		Greenhouse-Geisser	12.774	1.868	31.774	.000
		Huynh-Feldt	12.774	1.959	31.774	.000
		Lower-Bound	12.774	1.000	31.774	.000

Note: $N=40$.

Chapter 6   Discrepancies in Classroom Psychosocial Environment Perceptions

As shown in the results of the pair-wise comparisons in Table 6.4, it is found that there were significant differences at $p<0.001$ for all the six WIHIC scales between students' actual and preferred perceptions. With regard to the differences in the actual perceptions between students and instructors, three out of the six actual WIHIC scales were found to be perceived differently at $p<0.001$. These scales are "Teacher support", "Involvement", and "Task orientation". For the rest three scales, "Student cohesiveness", "Cooperation", and "Equity", there were no significant differences between the actual perceptions of students and instructors. It is also shown in Table 6.4 that there were significant differences in the preferred perceptions between students and instructors of "Student cohesiveness", "Teacher support", "Involvement", "Task orientation", and "Cooperation" at $p<0.001$ and "Equity" at $p<0.05$. At last, results in Table 6.4 show that instructors perceived the actual and preferred classroom psychosocial environments differently with statistical significance at $p<0.001$ for all the six WIHIC scales.

Table 6.4   Post-hoc tests of the six WIHIC scales among four forms

Measure	(I) Form	(J) Form	Mean Difference (I-J)	Std. Error	Sig.	95% Confidence Interval for Difference	
						Lower Bound	Upper Bound
SC	SA	SP	-.307***	.028	.000	-.384	-.230
	SA	IA	-.051	.083	1.000	-.282	.181
	SP	IP	-.323***	.044	.000	-.446	-.200
	IA	IP	-.579***	.080	.000	-.800	-.358
	SA	IP	-.630***	.048	.000	-.763	-.497
	IA	SP	-.257*	.083	.021	-.486	-.027
TS	SA	SP	-.789***	.042	.000	-.907	-.671
	SA	IA	-1.012***	.071	.000	-1.210	-.814
	SP	IP	-.621***	.066	.000	-.804	-.437
	IA	IP	-.398***	.047	.000	-.527	-.268
	SA	IP	-1.410***	.066	.000	-1.594	-1.226
	IA	SP	.223*	.075	.029	.015	.431

Continued

Measure	(I) Form	(J) Form	Mean Difference (I-J)	Std. Error	Sig.	95% Confidence Interval for Difference	
						Lower Bound	Upper Bound
IN	SA	SP	-.758***	.040	.000	-.869	-.647
	SA	IA	-.545***	.106	.000	-.840	-.251
	SP	IP	-.646***	.056	.000	-.801	-.490
	IA	IP	-.858***	.107	.000	-1.157	-.560
	SA	IP	-1.404***	.053	.000	-1.550	-1.258
	IA	SP	-.213	.109	.352	-.517	.091
TO	SA	SP	-.694***	.032	.000	-.783	-.606
	SA	IA	-.247**	.063	.002	-.423	-.071
	SP	IP	-.455***	.032	.000	-.543	-.368
	IA	IP	-.903***	.063	.000	-1.077	-.729
	SA	IP	-1.150***	.037	.000	-1.252	-1.048
	IA	SP	-.448***	.063	.000	-.624	-.272
CO	SA	SP	-.654***	.031	.000	-.739	-.568
	SA	IA	-.068	.090	1.000	-.317	.181
	SP	IP	-.425***	.062	.000	-.598	-.253
	IA	IP	-1.011***	.074	.000	-1.216	-.806
	SA	IP	-1.079***	.062	.000	-1.253	-.906
	IA	SP	-.586***	.093	.000	-.843	-.329
EQ	SA	SP	-.537***	.033	.000	-.629	-.445
	SA	IA	-.251	.101	.107	-.532	.031
	SP	IP	-.209*	.068	.024	-.399	-.019
	IA	IP	-.495***	.089	.000	-.742	-.248
	SA	IP	-.746***	.075	.000	-.954	-.537
	IA	SP	-.286*	.93	.041	-.573	-.001

Note: $N=40$; SA: student actual form; SP: student preferred form; IA: instructor actual form; IP: instructor preferred form; *$p<0.05$; ***$p<0.001$.

Figure 6.1 below is a simplified plot of significant differences in perceptions measured by the four forms of the WIHIC based on the descriptive statistics in Table 6.1 and results of paired comparisons in Table 6.4. Only the mean scores with significant differences ($p<0.05$) between the scales in pairs of different forms were considered in the figure in order to present a parsimonious

Chapter 6 Discrepancies in Classroom Psychosocial Environment Perceptions

picture of the differences. The scale means without significant differences between the pairs of different forms were considered as zero difference, and the average mean scores of the relevant item mean scores in the pairs were calculated and taken into account in the figure. In Figure 6.1, Line SA and Line SP represent students' perceptions of the actual and preferred CE classroom psychosocial environments respectively. Line IA and Line IP represent instructors' perceptions of the actual and preferred CE classroom psychosocial environments respectively. The six markers in each of the four lines represent the mean scores for the six environmental scales in the student actual form, the student preferred form, the instructor actual form, and the instructor preferred form respectively.

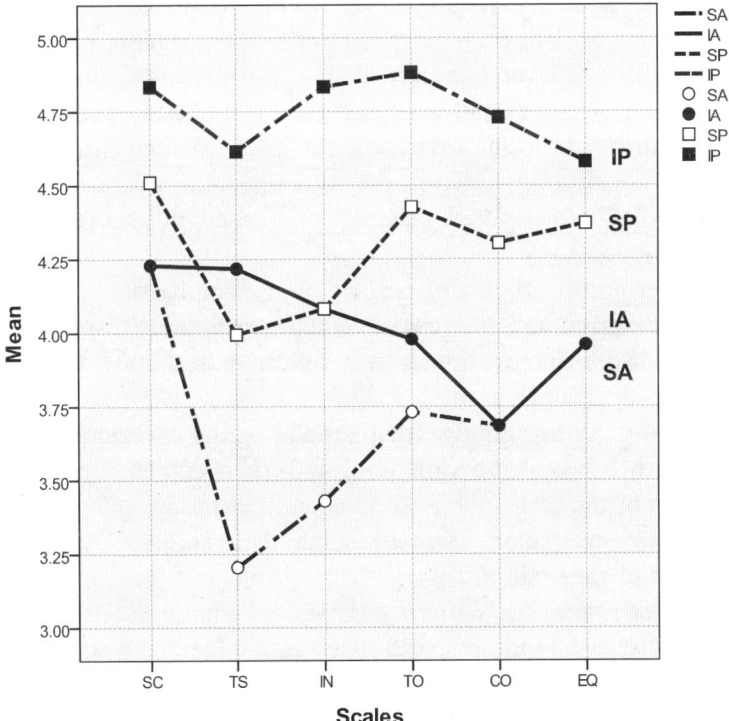

Figure 6.1 Differences in perceptions among student actual, student preferred, instructor actual, and instructor preferred forms

Figure 6.1 depicts that the perception scores of instructors' preferred perceptions of the six environmental scales were the highest followed by students' preferred perception scores, then instructors' actual perception scores, and students' actual perception scores. Two general patterns of discrepancies in perceptions between students and instructors emerged. The first general pattern was that both students and instructors would prefer a more favorable CE classroom psychosocial environment than what they were experiencing at present. The second general pattern was that instructors perceived both the actual and preferred CE classroom psychosocial environments more favorably than did their students. The two overall patterns of differences in classroom perceptions were consistent with the research findings of previous studies on classroom psychosocial environments (e.g. Chua et al., 2011; Fisher & Fraser, 1983a; Fraser, 1982, 1984; Fraser & Treagust, 1986; Sinclair & Fraser, 2002). Furthermore, the second pattern that instructors had better actual and preferred perceptions of classroom psychosocial environments than did their students is also a typical feature revealed in previous research, which has been named as the "rose-colored glasses" phenomenon by Fraser and Wubbles (1995: 141).

Furthermore, the differences and similarities between students' preferred and instructors' actual perceptions displayed in Figure 6.1 were noteworthy. It was reflected in Figure 6.1 that instructors perceived the existing classroom psychosocial environments so favorably that their actual perceptions of "Involvement" was at the same level with their students' preferred perceptions of the scale, while their actual perceptions of "Teacher support" was even more favorable than their students' preferred perceptions of the scale.

Another interesting pattern observed in Figure 6.1, together with reference to the mean scores listed in Table 6.1, was that the differences between instructors' actual and preferred perceptions of classroom psychosocial environments were generally greater in extent than those between students' actual and preferred perceptions. This implied that instructors anticipated greater improvements on

Chapter 6 Discrepancies in Classroom Psychosocial Environment Perceptions

their CE classroom psychosocial environments than did their students.

6.3 Differences between actual and preferred perceptions of students

As displayed by the significant differences in students' actual and preferred perceptions of the six WIHIC environmental scales in Figure 6.2 below, it could be inferred that students expected enhanced cohesiveness among themselves, more personal attention and academic support from their instructors, more active participation in classroom activities, greater commitment to learn, more cooperative roles for themselves, and more equal treatment by

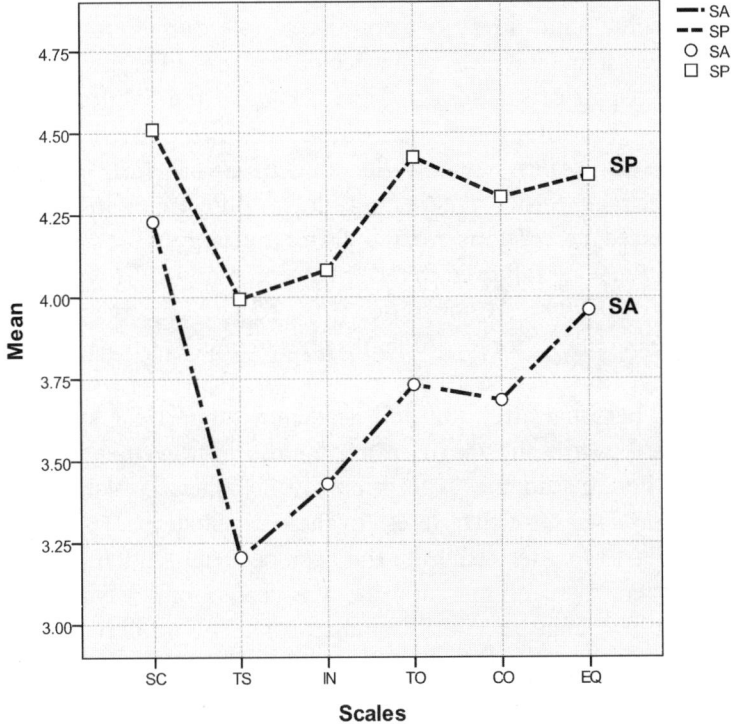

Figure 6.2 Differences in perceptions between students' actual and preferred forms

their instructors in class, though they were actually experiencing a positive CE classroom psychosocial environment indicated by a high level of perception for four WIHIC scales and a medium level of perception for two WIHIC scales.

The similar findings that students would prefer a more favorable classroom psychosocial environment have also been reported in previous studies on the differences between the actual and preferred classroom psychosocial environments perceived by Singaporean secondary students in Chinese language classes by Chua *et al.*(2011), Indonesian secondary students in science classes by Wahyudi and Treagust (2006), and Australian students in the early childhood classes by Fisher, Fraser, and Bassett (1995), to name just a few.

Furthermore, it was observed that the differences between students' actual and ideal perceptions of the six environmental scales varied in magnitude, as indicated by the different distance between each pair of markers in Line SA and Line SP graphed in Figure 6.2. According to the item mean differences listed in Table 6.3 for the six scales between the student actual form and the student preferred form, the magnitude of differences in student actual-preferred perceptions ranked from the largest for "Teacher support" (0.79), followed by "Involvement" (0.76), "Task orientation" (0.70), "Cooperation" (0.65), "Equity" (0.54) and to the smallest for "Student cohesiveness" (0.31). This suggests that the largest room existed for the improvement of instructors' personal attention and academic support for students, while there was still substantial room for the improvement of peer relations, though students' perceptions of the cohesive relationships among themselves were the closest to their expectations.

In order to further elaborate the gaps between students' actual and preferred perceptions of the CE classroom psychosocial environments, analyses and comparisons of differences in perceptions of each aspect within the six WIHIC scales were examined respectively through paired samples t-tests.

6.3.1 Differences between students' actual and preferred perceptions of SC

Results of paired comparisons listed in Table 6.5 on the next page show that there were significant differences ($p < 0.001$) between students' actual and preferred perceptions of all the six aspects of "Student cohesiveness". These differences in perceptions are graphically presented in Figure 6.3 on the next page.

As represented in Figure 6.3, students' preferred perception scores were higher than their actual perception scores for all the items in "Student cohesiveness" scale except for Item 7. This implied that students would expect a closer and friendlier interpersonal relationship among classmates with regard to the aspects measured in the five items of "Student cohesiveness"; however, they would prefer a less degree of familiarity among classmates as assessed by Item 7 than what was being experienced. One of the possible reasons accounted for such lower-than-actual expectation on familiarity for an ideal classroom psychosocial environment for students might come from the overmuch intimacy in their daily lives on campus. Students in the same class usually live in the same or nearby dormitories and mainly attend similar courses for the first two years of study, and thus most of them know each other so well that such intense familiarity for students might be a bit beyond the necessity for learning, and consequently, they would expect more personal distance and room for privacy in the ideal classroom psychosocial environments. In addition, it was observed that though students' preferred perceptions of familiarity was not as high as their actual perceptions, they were still in favor of a high level of familiarity in the ideal CE classroom psychosocial environments, as indicated by the preferred perception score ($M = 4.51$) of Item 7 shown in Table 6.5.

Table 6.5 Differences between students' actual and preferred perceptions of SC

Questionnaire Item		Mean			T	Sig.
		SA	SP	SA−SP		
Pair 1 (Item 1)	I make/would make friendships among students in this class.	3.96	4.48	−.52***	−8.021	.000
Pair 2 (Item 7)	I know/would know other students in this class.	4.61	4.51	.09***	3.099	.004
Pair 3 (Item 13)	I am/would be friendly to members of this class.	4.54	4.61	−.07***	−2.869	.007
Pair 4 (Item 19)	Members of the class are/would be my friends.	4.21	4.54	−.33***	−10.439	.000
Pair 5 (Item 25)	I work/would work well with other class members.	4.06	4.49	−.43***	−11.379	.000
Pair 6 (Item 37)	Students in this class like/would like me.	3.06	4.03	−.58***	−14.951	.000

Note: $N=40$; *** $p<0.001$.

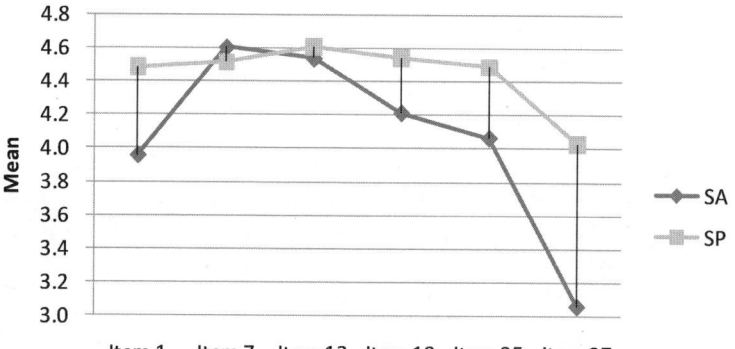

Figure 6.3 Differences between students' actual and preferred perceptions of SC

Another noteworthy feature spotted in Figure 6.3 is that the differences in student actual-preferred perceptions of the six aspects of "Student cohesiveness" varied in magnitude, indicating different degrees of improvements for the six aspects. The smallest difference occurs for Item 13, while the largest gap is found for Item 27. Meanwhile, the actual perception score of Item 27 (M = 3.06) in Table 6.5 indicates a medium level of perception, which might suggest that students held a conservative estimate about how their classmates took them as friends in class. The largest actual-ideal perception gap also reflects the strongest desire of students for the increase of acceptance and popularity among their classmates. While in contrast, it is interesting to find that the smallest gap of actual-preferred perceptions of Item 13 reflects that student felt positive or certain about their own affections for other classmates.

6.3.2 Differences between students' actual and preferred perceptions of TS

As shown by the results of paired samples t-tests in Table 6.6, all of the ten aspects of "Teacher support" were perceived differently by students between the actual and preferred forms with significance at $p<0.001$. These significant differences in perceptions of the ten aspects are presented in Figure 6.4.

It is shown in Figure 6.4 that students' preferred perception scores of the ten items in "Teacher support" scale were higher than their actual perception scores. It could be inferred that students would expect improvements for all the ten aspects of support provided by their instructors. To be specific, on the one hand, students would expect greater efforts of their instructors to provide more academic and personal support; on the other hand, students would prefer more opportunities ensured for them to interchange ideas with instructors.

In addition, the different gaps in actual-ideal perceptions of the ten items in "Teacher support" scale indicated different expectations of students on the improvements of the ten aspects, with the largest room of improvement on the efforts of instructors to provide support for them, and the smallest room of improvement on the provision of opportunities to express their ideas and opinions to their instructors.

Table 6.6　Differences between students' actual and preferred perceptions of TS

	Questionnaire Item	Mean			T	Sig.
		SA	SP	SA-SP		
Pair 1 (Item 2)	The teacher takes/would take a personal interest in me.	2.92	3.70	-.78***	-13.834	.000
Pair 2 (Item 8)	The teacher makes/would make an extra effort to help me.	2.56	3.74	-1.19***	-20.568	.000
Pair 3 (Item 15)	The teacher asks/would ask me questions.	3.66	3.95	-.29***	-6.437	.000
Pair 4 (Item 21)	My ideas and suggestions are/would be used during classroom discussions.	3.36	4.15	-.79***	-16.328	.000
Pair 5 (Item 26)	The teacher talks/would talk with me.	3.39	4.00	-.61***	-10.027	.000
Pair 6 (Item 27)	I ask/would ask the teacher questions.	3.06	4.03	-.97***	-17.192	.000
Pair 7 (Item 32)	The teacher is/would be interested in my problems.	3.24	4.11	-.87***	-15.613	.000
Pair 8 (Item 38)	The teacher moves/would move about the class to talk with me.	2.91	3.83	-.92***	-13.815	.000
Pair 9 (Item 44)	The teacher's questions help/would help me to understand.	3.88	4.44	-.56***	-13.507	.000
Pair 10 (Item 45)	I am/would be asked to explain how I solve problems.	3.07	3.98	-.91***	-21.492	.000

Note: $N=40$; *** $p<0.001$.

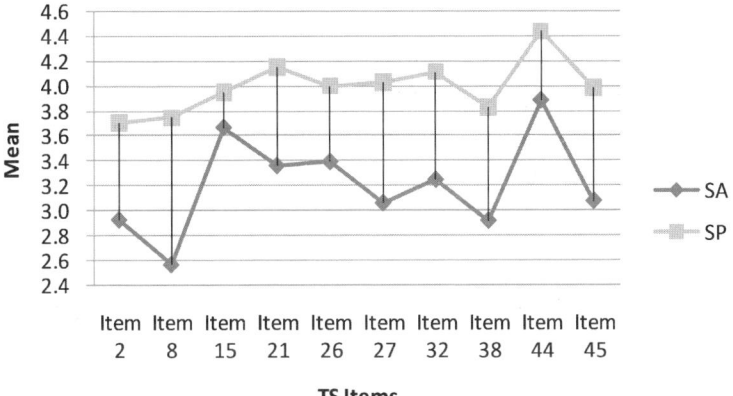

Figure 6.4 Differences between students' actual and preferred perceptions of TS

6.3.3 Differences between students' actual and preferred perceptions of IN

Results of paired samples t-tests listed in Table 6.7 below show that there were significant differences at $p<0.001$ between students' actual and preferred perceptions of all the three aspects of "Involvement". Students' preferred perception scores of the three aspects were all higher than their actual perception scores for the corresponding items. These significant differences in perceptions of the aspects in "Involvement" scale are presented in Figure 6.5.

Table 6.7 Differences between students' actual and preferred perceptions of IN

	Questionnaire Item	Mean			T	Sig.
		SA	SP	SA−SP		
Pair 1 (Item 3)	I discuss/would discuss ideas in class.	3.39	4.18	−.79***	−16.939	.000
Pair 2 (Item 9)	I give/would give my opinions during class discussions.	3.44	4.19	−.75***	−16.265	.000
Pair 3 (Item 33)	I explain/would explain my ideas to other students.	3.46	4.20	−.74***	−17.594	.000

Note: $N=40$; *** $p<0.001$.

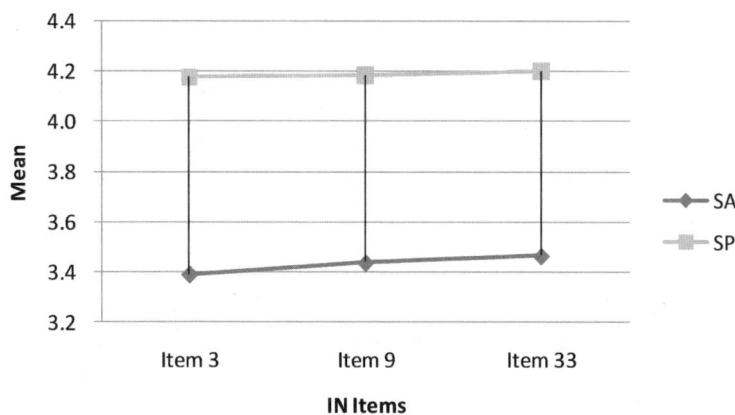

Figure 6.5 Differences between students' actual and preferred perceptions of IN

As noted in Figure 6.5, it could be summarized that students would like to get more involved in class through more active participation and more contributions of ideas in class discussions. Furthermore, Figure 6.5 illustrates that there were similar gaps between the actual and preferred perceptions of the three aspects of "Involvement", implying students' similar expectations of improvements in the three aspects.

6.3.4 Differences between students' actual and preferred perceptions of TO

Results of pair-wise comparisons listed in Table 6.8 on the next page show that there were significant differences at $p < 0.001$ between students' actual and preferred perceptions for all the eight items in "Task orientation" scale. The preferred perception scores of the eight items were all higher than the actual perception scores of the corresponding items. Figure 6.6 represents these significant differences between the actual and preferred perceptions of the eight aspects of "Task orientation".

Chapter 6 Discrepancies in Classroom Psychosocial Environment Perceptions

Table 6.8 Differences between students' actual and preferred perceptions of TO

	Questionnaire Item	Mean			T	Sig.
		SA	SP	SA-SP		
Pair 1 (Item 4)	Getting a certain amount of work done is/would be important to me.	3.77	4.17	-.40***	-10.773	.000
Pair 2 (Item 10)	I do/would do as much as I set out to do.	3.37	4.35	-.98***	-23.896	.000
Pair 3 (Item 16)	I know/would know the goals for this class.	3.42	4.44	-1.02***	-20.512	.000
Pair 4 (Item 22)	I am/would be ready to start this class on time.	4.15	4.55	-.40***	-10.572	.000
Pair 5 (Item 28)	I know/would know what I am trying to accomplish in this class.	3.48	4.47	-.99***	-18.835	.000
Pair 6 (Item 34)	I pay/would pay attention during this class.	3.99	4.51	-.52***	-13.796	.000
Pair 7 (Item 40)	I try/would try to understand the work in this class.	3.95	4.50	-.55***	-14.884	.000
Pair 8 (Item 46)	I know/would know how much work I have to do.	3.72	4.42	-.70***	-15.572	.000

Note: $N=40$; *** $p<0.001$.

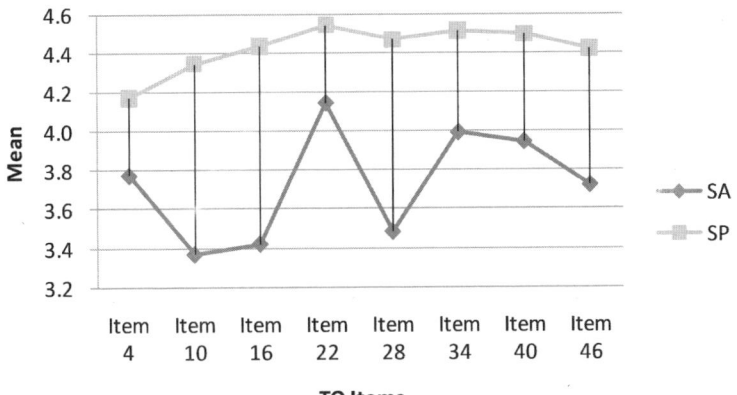

Figure 6.6 Differences between students' actual and preferred perceptions of TO

As shown in Figure 6.6, students would prefer a more task oriented classroom environment in terms of all the eight aspects assessed in "Task orientation" scale. It is also represented in Figure 6.6 that the differences in actual-ideal perceptions of the eight aspects varied in magnitude. Among these aspects, there was larger room for improvement in getting students know clear goals of this class, while smaller room existed for the improvements in students' awareness of the importance of getting class work done and starting class on time.

6.3.5 Differences between students' actual and preferred perceptions of CO

Results of paired samples t-tests in Table 6.9 below indicated that students' preferred perceptions of the eleven items in "Cooperation" scale were all significantly higher at $p<0.001$ than their actual perception scores of the corresponding items. Significant differences in the actual and preferred perceptions of the items in "Cooperation" scale are represented in Figure 6.7.

Table 6.9 Differences between students' actual and preferred perceptions of CO

	Questionnaire Item	Mean			T	Sig.
		SA	SP	SA-SP		
Pair 1 (Item 5)	I cooperate/would cooperate with other students when doing assignment work.	3.44	4.17	-.73***	-14.850	.000
Pair 2 (Item 11)	I share/would share my books and resources with other students when doing assignments.	3.47	4.18	-.71***	-17.542	.000
Pair 3 (Item 17)	When I work in groups in this class, there is/would be teamwork.	4.03	4.39	-.36***	-9.942	.000
Pair 4 (Item 23)	I work/would work with other students on projects in this class.	3.80	4.32	-.52***	-13.216	.000

Chapter 6 Discrepancies in Classroom Psychosocial Environment Perceptions

Continued

	Questionnaire Item	Mean			T	Sig.
		SA	SP	SA−SP		
Pair 5 (Item 29)	I learn/would learn from other students in this class.	3.77	4.43	−.66***	−19.335	.000
Pair 6 (Item 31)	I help/would help other class members who are having trouble with their work.	3.27	4.29	−1.02***	−22.577	.000
Pair 7 (Item 35)	I work/would work with other students in this class.	3.85	4.37	−.52***	−12.783	.000
Pair 8 (Item 39)	Students discuss/would discuss with me how to go about solving problems.	3.37	4.22	−.85***	−17.673	.000
Pair 9 (Item 41)	I cooperate/would cooperate with other students on class activities.	3.91	4.39	−.48***	−13.848	.000
Pair 10 (Item 43)	In this class, I get/would get help from other students.	3.64	4.26	−.61***	−17.703	.000
Pair 11 (Item 47)	Students work/would work with me to achieve class goals.	3.61	4.32	−.71***	−16.722	.000

Notes: $N=40$; *** $p<0.001$.

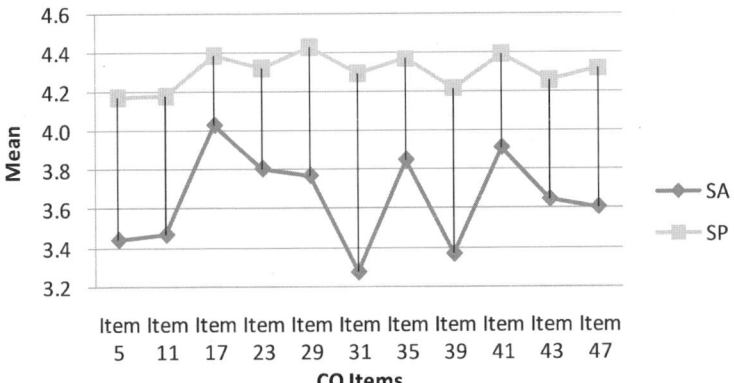

Figure 6.7 Differences between students' actual and preferred perceptions of CO

As illustrated in Figure 6.7, students would like to experience greater cooperation among classmates with regard to all the eleven aspects assessed in "Cooperation" scale. Among these aspects, there was less room for improvement in teamwork than the other aspects as indicated by the smallest gap between students' actual and preferred perceptions of Item 17. The largest gap between students' actual and preferred perceptions of Item 31 reflected that the greatest reality-ideal contrast among students occurred in their provision of help to other class members. It might be explained that though students were sincere to help classmates solve problems, they did not usually have such kind of experience in reality in that either their classmates seldom had trouble with their work or they were reluctant to tell others when in trouble.

6.3.6 Differences between students' actual and preferred perceptions of EQ

Results of paired samples t-tests listed in Table 6.10 revealed that students' preferred perceptions were more favorable than their actual perceptions with statistical significance at $p<0.001$ for all the ten items of "Equity". Figure 6.8 provides a graph of these differences between the actual and preferred perceptions of "Equity".

It is shown in Figure 6.8 that students would like to access more opportunities to be equally treated by their instructors concerning all the ten aspects of "Equity" assessed in the scale. The improvements in the ten aspects of "Equity" expected by students were found to be different in degrees. The greatest expectation of students on improvement, as indicated by the largest gap in the perceptions of Item 18, was to be provided with more opportunities to have the same amount of say in class as other classmates, while relatively less was needed to be done in order to improve the general feelings of students as being treated the same with other students, since their actual perception score for Item 24 was closer to their preferred perception score in comparison with the other Items in "Equity" scale.

Chapter 6 Discrepancies in Classroom Psychosocial Environment Perceptions

Table 6.10 Differences between students' actual and preferred perceptions of EQ

	Questionnaire Item	Mean			T	Sig.
		SA	SP	SA–SP		
Pair 1 (Item 6)	The teacher gives/would give as much attention to my questions as to other students' questions.	4.02	4.36	−.34***	−7.758	.000
Pair 2 (Item 12)	I get/would get the same amount of help from the teacher as do other students.	3.65	4.34	−.69***	−19.960	.000
Pair 3 (Item 14)	The teacher considers/would consider my feelings.	3.82	4.31	−.48***	−8.691	.000
Pair 4 (Item 18)	I have/would have the same amount of say in this class as other students.	3.51	4.33	−.82***	−18.502	.000
Pair 5 (Item 20)	The teacher helps/would help me when I have trouble with the work.	3.90	4.38	−.48***	−10.158	.000
Pair 6 (Item 24)	I am/would be treated the same as other students in this class.	4.27	4.51	−.25***	−8.137	.000
Pair 7 (Item 30)	I receive/would receive the same encouragement from the teacher as other students do.	3.75	4.39	−.64***	−12.633	.000
Pair 8 (Item 36)	I get/would get the same opportunity to contribute to class discussions as other students.	3.86	4.38	−.52***	−12.016	.000
Pair 9 (Item 42)	My work receives/would receive as much praise as other students' work.	3.55	4.33	−.78***	−16.060	.000
Pair 10 (Item 48)	I get/would get the same opportunity to answer questions as other students.	4.01	4.38	−.36***	−10.761	.000

Note: $N=40$; *** $p<0.001$.

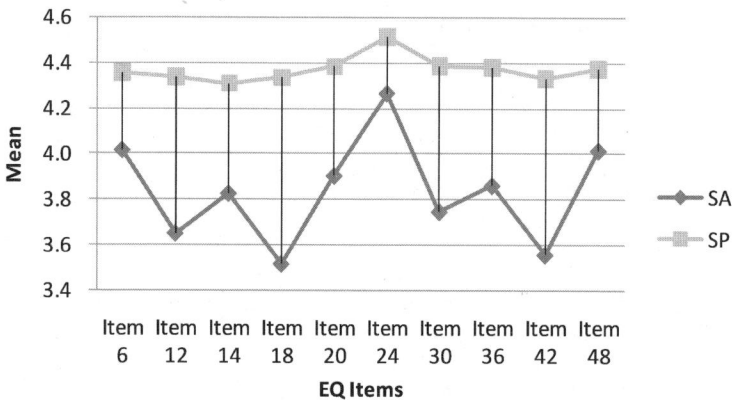

Figure 6.8 Differences between students' actual and preferred perceptions of EQ

6.4 Differences between instructors' actual and preferred perceptions

Results of the comparisons between instructors' actual and preferred perceptions graphed in Figure 6.9 show that instructors' preferred perception scores were all significantly ($p<0.001$) higher than their actual perception scores for all the six WIHIC scales. Different distances between markers of the six WIHIC scales in Line IA and Line IP in Figure 6.9 indicate that the differences between instructors' actual and ideal perceptions of the six environmental scales varied in magnitude. The item mean differences listed in Table 6.1 indicate that actual-ideal perception gaps for instructors ranged from the largest for "Cooperation" (1.01), followed by "Task orientation" (0.90), "Involvement" (0.86), "Student cohesiveness" (0.58), "Equity" (0.50), and to the smallest for "Teacher support" (0.40). This implies that instructors would like to see the greatest improvement in cooperation among students while the smallest improvement in the personal and academic support of instructors in order to create an ideal classroom psychosocial environment.

Chapter 6   Discrepancies in Classroom Psychosocial Environment Perceptions

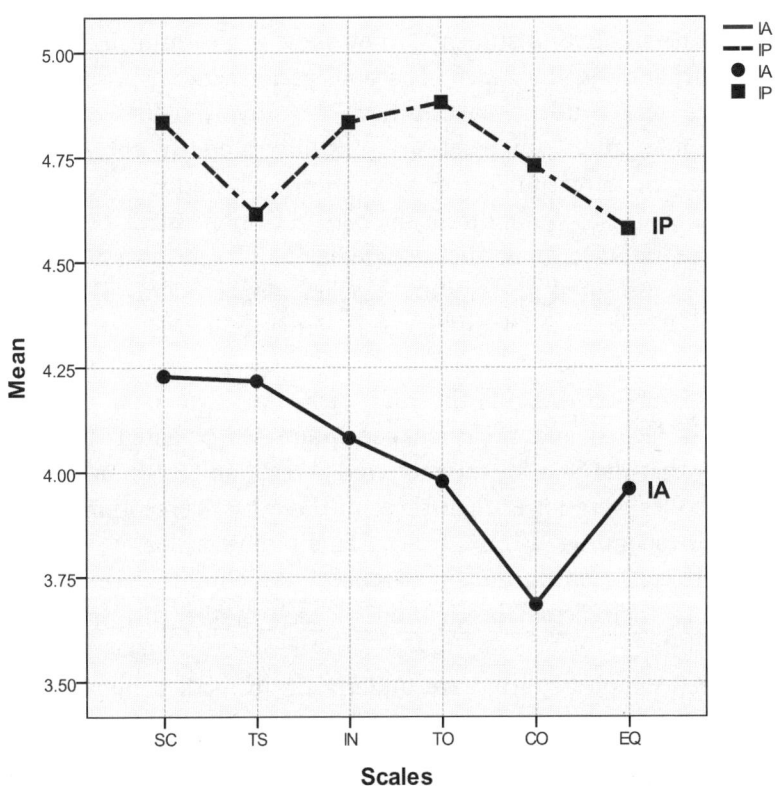

Figure 6.9   Differences in perceptions between instructors' actual and preferred forms

In addition, another noteworthy feature emerges from the closer inspection of item mean differences listed in Table 6.1 for students' actual-preferred perception gaps against those for instructors' actual-preferred perception gaps. The comparison results reveal that the differences between instructors' actual and preferred perceptions were greater than those between their students' actual and preferred perceptions for scales "Student cohesiveness", "Involvement", "Task orientation", and "Cooperation", while smaller for scales "Teacher support" and "Equity". This feature of the discrepancies in perceptions of the CE classroom psychosocial environments could be interpreted and understood from the different perspectives of students and instructors. Viewed from the perspective of students, they show more enthusiasm than their instructors in their own classroom performance as assessed in the scales of "Student cohesiveness", "Involvement", "Task orientation", and "Cooperation", as indicated by the smaller differences in actual-preferred perceptions of students on these scales. In contrast, viewed from the perspective of instructors, they were more satisfied than their students with their own teaching practices as measured in scales of "Teacher support" and "Equity", as implied by the smaller difference in actual-preferred perceptions of instructors on the two scales.

The comparisons of the SDs for the two data sets of instructors' actual and preferred perception scores listed in Table 6.1 show that the SDs for the preferred perception scores for the six WIHIC scales were lower than those of the actual perception scores of the corresponding WIHIC scales. This indicates that instructors were more consistent in their preferences for each of the six WIHIC scales than their actual perceptions of each of the corresponding WIHIC scales.

Paired samples t-tests were undertaken to further analyze and investigate the gaps between instructors' actual and preferred perceptions of each aspect in the six WIHIC environmental scales in the CE classroom psychosocial environments.

6.4.1 *Differences between instructors' actual and preferred perceptions of SC*

Results of paired samples t-tests listed in Table 6.11 show that five out of the six items in "Student cohesiveness" scale were perceived by instructors significantly ($p < 0.001$) higher in the preferred classroom psychosocial environments than those in the actual classroom psychosocial environments. For Item 7, there was no statistically significant difference between instructors' actual and preferred perceptions.

The significant differences in the actual-preferred perceptions of the five items are illustrated in Figure 6.10. In Figure 6.10, the

Chapter 6 Discrepancies in Classroom Psychosocial Environment Perceptions

nonsignificant difference in perceptions of Item 7 is represented as a zero difference by averaging its actual and preferred item scores.

As shown in Figure 6.10, instructors would prefer a greater level of cohesiveness among students in terms of all the aspects as measured in "Teacher support" scale except for the familiarity among students assessed in Item 7. In addition, the congruence in instructors' actual and ideal perceptions of Item 7, together with the difference discovered in section 6.3.1 about students' actual and ideal perceptions of Item 7, further confirmed the distinctive feature of the actual CE classroom psychosocial environments in the present study that students were in such good familiarity with each other that there was no need for enhancement as perceived by both students and instructors.

Table 6.11 Differences between instructors' actual and preferred perceptions of SC

	Questionnaire Item	Mean			T	Sig.
		IA	IP	IA−IP		
Pair 1 (Item 1)	Students make/would make friendships among one another in this class.	4.13	4.80	−.68***	−4.521	.000
Pair 2 (Item 7)	Students know/would know other members in this class.	4.70	4.88	−.18***	−1.740	.090
Pair 3 (Item 13)	Students are/would be friendly to other members in this class.	4.30	4.88	−.58***	−5.718	.000
Pair 4 (Item 19)	Members of the class are/would be friends.	4.23	4.88	−.65***	−6.208	.000
Pair 5 (Item 25)	Students work/would work well with other class members.	4.15	4.90	−.75***	−6.389	.000
Pair 6 (Item 37)	Students in this class like/would like other members of this class.	4.03	4.68	−.65***	−5.874	.000

Note: $N=40$; *** $p<0.001$.

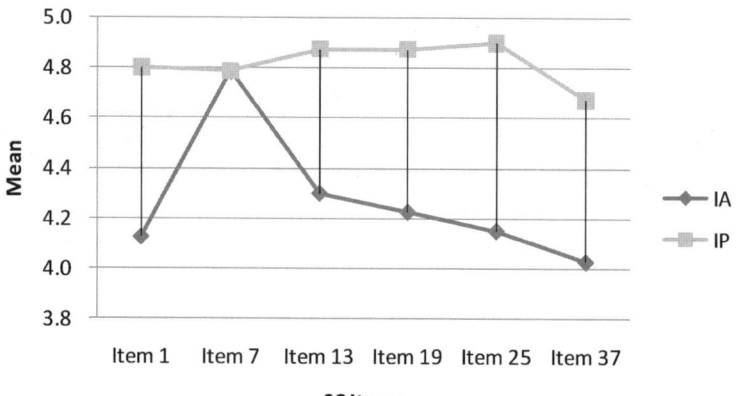

Figure 6.10 Differences between instructors' actual and preferred perceptions of SC

6.4.2 Differences between instructors' actual and preferred perceptions of TS

Results of pair-wise comparisons in Table 6.12 below show that the preferred perception scores of eight out of the ten items in "Teacher support" scale were found to be significantly higher than their corresponding actual perception scores. No significant differences were found between instructors' actual and ideal perceptions of Item 1 and Item 3. These significant differences are plotted in Figure 6.11, in which the nonsignificant differences for Item 1 and Item 3 are depicted as zero differences.

Table 6.12 Differences between instructors' actual and preferred perceptions of TS

	Questionnaire Item	Mean			T	Sig. (2-tailed)
		IA	IP	IA−IP		
Pair 1 (Item 2)	*I take/would take a personal interest in students.*	4.18	4.13	.050	.280	.781
Pair 2 (Item 8)	*I make/would make an extra effort to help students.*	4.10	4.63	−.53***	−5.188	.000

Chapter 6 Discrepancies in Classroom Psychosocial Environment Perceptions

Continued

	Questionnaire Item	Mean			T	Sig. (2-tailed)
		IA	IP	IA−IP		
Pair 3 (Item 15)	I call/would call on individual student to answer questions.	4.43	4.45	−.03	−.206	.838
Pair 4 (Item 21)	Students' ideas and suggestions are/would be used during classroom discussions.	3.98	4.40	−.43***	−4.523	.000
Pair 5 (Item 26)	I talk/would talk with students.	4.50	4.90	−.40***	−4.639	.000
Pair 6 (Item 27)	Students ask/would ask me questions.	4.18	4.80	−.63***	−5.922	.000
Pair 7 (Item 32)	I am/would be interested in students' problems.	4.25	4.75	−.50***	−4.655	.000
Pair 8 (Item 38)	I move/would move about the class to talk with students.	4.13	4.70	−.58***	−4.867	.000
Pair 9 (Item 44)	My questions help/would help students to understand.	4.45	4.85	−.40**	−3.399	.002
Pair 10 (Item 45)	Students are/would be asked to explain how they solve problems.	4.00	4.55	−.55***	−3.973	.000

Note: $N=40$; ** $p<0.01$; *** $p<0.001$.

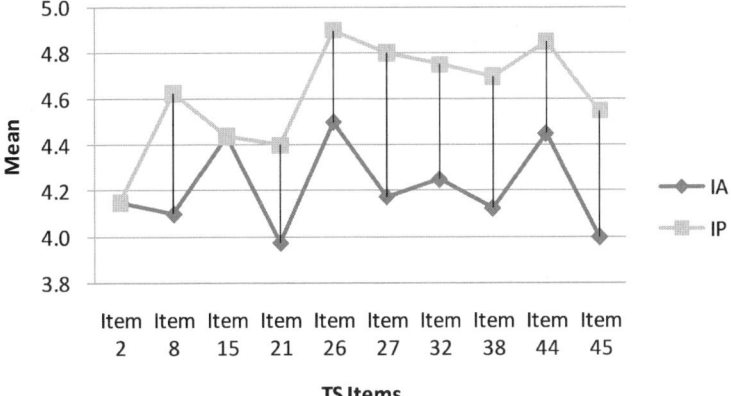

Figure 6.11 Differences between instructors' actual and preferred perceptions of TS

It is observed in Figure 6.11 that instructors would prefer to take more measures to provide more teacher support for students in CE classes with regard to eight out of ten aspects assessed in "Teacher support" scale. However, the congruence in instructors' actual-ideal perceptions of Item 2 and Item 15 indicates that instructors were satisfied with the personal attention and concerns they provided for students in class.

6.4.3 Differences between instructors' actual and preferred perceptions of IN

Differences between instructors' actual and preferred perceptions are found to be significantly different at $p<0.001$ for all the three items of "Involvement", as shown in Table 6.13 below. The results of differences in perceptions are represented in Figure 6.12.

Table 6.13 Differences between instructors' actual and preferred perceptions of IN

	Questionnaire Item	Mean			T	Sig.
		IA	IP	IA−IP		
Pair 1 (Item 3)	Students discuss/would discuss ideas in class.	3.90	4.75	−.85***	−6.224	.000
Pair 2 (Item 9)	Students give/would give their opinions during class discussions.	4.23	4.95	−.73***	−5.230	.000
Pair 3 (Item 33)	Students explain/would explain their ideas to other members.	3.80	4.80	−1.00***	−8.062	.000

Note: $N=40$; *** $p<0.001$.

As shown in Figure 6.12, instructors' preferred perception scores of the three items of "Involvement" were all higher than their actual perception scores. This implies that instructors would expect more active classroom involvement of students in class by taking more active part in classroom discussions and contributing more ideas to group discussions.

Chapter 6   Discrepancies in Classroom Psychosocial Environment Perceptions

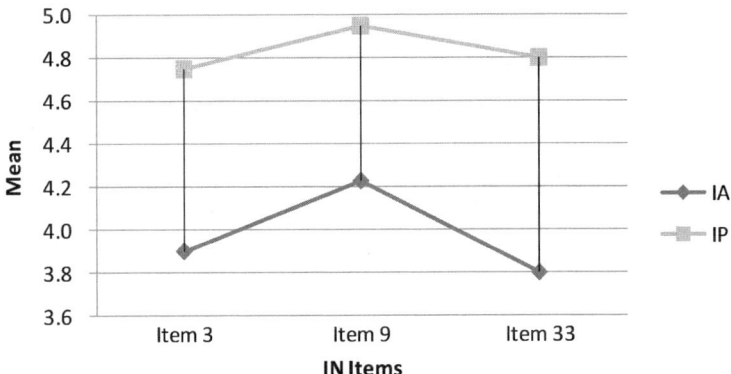

Figure 6.12   Differences between instructors' actual and preferred perceptions of IN

6.4.4   Differences between instructors' actual and preferred perceptions of TO

Results of paired samples t-tests in Table 6.14 show that there were significant differences ($p<0.001$) between instructors' actual and preferred perceptions of all the eight items in "Task orientation" scale. The significant differences between instructors' actual and ideal perceptions of items in "Task orientation" scale are plotted in Figure 6.13.

Table 6.14   Differences between instructors' actual and preferred perceptions of TO

	Questionnaire Item	Mean			T	Sig.
		IA	IP	IA−IP		
Pair 1 (Item 4)	*Getting a certain amount of work done is/would be important to students.*	4.48	4.90	−.43***	−4.226	.000
Pair 2 (Item 10)	*Students do/would do as much as they set out to do.*	3.48	4.75	−1.28***	−13.471	.000
Pair 3 (Item 16)	*Students know/would know the goals for this class.*	3.90	4.95	−1.05***	−8.862	.000

Continued

	Questionnaire Item	Mean			T	Sig.
		IA	IP	IA-IP		
Pair 4 (Item 22)	Students are/would be ready to start this class on time.	4.10	4.95	-.85***	-6.224	.000
Pair 5 (Item 28)	Students know/would know what they are trying to accomplish in this class.	3.83	4.90	-1.08***	-11.046	.000
Pair 6 (Item 34)	Students pay/would pay attention during this class.	4.13	4.95	-.83***	-7.328	.000
Pair 7 (Item 40)	Students try/would try to understand the work in this class.	4.08	4.88	-.80***	-8.973	.000
Pair 8 (Item 46)	Students know/would know how much work they have to do.	3.85	4.78	-.93***	-8.432	.000

Notes: $N=40$; *** $p<0.001$.

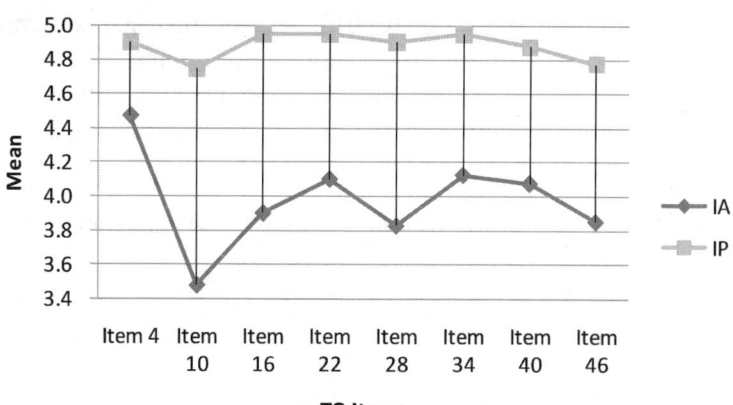

Figure 6.13 Differences between instructors' actual and preferred perceptions of TO

It is shown in Figure 6.13 that instructors would expect improvements for all the eight aspects of "Task orientation". Instructors, in particular, expected that their students could be more perseverant with their work, as indicated by the largest gap in their actual-ideal perceptions of Item 10. Besides, the narrowest gap between instructors' actual and preferred perceptions of Item 4 reveals that instructors were relatively more satisfied with students' awareness of task importance than the other aspects of "Task orientation". In addition, as revealed in section 6.3.4, students were also more satisfied with their awareness of task importance as assessed in Item 4 in comparison with the other aspects in "Task orientation" scale.

6.4.5 Differences between instructors' actual and preferred perceptions of CO

Differences between instructors' actual and preferred perceptions of "Cooperation" were found to be significant at $p < 0.001$ for all the eleven items assessed, as shown by the results of paired samples t-tests in Table 6.15. These significant differences in perceptions are represented in Figure 6.14 on the next page.

Table 6.15 Differences between instructors' actual and preferred perceptions of CO

	Questionnaire Item	Mean			T	Sig.
		IA	IP	IA−IP		
Pair 1 (Item 5)	Students cooperate/would cooperate with others when doing assignment work.	3.63	4.55	−.93***	−6.586	.000
Pair 2 (Item 11)	Students share/would share their books and resources with others when doing assignments.	3.38	4.68	−1.30***	−10.395	.000
Pair 3 (Item 17)	When students work/would work in groups in this class, there is teamwork.	3.88	4.85	−.98***	−9.347	.000
Pair 4 (Item 23)	Students work/would work with other members on projects in this class.	3.93	4.75	−.83***	−6.683	.000
Pair 5 (Item 29)	Students learn/would learn from other members in this class.	3.74	4.75	−1.03***	−11.239	.000

Continued

	Questionnaire Item	Mean			T	Sig.
		IA	IP	IA-IP		
Pair 6 (Item 31)	*Students help/would help other class members who are having trouble with their work.*	3.48	4.65	-1.18***	-9.141	.000
Pair 7 (Item 35)	*Students work/would work with other members in this class.*	3.85	4.73	-.88***	-7.306	.000
Pair 8 (Item 39)	*Students discuss/would discuss with others how to go about solving problems.*	3.65	4.75	-1.10***	-10.356	.000
Pair 9 (Item 41)	*Students cooperate/would cooperate with other members on class activities.*	3.85	4.93	-1.08***	-9.799	.000
Pair 10 (Item 43)	*In this class, students get/would get help from other members.*	3.75	4.75	-1.00***	-8.421	.000
Pair 11 (Item 47)	*Students work/would work with others to achieve class goals.*	3.80	4.65	-.85***	-7.309	.000

Note: $N=40$; *** $p<0.001$.

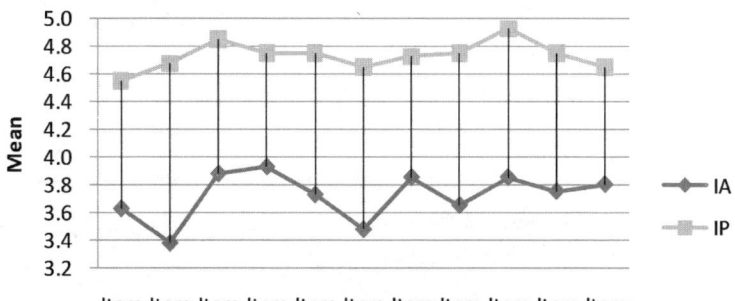

Figure 6.14 Differences between instructors' actual and preferred perceptions of CO

Chapter 6   Discrepancies in Classroom Psychosocial Environment Perceptions

As illustrated in Figure 6.14, instructors would prefer better cooperation among students at all the eleven aspects assessed in "Cooperation" scale. Instructors particularly would like to see the greatest change for students to become more cooperative in sharing books and resources when doing assignment work, as instructors' actual and preferred perceptions of Item 11 were found to differ most greatly than the other items. However, the largest gap in the actual-ideal perceptions of Item 11 might be explained by another reason. Since Item 11 measured the cooperation among students when doing assignment work, most instructors expressed that they were not quite sure about the situation since they had limited contact with students after class, so instructors assumed that students on average "sometimes" shared books and resources as indicated by the average mean score of 3.38 for Item 11 in the instructor actual form, but instructors emphasized the importance of resources sharing among students as suggested by the average mean score of 4.68 for Item 11 in the instructor preferred form.

6.4.6   *Differences between instructors' actual and preferred perceptions of EQ*

Results of paired samples t-tests in Table 6.16 below show that instructors' preferred perception scores of "Equity" were significantly ($p<0.05$) higher than those of actual perceptions for all the items in "Equity" scale except for Item 14. No significant difference was found for this item. These significant differences in the perceptions of nine items as well as the zero difference in the perception of one item are plotted in Figure 6.15.

Table 6.16   Differences between instructors' actual and preferred perceptions of EQ

	Questionnaire Item	Mean			T	Sig.
		IA	IP	IA−IP		
Pair 1 (Item 6)	I give/would give the same attention to the questions asked by each student.	4.25	4.60	−.35*	−2.655	.011

Continued

	Questionnaire Item	Mean			T	Sig.
		IA	IP	IA-IP		
Pair 2 (Item 12)	I give/would give the same amount of help to all the students in this class.	3.55	4.45	-.90***	-7.649	.000
Pair 3 (Item 14)	I consider/would consider students' feelings.	4.45	4.58	-.13	-1.044	.303
Pair 4 (Item 18)	All students have/would have the same amount of say in this class.	3.55	4.63	-1.08***	-7.200	.000
Pair 5 (Item 20)	I help/would help students when they have trouble with their work.	4.35	4.68	-.33**	-2.962	.005
Pair 6 (Item 24)	All students are/would be treated the same in this class.	4.23	4.63	-.40**	-3.399	.002
Pair 7 (Item 30)	All students receive/would receive the same encouragement from me.	4.08	4.40	-.33*	-2.177	.036
Pair 8 (Item 36)	Students get/would get the same opportunity to contribute to class discussions.	4.13	4.70	-.58***	-4.309	.000
Pair 9 (Item 42)	Student's work receives/would receive as much praise as other class members from me.	4.10	4.48	-.38*	-2.303	.027
Pair 10 (Item 48)	All students get/would get the same opportunity to answer questions.	4.18	4.68	-.50**	-2.977	.005

Note: $N=40$; *$p<0.05$; **$p<0.01$; ***$p<0.001$.

As shown in Figure 6.15, instructors would anticipate betterment in their equal treatment of students in class in terms of the nine aspects of "Equity" scale, in particular, by ensuring equal opportunities for students to express their thoughts, opinions, or suggestions in class, since the gaps of actual-preferred perceptions of Item 18 and Item 12 were relatively larger than the other items of "Equity" scale. In addition, though in general instructors would prefer more practices of equal treatment in class, the congruence in instructors' actual and preferred perceptions of Item 14 reveals that instructors were satisfied with their treatment of students' feelings with equal concerns, indicating no need for improvement.

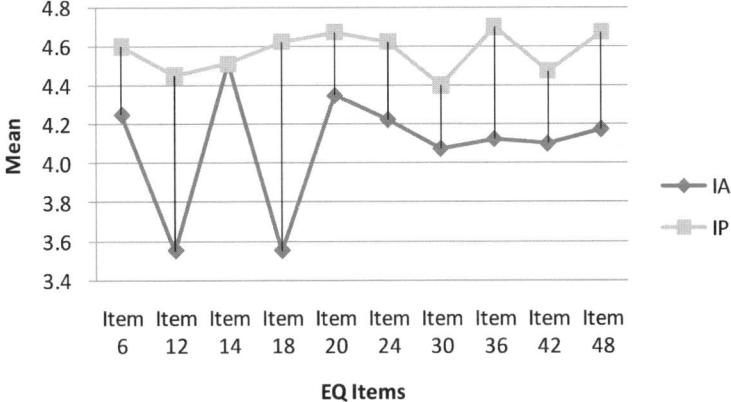

Figure 6.15 Differences between instructors' actual and preferred perceptions of EQ

6.5 Differences in actual perceptions between students and instructors

Comparison results of differences in the actual perceptions between students and instructors depicted in Figure 6.16 show that instructors perceived significantly more favorably on three WIHIC scales, namely, "Teacher support", "Involvement", and "Task orientation", than did their students in the same CE classroom. As for "Student cohesiveness", "Cooperation", and "Equity", the three environmental scales were perceived similarly by students and instructors in the existing CE classrooms.

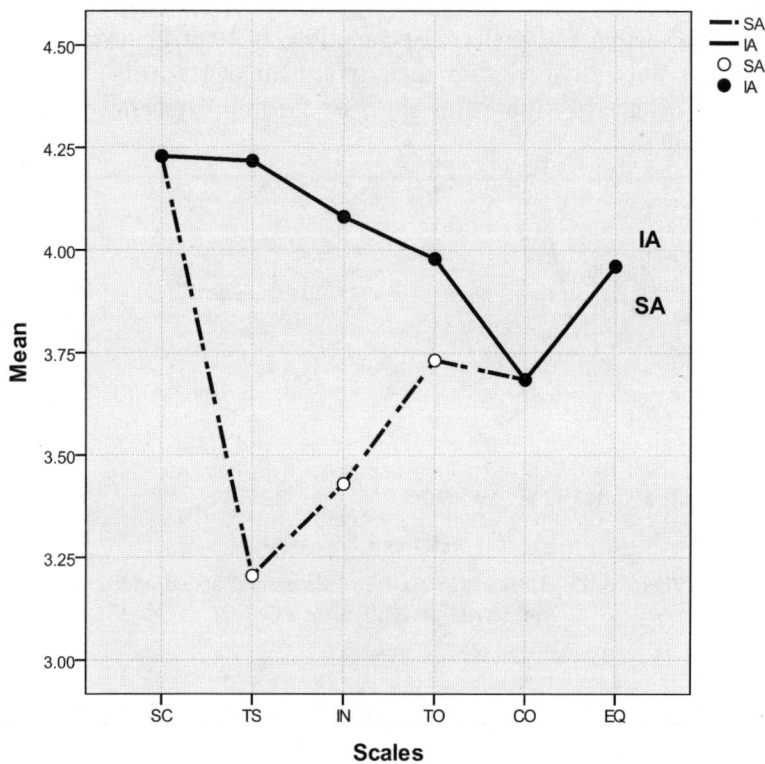

Figure 6.16 Differences in perceptions between student actual and instructor actual forms

With reference to the item mean differences listed in Table 6.1, it can be observed that the differences in student-instructor actual perceptions ranged from the greatest for "Teacher support" (1.01), followed by "Involvement" (0.55), and to the smallest for "Task Orientation" (0.25). Consistent research findings were also reported in the studies of Chua et al. (2011), Sun (2009, 2010), and Sun and Lin (2008) that students and instructors differed most in their perceptions of "Teacher support" in the existing CE classroom psychosocial environments.

More detailed analyses were performed on the significant differences in the student-instructor actual perceptions of "Teacher support", "Involvement", and "Task orientation". The results of analyses were reported and interpreted in the sections below.

6.5.1 Differences in actual perceptions of TS between students and instructors

Results of paired sample t-tests in Table 6.17 show that the actual perception scores of instructors were all significantly higher ($p<0.001$) than those of students for all the ten items in "Teacher support" scale. In other words, instructors felt that they were providing more teacher support in class than what their students received in terms of all the ten aspects assessed in the scale. These significant differences are depicted in Figure 6.17.

Table 6.17 Differences in actual perceptions of TS between students and instructors

	Questionnaire Item		Mean		
	SA	IA	SA	IA	SA-IA
Pair 1 (Item 2)	The teacher takes a personal interest in me.	I take a personal interest in students.	2.92	4.18	-1.25***
Pair 2 (Item 8)	The teacher makes an extra effort to help me.	I make an extra effort to help students.	2.56	4.10	-1.54***
Pair 3 (Item 15)	The teacher asks ask me questions.	I call on individual student to answer questions.	3.67	4.43	-.76***
Pair 4 (Item 21)	My ideas and suggestions are used during classroom discussions.	Students' ideas and suggestions are used during classroom discussions.	3.36	3.98	-.62***
Pair 5 (Item 26)	The teacher talks with me.	I talk with students.	3.39	4.50	-1.11***
Pair 6 (Item 27)	I ask the teacher questions.	Students ask me questions.	3.06	4.18	-1.12***
Pair 7 (Item 32)	The teacher is interested in my problems.	I am interested in students' problems.	3.24	4.25	-1.01***
Pair 8 (Item 38)	The teacher moves about the class to talk with me.	I move about the class to talk with students.	2.91	4.13	-1.21***

Continued

	Questionnaire Item		Mean		
	SA	IA	SA	IA	SA-IA
Pair 9 (Item 44)	The teacher's questions help me to understand.	My questions help students to understand.	3.88	4.45	-.57***
Pair 10 (Item 45)	I am asked to explain how I solve problems.	Students are asked to explain how they solve problems.	3.07	4.00	-.93***

Note: $N=40$; *** $p<0.001$.

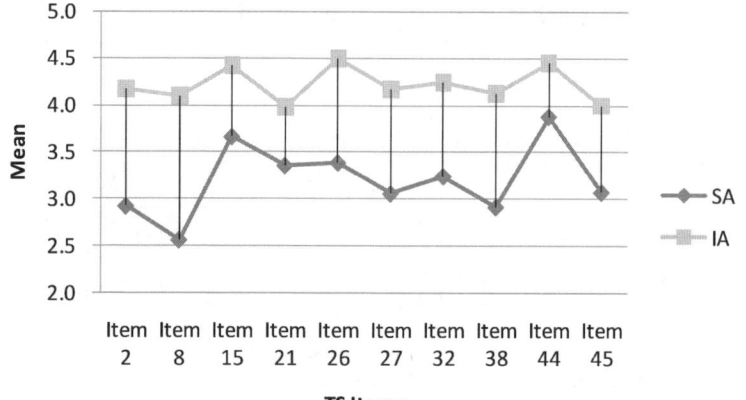

Figure 6.17 Differences in actual perceptions of TS between students and instructors

As shown in Figure 6.17, the differences in actual perceptions of "Teacher support" between students and instructors varied in magnitude for the ten aspects assessed in the scale. Among these items, students and instructors differed most in their perceptions of the amount of extra effort made by instructors to help students, as indicated by the largest gap between the perception scores of Item 8, while students and instructors tended to agree most on their perceptions of the assistance of teachers' questions in helping students to understand, implied by the smallest gap between the perception scores of Item 44.

It has been reported in some past studies that teachers

perceived more teacher support than did their students in various classes, such as Chinese language classes in Singaporean secondary schools (Chua et al., 2011), science classes in Indonesian secondary schools (Wahyudi & Treagust, 2003), both Comprehensive English classes and Oral English classes for non-English majors in some Chinese key universities (Sun, 2009, 2010; Sun & Lin, 2008).

Chua et al. (2011) proposed that one of the possible reasons for the more favorable perceptions of "Teacher support" by instructors than their students might be the low teacher-student ratio of 1 : 30 in the Chinese language classes in the Singaporean context. According to Chua et al. (2011), since the teacher had to attend to many students, the teacher might feel he/she frequently provided support for student in class activities, but some students might feel that they only sometimes receive the support of their teacher, especially when the teacher has to focus on a group of weaker students in order to help them to prepare for examinations. In fact, this is also the case in CE classes for English majors in the Chinese context with a similar low teacher-student ratio of 1 : 30, and this might also result in the asymmetrical perceptions of the personal and academic support provided by instructors between students and instructors in the same classroom.

6.5.2 *Differences in actual perceptions of IN between students and instructors*

Results of paired samples t-tests in Table 6.18 show that there were significant differences between the actual perceptions of students and instructors of Item 3 and Item 33 at $p<0.01$, and Item 9 at $p<0.001$. These differences in perceptions of "Involvement" between students and instructors are illustrated in Figure 6.18.

Table 6.18 Differences in actual perceptions of IN between students and instructors

	Questionnaire Item		Mean		
	SA	IA	SA	IA	SA–IA
Pair 1 (Item 3)	I discuss ideas in class.	Students discuss ideas in class.	3.39	3.91	-.52**
Pair 2 (Item 9)	I give my opinions during class discussions.	Students give their opinions during class discussions.	3.44	4.23	-.79***
Pair 3 (Item 33)	I explain my ideas to other students.	Students explain their ideas to other members.	3.46	3.80	-.34**

Note: $N=40$; ** $p<0.01$; *** $p<0.001$.

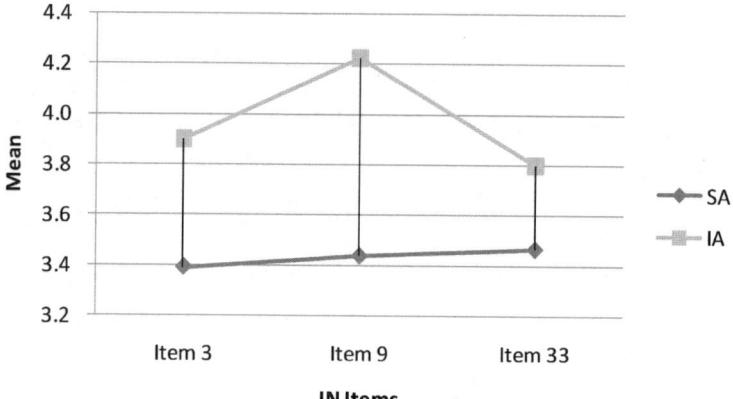

Figure 6.18 Differences in actual perceptions of IN between students and instructors

It is shown in Figure 6.18 that instructors held more favorable views of students' classroom involvement than did their students themselves with regard to all the three aspects assessed in "Involvement" scale. In the studies of Chua *et al.* (2011), Fraser and Treagust (1986), Sun (2009, 2010) and Sun & Lin (2008), students were also found to be more actively involved in class activities as perceived by their teachers than the students themselves in the same classroom.

Such different views on "Involvement" between students and

instructors might occur due to the different perspectives perceived by students and instructors in class. Instructors viewed students' involvement in class activities from a macroscopic view of observing the class as a whole, in which a high level of student involvement could be characterized by the active participation of most students rather than every single student, whereas students focused more on their own participation of class activities as an individual from a microscopic view.

6.5.3 Differences in actual perceptions of TO between students and instructors

As shown by the results of paired samples t-tests in Table 6.19, statistically significant differences occurred for students' and instructors' actual perceptions of Item 4 at $p<0.001$, and both Item 16 and Item 28 at $p<0.01$. There were no statistical differences between their perceptions of Item 10, Item 22, Item 34, Item 40, and Item 46, though in general "task orientation" scale was perceived by students and instructors with substantial difference. Figure 6.19 is plotted to show these differences in perceptions of the eight items in "task orientation" scale with significant and nonsignificant differences.

Table 6.19 Differences in actual perceptions of TO between students and instructors

	Questionnaire Item		Mean		
	SA	IA	SA	IA	SA-IA
Pair 1 (Item 4)	Getting a certain amount of work done is important to me.	Getting a certain amount of work done is important to students.	3.78	4.48	-.70***
Pair 2 (Item 10)	I do as much as I set out to do.	Students do as much as they set out to do.	3.37	3.48	-.11
Pair 3 (Item 16)	I know the goals for this class.	Students know the goals for this class.	3.42	3.90	-.48**
Pair 4 (Item 22)	I am ready to start this class on time.	Students are ready to start this class on time.	4.15	4.10	.05

Continued

	Questionnaire Item		Mean		
	SA	IA	SA	IA	SA-IA
Pair 5 (Item 28)	I know what I am trying to accomplish in this class.	Students know what they are trying to accomplish in this class.	3.48	3.83	-.34**
Pair 6 (Item 34)	I pay attention during this class.	Students pay attention during this class.	3.99	4.13	-.13
Pair 7 (Item 40)	I try to understand the work in this class.	Students try to understand the work in this class.	3.95	4.08	-.13
Pair 8 (Item 46)	I know how much work I have to do.	Students know how much work they have to do.	3.72	3.85	-.13

Note: $N=40$; ** $p<0.01$; *** $p<0.001$.

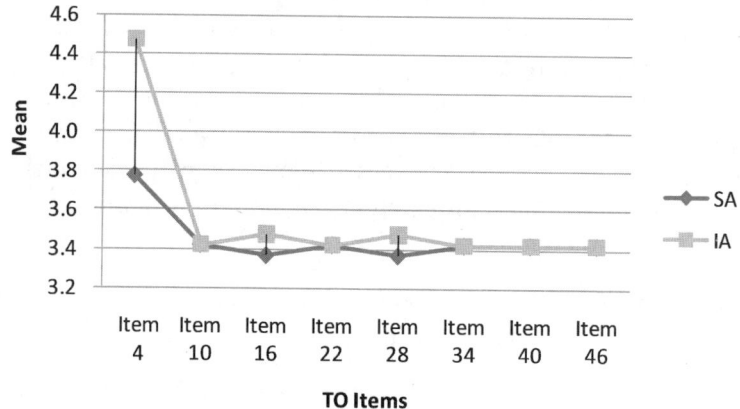

Figure 6.19 Differences in actual perceptions of TO between students and instructors

As shown in Figure 6.19, in the actual CE classroom psychosocial environments, instructors saw more task-oriented students than what the students perceived themselves to be, with more positive attitudes to getting work done and clearer class goals and objectives. Moreover, students were also reported to be more task-oriented as perceived by their instructors than by themselves in the studies of Fraser and Treagust (1986), Sun (2009, 2010;

Sun & Lin, 2008), Wahyudi and Treagust (2003).

Nevertheless, the largest gap in perceptions of Item 4 in "Task orientation" scale between students and instructors revealed in the present study reminded educators that they should avoid being over-optimistic about students' attitudes to accomplishing learning tasks, in particular.

6.6 Differences in preferred perceptions between students and instructors

Differences in the preferred perceptions between students and instructors depicted in Figure 6.20 show that instructors had statistically significant greater expectations and higher standards of the ideal CE classroom psychosocial environments than did their students on all the six WIHIC environmental dimensions.

The item mean differences listed in Table 6.1 show that the gaps of differences between student-instructor preferred perceptions ranged from the largest for "Involvement" (0.65), followed closely by "Teacher Support" (0.62), "Task orientation" (0.46), "Cooperation" (0.43), "Student cohesiveness" (0.32), and to the narrowest for "Equity" (0.21). The degree of differences could also be roughly observed from the various distances between the markers of the six scales in Line SP and Line IP presented in Figure 6.20.

Figure 6.20 showed that students and instructors differed most on their emphasis on students' classroom involvement in CE classes, though basically both of them agreed on the high level perception of "Involvement". Being second to "Involvement" in degree of emphasis, "Teacher support" was also more stressed by instructors than their students. Among the six WIHIC scales, students and instructors tended to be in more agreement on the level of equity in class in comparison with the other five scales, though instructors still had substantially higher expectation on equity than their students.

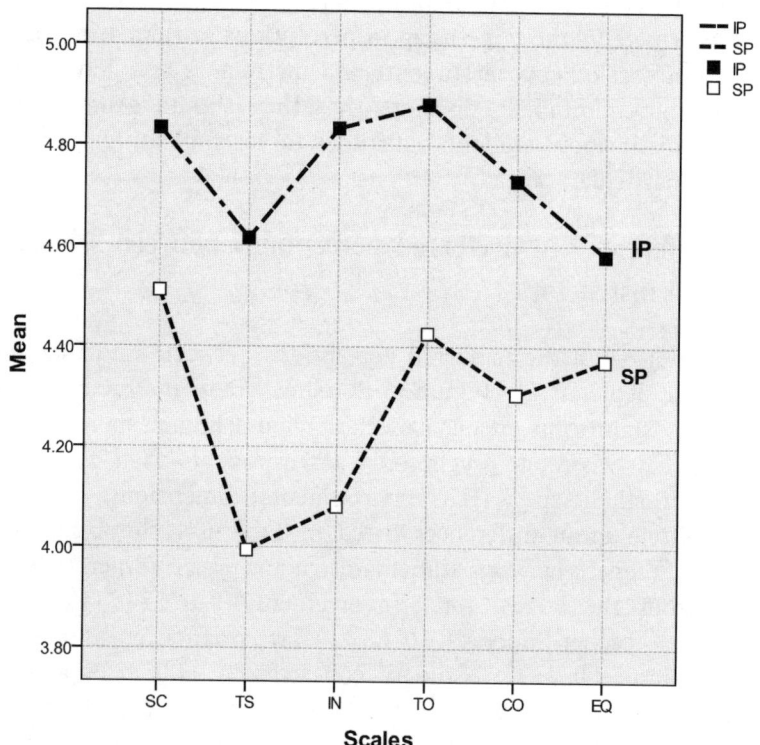

Figure 6.20 Differences in perceptions between students' preferred and instructor preferred forms

More differences in the preferences of a preferred CE classroom psychosocial environment in terms of the six WIHIC scales between students and instructors were explored and reported in the sections below.

6.6.1 Differences in preferred perceptions of SC between students and instructors

Results of paired samples t-tests in Table 6.20 show that there were significant differences in the preferred perceptions of Item 1, Item 7, Item 13, Item 19, and Item 25 at $p<0.001$, and Item 37 at

Chapter 6 Discrepancies in Classroom Psychosocial Environment Perceptions

$p<0.01$ between students and instructors. In other words, all the six aspects of "Student cohesiveness" were perceived differently with statistical significance by students and instructors in an ideal CE classroom psychosocial environment. These differences are illustrated in Figure 6.21.

Table 6.20 Differences in preferred perceptions of SC between students and instructors

	Questionnaire Item		Mean		
	SP	IP	SP	IP	SP-IP
Pair 1 (Item 1)	I would make friendships among students in this class.	Students would make friendships among one another in this class.	4.48	4.80	-.32***
Pair 2 (Item 7)	I would know other students in this class.	Students would know other members in this class.	4.51	4.88	-.36***
Pair 3 (Item 13)	I would be friendly to members of this class.	Students would be friendly to other members in this class.	4.61	4.88	-.26***
Pair 4 (Item 19)	Members of the class would be my friends.	Members of the class would be friends.	4.54	4.88	-.33***
Pair 5 (Item 25)	I would work well with other class members.	Students would work well with other class members.	4.49	4.90	-.41***
Pair 6 (Item 37)	Students in this class would like me.	Students in this class would like other members of this class.	4.42	4.68	-.25**

Note: $N=40$; ** $p<0.01$; *** $p<0.01$.

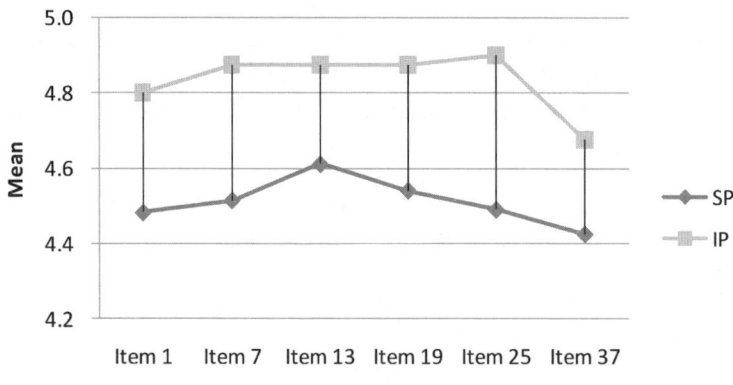

Figure 6.21 Differences in preferred perceptions of SC between students and instructors

Figure 6.21 shows that instructors anticipated better relationships among students than their students did concerning all the six aspects of "Student cohesiveness". Differences in perceptions of the six aspects were similar in magnitude, with the relatively largest gap occurred for Item 25 and the smallest for Item 37.

6.6.2 *Differences in preferred perceptions of TS between students and instructors*

It is shown in Table 6.21 that differences between students' and instructors' preferred perceptions of "Teacher support" were found to be statistically significant for Item 21 at $p<0.05$ and other eight items at $p<0.001$, namely, Item 8, Item 15, Item 26, Item 27, Item 32, Item 38, Item 44, and Item 45. No significant difference in perceptions between students and instructors was found for Item 2. The differences in perceptions are illustrated in Figure 6.22.

Chapter 6   Discrepancies in Classroom Psychosocial Environment Perceptions

Table 6.21   Differences in preferred perceptions of TS between students and instructors

	Questionnaire Item		Mean		
	SP	IP	SP	IP	SP-IP
Pair 1 (Item 2)	The teacher would take a personal interest in me.	I would take a personal interest in students.	3.70	4.13	-.42
Pair 2 (Item 8)	The teacher would make an extra effort to help me.	I would make an extra effort to help students.	3.74	4.63	-.88***
Pair 3 (Item 15)	The teacher would ask me questions.	I would call on individual student to answer questions.	3.95	4.45	-.50***
Pair 4 (Item 21)	My ideas and suggestions would be used during classroom discussions.	Students' ideas and suggestions would be used during classroom discussions.	4.15	4.40	-.25*
Pair 5 (Item 26)	The teacher would talk with me.	I would talk with students.	4.00	4.90	-.90***
Pair 6 (Item 27)	I would ask the teacher questions.	Students would ask me questions.	4.03	4.80	-.77***
Pair 7 (Item 32)	The teacher would be interested in my problems.	I would be interested in students' problems.	4.11	4.75	-.64***
Pair 8 (Item 38)	The teacher would move about the class to talk with me.	I would move about the class to talk with students.	3.83	4.70	-.87***
Pair 9 (Item 44)	The teacher's questions would help me to understand.	My questions would help students to understand.	4.44	4.85	-.41***
Pair 10 (Item 45)	I would be asked to explain how I solve problems.	Students would be asked to explain how they solve problems.	3.98	4.55	-.57***

Note: $N=40$, ** $p<0.01$, *** $p<0.01$.

It was shown in Figure 6.22 that instructors would expect

more teacher support than their students with respect to nine out of the ten items in "teacher support" scale. Among the nine items, students and instructors varied most on their stress on the communication of instructors with students as assessed in Item 26, while they tended to have more similar views on the support of instructors by taking students' ideas and suggestions during classroom discussions as measured in Item 4 than the other aspects of "teacher support". In addition, the zero difference in perceptions of Item 2 between students and instructors implies that they were consistent in their emphasis and expectations on the support of instructors in terms of taking personal interests in students.

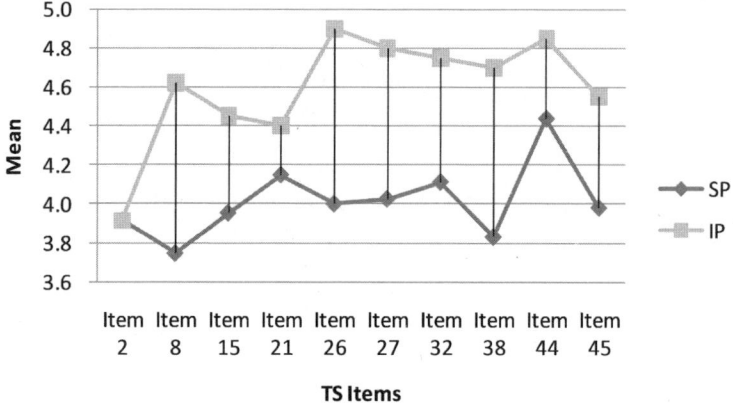

Figure 6.22 Differences in preferred perceptions of TS between students and instructors

6.6.3 *Differences in preferred perceptions of IN between students and instructors*

Results of paired samples t-tests in Table 6.22 show that there were significant differences at $p < 0.001$ between students' and instructors' perceptions of all the three items in "Involvement" scale. The differences in perceptions are plotted in Figure 6.23.

Chapter 6 Discrepancies in Classroom Psychosocial Environment Perceptions

Table 6.22 Differences in preferred perceptions of IN between students and instructors

	Questionnaire Item		Mean		
	SP	IP	SP	IP	SP−IP
Pair 1 (Item 3)	I would discuss ideas in class.	Students would discuss ideas in class.	4.18	4.75	−.57***
Pair 2 (Item 9)	I would give my opinions during class discussions.	Students would give their opinions during class discussions.	4.19	4.95	−.76***
Pair 3 (Item 33)	I would explain my ideas to other students.	Students would explain their ideas to other members.	4.20	4.80	−.60***

Note: $N=40$; *** $p<0.01$.

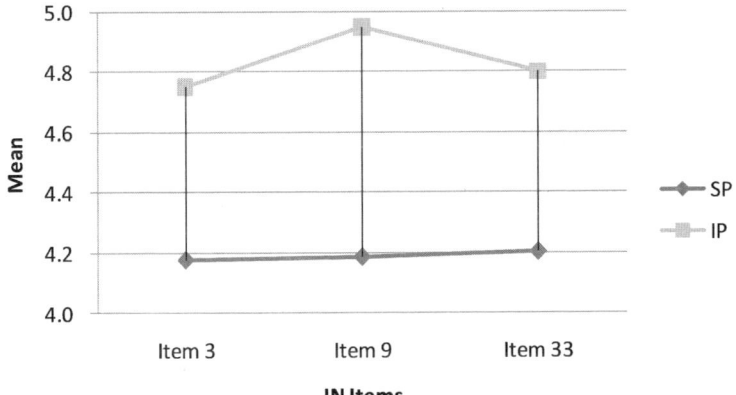

Figure 6.23 Differences in preferred perceptions of IN between students and instructors

Figure 6.23 shows that instructors emphasized the important role of student classroom engagement more greatly than did their students with respect to all the three aspects of "Involvement", particularly on the active role of students in expressing ideas during class discussions as indicated by the relatively largest gap in perceptions of Item 9.

6.6.4 Differences in preferred perceptions of TO between students and instructors

Statistically significant differences at $p < 0.001$ were found between students' and instructors' preferred perceptions of all the eight items in "Task orientation" scale (see Table 6.23). The differences in perceptions are illustrated in Figure 6.24.

It is shown in Figure 6.24 that instructors had greater expectations than their students on all the eight aspects of "Task orientation" in the ideal CE classroom psychosocial environments. Among these aspects, students and instructors differed most on the stress laid on the importance of getting class work done for students as assessed in Item 4. As revealed in section 6.5.3, the largest gap also occurred in the actual perceptions of Item 4 between students and instructors. Therefore, more concerns and efforts were required for educators to narrow or eliminate the gap between the different views of students and instructors on the importance of getting class work done in order to create a more congruent classroom psychosocial environment conducive to learning.

Table 6.23 Differences in preferred perceptions of TO between students and instructors

	Questionnaire Item		Mean		
	SP	IP	SP	IP	SP-IP
Pair 1 (Item 4)	Getting a certain amount of work done would be important to me.	Getting a certain amount of work done would be important to students.	4.17	4.90	-.73***
Pair 2 (Item 10)	I would do as much as I set out to do.	Students would do as much as they set out to do.	4.35	4.75	-.40***
Pair 3 (Item 16)	I would know the goals for this class.	Students would know the goals for this class.	4.44	4.95	-.51***
Pair 4 (Item 22)	I would be ready to start this class on time.	Students would be ready to start this class on time.	4.55	4.95	-.40***

Chapter 6 Discrepancies in Classroom Psychosocial Environment Perceptions

Continued

	Questionnaire Item		Mean		
	SP	IP	SP	IP	SP–IP
Pair 5 (Item 28)	I would know what I am trying to accomplish in this class.	Students would know what they are trying to accomplish in this class.	4.47	4.90	−.43***
Pair 6 (Item 34)	I would pay attention during this class.	Students would pay attention during this class.	4.51	4.95	−.44***
Pair 7 (Item 40)	I would try to understand the work in this class.	Students would try to understand the work in this class.	4.50	4.88	−.38***
Pair 8 (Item 46)	I would know how much work I have to do.	Students would know how much work they have to do.	4.42	4.78	−.35***

Note: $N=40$; *** $p<0.01$.

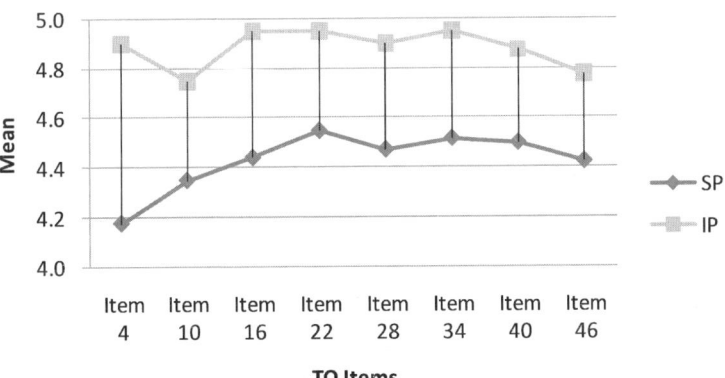

Figure 6.24 Differences in preferred perceptions of TO between students and instructors

6.6.5 *Differences in preferred perceptions of CO between students and instructors*

Results of paired samples *t*-tests in Table 6.24 show that there were significant differences between students' and instructors' preferred perceptions of Item 5 and Item 35 at $p<0.01$, Item 11, Item 17, Item 23, Item 29, Item 31, Item 39, Item 41, Item 43, and Item 47 at $p<0.001$. These differences in perceptions are graphed in Figure 6.25.

As shown in Figure 6.25, instructors placed greater value on cooperation among students than did their students regarding all the eleven aspects in "Cooperation" scale. Among these aspects, differences in the stress laid on cooperation among students on problems solving and class activities were greater than the other aspects of cooperation.

Table 6.24 Differences in preferred perceptions of CO between students and instructors

	Questionnaire Item		Mean		
	SA	IP	SA	IP	SA−IP
Pair 1 (Item 5)	I would cooperate with other students when doing assignment work.	Students would cooperate with others when doing assignment work.	4.17	4.55	−.38**
Pair 2 (Item 11)	I would share my books and resources with other students when doing assignments.	Students would share their books and resources with others when doing assignments.	4.18	4.68	−.49***
Pair 3 (Item 17)	When I work in groups in this class, there would be teamwork.	When students work in groups in this class, there would be teamwork.	4.39	4.85	−.46***
Pair 4 (Item 23)	I would work with other students on projects in this class.	Students would work with other members on projects in this class.	4.32	4.75	−.43***
Pair 5 (Item 29)	I would learn from other students in this class.	Students would learn from other members in this class.	4.43	4.75	−.32***
Pair 6 (Item 31)	I would help other class members who are having trouble with their work.	Students would help other class members who are having trouble with their work.	4.29	4.65	−.36***

Continued

	Questionnaire Item		Mean		
	SA	IP	SA	IP	SA−IP
Pair 7 (Item 35)	I would work with other students in this class.	Students would work with other members in this class.	4.37	4.73	−.36**
Pair 8 (Item 39)	Students would discuss with me how to go about solving problems.	Students would discuss with others how to go about solving problems.	4.22	4.75	−.53***
Pair 9 (Item 41)	I would cooperate with other students on class activities.	Students would cooperate with other members on class activities.	4.39	4.93	−.53***
Pair 10 (Item 43)	In this class, I would get help from other students.	In this class, students would get help from other members.	4.26	4.75	−.49***
Pair 11 (Item 47)	Students would work with me to achieve class goals.	Students would work with others to achieve class goals.	4.32	4.65	−.33***

Note: $N=40$; ** $p<0.01$; *** $p<0.01$.

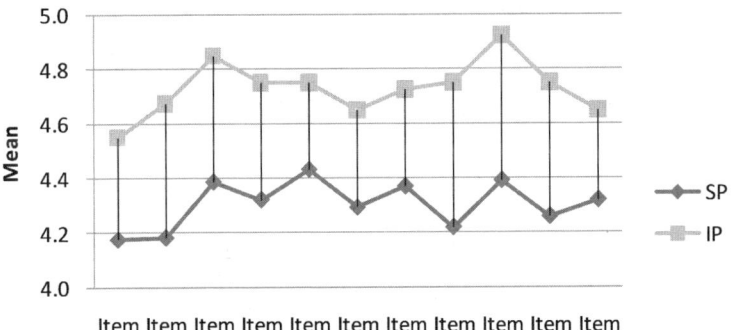

Figure 6.25 Differences in preferred perceptions of CO between students and instructors

6.6.6 Differences in preferred perceptions of EQ between students and instructors

As shown by the results of paired samples t-tests in Table 6.25, statistically differences between students' and instructors' preferred perceptions of "Equity" were found for Item 36 at $p < 0.001$, Item 14, Item 18, Item 20, and Item 48 at $p < 0.01$, and Item 6 at $p < 0.05$. There were no significant differences in perceptions of Item 12, Item 24, Item 30, and Item 42. Figure 6.26 illustrates these significant and nonsignificant differences.

Table 6.25 Differences in preferred perceptions of EQ between students and instructors

	Questionnaire Item		Mean		
	SP	IP	SP	IP	SP–IP
Pair 1 (Item 6)	The teacher would give as much attention to my questions as to other students' questions.	I would give the same attention to the questions asked by each student.	4.36	4.60	−.24*
Pair 2 (Item 12)	I would get the same amount of help from the teacher as do other students.	I would give the same amount of help to all the students in this class.	4.34	4.45	−.11
Pair 3 (Item 14)	The teacher would consider my feelings.	I would consider students' feelings.	4.31	4.58	−.27**
Pair 4 (Item 18)	I would have the same amount of say in this class as other students.	All students would have the same amount of say in this class.	4.34	4.63	−.29**
Pair 5 (Item 20)	The teacher would help me when I have trouble with the work.	I would help students when they have trouble with their work.	4.38	4.68	−.29**
Pair 6 (Item 24)	I would be treated the same as other students in this class.	All students would be treated the same in this class.	4.51	4.63	−.11

Continued

	Questionnaire Item		Mean		
	SP	IP	SP	IP	SP-IP
Pair 7 (Item 30)	I would receive the same encouragement from the teacher as other students do.	All students would receive the same encouragement from me.	4.39	4.40	-.015
Pair 8 (Item 36)	I would get the same opportunity to contribute to class discussions as other students.	Students would get the same opportunity to contribute to class discussions.	4.38	4.70	-.32***
Pair 9 (Item 42)	My work would receive as much praise as other students' work.	Student's work would receive as much praise as other class members from me.	4.33	4.48	-.14
Pair 10 (Item 48)	I would get the same opportunity to answer questions as other students.	All students would get the same opportunity to answer questions.	4.38	4.68	-.30**

Note: $N=40$ *$p<0.05$; **$p<0.01$; ***$p<0.01$.

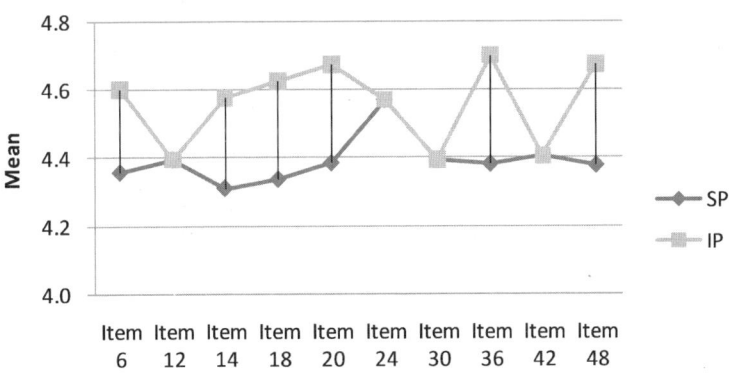

Figure 6.26 Differences in preferred perceptions of EQ between students and instructors

As shown in Figure 6.26, instructors would prefer more

"Equity" than what was expected by their students in terms of the six aspects measured in the scale. However, though the overall preferred perceptions of "Equity" scale were found to be significantly different between students and instructors, there was still agreement in their preferences of some aspects of "Equity", such as the equal treatment by providing/receiving the same amount of help, encouragement, and praise as assessed in Item 12, Item 20, Item 24, and Item 42.

6.7 Summary

This chapter has provided the analyses and interpretations of discrepancies in students' and instructors' actual and preferred perceptions of their CE classroom environments so as to reveal the psychosocial features of the classroom environments. Initially, two general patterns of discrepancies between students' and instructors' perceptions of their actual and preferred classroom environments were revealed by performing the one-way repeated measures MANOVA. First, it is found that both students and instructors would prefer a more favorable CE classroom environment in comparison with what they were experiencing at present. Second, both the actual and preferred CE classroom environments were perceived more positively by instructors than their students. The two general patterns of CE classroom psychosocial environments are in support of the research findings reported in previous studies.

Four pairs of comparisons by performing a series of t-tests for paired samples between the actual and preferred perceptions of both students and instructors further explored and revealed the psychosocial characteristics of CE classroom environments.

Comparisons between the actual and preferred perceptions of students in Section 6.3 and instructors in Section 6.4 indicated that both students and instructors had preferences for a more favorable classroom in terms of all the six WIHIC environmental scales. They would like to see improvements in all the six WIHIC scales with varied magnitude. Further closer examination on differences in perceptions of the items within each WIHIC scale

Chapter 6   Discrepancies in Classroom Psychosocial Environment Perceptions

showed that both students and instructors had different expectations for the improvements of aspects within each scale.

Comparisons between students' and instructors' actual perceptions in Section 6.5 showed that instructors perceived more "Teacher support", "Involvement" and "Task orientation" than their students in the same classes. Further inspection on the items within each of the three scales showed that all the items in "Teacher support" and "Involvement" were perceived more positively by instructors, while perceptions of instructors and students differed for three out of the ten items in "Task orientation" scale.

The last pair of comparisons between students' and instructors' preferred perceptions in Section 6.6 showed that instructors would expect a more favorable CE classroom environment than their students on all the six WIHIC scales. Furthermore, it is found that instructors had higher expectations for all the items within the six WIHIC scales except for the agreement between them on the preferences for certain aspects of "Equity".

Chapter 7
Gender Differences in CE Classroom Psychosocial Environment Perceptions

7.1 Introduction

Gender has been considered as an important factor influencing second language (L2) teaching and learning. In the present study, gender is also regarded as one of the factors to influence students' perceptions of classroom psychosocial environments. This chapter sets out to explore the nature of Comprehensive English (CE) classroom psychosocial environments from the comparisons of male and female students' perceptions of both their actual and preferred CE classroom psychosocial environments. Gender differences in perceptions of both the actual and preferred CE classroom psychosocial environments are analyzed and discussed at the level of "What Is Happening In this Class?" (WIHIC) environmental scales and more subtle gender differences in perceptions are further investigated and revealed at the level of the aspects measured in each WIHIC environmental scale.

7.2 Data analysis of gender differences in classroom environment perceptions

Differences between male and female students' actual and preferred perceptions of their CE classroom psychosocial environments were investigated using sex subgroup item means of each class as the unit of analysis, namely, male subgroup mean and female subgroup mean. Four sets of data (i.e. male actual mean, female actual mean, male preferred mean, and female preferred mean) were calculated across the 40 classes to compare the male students' and female students' actual and preferred perceptions of the classroom environments. Table 7.1 below reports the item means and standard deviations (SDs) for the actual and preferred perception scores of each scale for male and female students in the 40 classes.

Table 7.1 Means and SDs for actual and preferred perception scores of male and female students

Environment scale	No. of items	Male actual		Female actual		Male preferred		Female preferred	
		Mean	SD	Mean	SD	Mean	SD	Mean	SD
SC	6	3.96	0.35	4.27	0.15	4.28	0.33	4.56	0.16
TS	10	3.37	0.39	3.17	0.29	3.90	0.37	4.02	0.19
IN	3	3.39	0.44	3.44	0.25	4.05	0.39	4.22	0.19
TO	8	3.61	0.33	3.77	0.18	4.25	0.33	4.47	0.16
CO	11	3.55	0.33	3.67	0.20	4.15	0.28	4.34	0.16
EQ	10	3.82	0.40	3.84	0.24	4.24	0.33	4.40	0.15

Note: $N=40$; "Almost never" =1; "Seldom" =2; "Sometimes" =3; "Often" =4; "Almost always" =5.

One-way multivariate analysis of variance (MANOVA) for repeated measures was performed to analyze the four sets of data for gender differences in perceptions of the twelve WIHIC scales (i.e. six actual scales and six preferred scales). The result of MANOVA yielded a significant result ($p<0.001$) in terms of Wilks' lambda criterion (Wilks' lambda $=0.152$), indicating that there were statistically significant gender differences in the set of criterion variables as a whole. Post-hoc tests with Bonferroni correction were run by SPSS 19.0 for the twelve dependent variables. The results of the post-hoc tests are displayed in Table 7.2 on the next page.

Results in Table 7.2 show that significant gender differences ($p<0.05$) in students' actual perceptions occurred on four out of the six WIHIC scales, namely "Student cohesiveness", "Teacher support", "Task orientation", and "Cooperation". No significant differences were found in their actual perceptions of "Involvement" and "Equity" scales. As for their preferences for the CE classroom psychosocial environments, five out of the six WIHIC scales were perceived significantly differently ($p < 0.05$) between male and female students, namely, "Student cohesiveness", "Involvement", "Task orientation", "Cooperation", and "Equity". No significant difference was found for the preferred perceptions of "Teacher support" between male and female students.

Table 7.2 Post-hoc tests of perceptions of the twelve WIHIC scales between male and female students

Measure	(I) Sex	(J) Sex	Mean Difference (I-J)	Std. Error	Sig.	95% Confidence Interval for Difference	
						Lower Bound	Upper Bound
SC_SA	M	F	-.307***	.053	.000	-.415	-.199
TS_SA	M	F	.207***	.051	.000	.103	.310
IN_SA	M	F	-.043	.065	.513	-.174	.088
TO_SA	M	F	-.157**	.052	.004	-.262	-.052
CO_SA	M	F	-.124*	.048	.014	-.221	-.026
EQ_SA	M	F	-.020	.057	.731	-.134	.095
SC_SP	M	F	-.288***	.056	.000	-.401	-.174
TS_SP	M	F	-.113	.062	.074	-.238	.011
IN_SP	M	F	-.174*	.067	.014	-.310	-.038
TO_SP	M	F	-.219***	.050	.000	-.320	-.119
CO_SP	M	F	-.186***	.045	.000	-.277	-.095
EQ_SP	M	F	-.158**	.058	.009	-.275	-.041

Note: $N=40$; *$p<0.05$; **$p<0.01$; ***$p<0.001$.

With reference to the perception scores and results of differences obtained in Table 7.1, the significant differences between male and female students' actual perceptions of CE classroom psychosocial environments are plotted in Figure 7.1 below, and the significant differences between male and female students' preferred perceptions of CE classroom psychosocial environments are illustrated in Figure 7.6 in section 7.4. In order to present a parsimonious picture of the differences, only mean scores with significant differences ($p < 0.05$) in perceptions are included in both Figure 7.1 and Figure 7.6. As for the scales with nonsignificant differences in perceptions, average mean scores of the relevant item mean scores in the pairs are calculated and taken into account in the two figures.

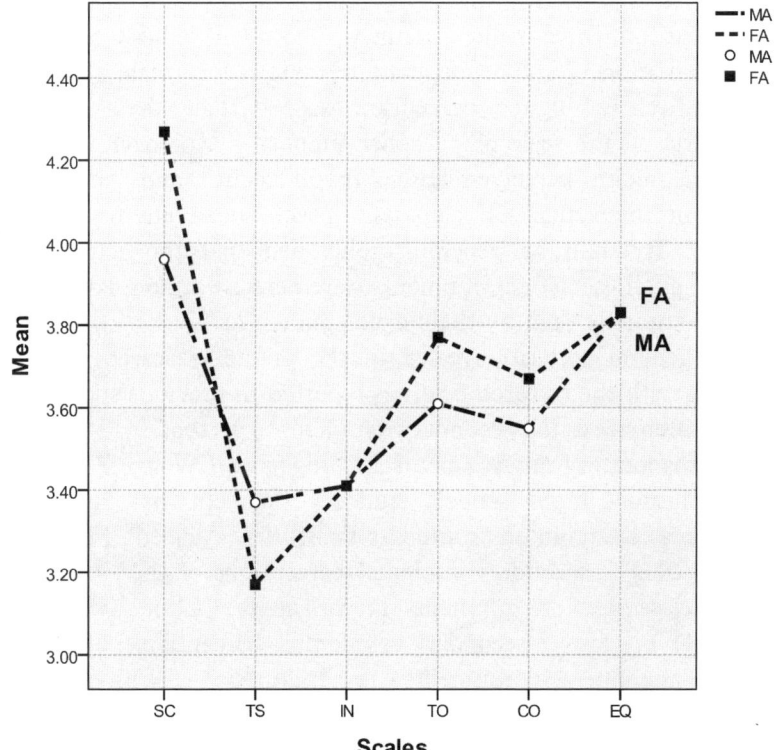

Figure 7.1 Gender differences in actual CE classroom environment perceptions

7.3 Gender differences in actual classroom environment perceptions

7.3.1 General pattern of gender differences in actual perceptions

Figure 7.1 provides a graph of the differences in perceptions of actual CE classroom psychosocial environments between male and female students. As shown in Figure 7.1, on the whole, female students had significantly higher perception scores than their male counterparts on three scales, namely, "Student cohesiveness", "Task orientation", and "Cooperation". However, male students had significantly higher perception scores than their female counterparts on the scale of "Teacher support". Moreover, female and male students perceived both "Involvement" and "Equity" similarly in the actual CE classroom psychosocial environments. Therefore, it could be generally concluded that the actual CE classroom psychosocial environments were perceived more favorably by female students than by their male counterparts.

The general pattern revealed in the present research was in agreement with the research findings reported in previous studies of gender differences in secondary students' perceptions of the chemistry laboratory environments in Singapore (Wong & Fraser, 1994), junior high school students' perceptions of their mathematics classroom environments in Brunei (Majeed, Fraser & Aldridge, 2002), secondary students' perceptions of their Chinese language classroom environments in Singapore (Chua, Wong & Chen, 2011), lower secondary students' perceptions of their science classroom environments in Indonesia (Wuhyudi & Treagust, 2003), students' perceptions of their science classroom environments in Indian (Koul & Fisher, 2006), elementary students' perceptions of their mathematics classroom environments in Singapore (Goh & Fraser, 1995), and students' perceptions of their English reading and mathematics classrooms at three levels of schooling (elementary, middle, high) in the United States

(Waxman & Huang, 1998). However, the findings of the present study are different from the result reported by Nair (2002) that first-year university female and male students similarly perceived their classroom environments of chemistry, physics, biology, computer science, mathematics and geography in Canadian and Australian institutions.

It was worth noticing that the general pattern of the present study that female students perceived the existing CE classroom environments more favorably than male students was also in contrast to the similarity in perceptions between male and female non-English majors of their CE classroom environments in Chinese colleges and universities reported by Sun et al. (2010). However, close examination exhibited the consistent findings between the present study and the study of Sun et al. (2010) that the three scales, namely, "Student cohesiveness" (SC), "Task orientation" (TO), and "Cooperation" (CO), were perceived more positively by female students than their male counterparts.

In an attempt to further reveal the differences in perceptions between male and female students towards the specific aspects within actual and preferred WIHIC environmental scales, a series of paired samples t-tests were performed. The following sections presented, analyzed, and interpreted the results of these pair-wise comparisons.

7.3.2 Gender differences in students' actual perceptions of SC

Results of paired samples t-tests listed in Table 7.3 on the next page show that there were significant gender differences in students' actual perceptions of Item 1, Item 7, Item 19, and Item 25 at $p < 0.001$, Item 13 at $p < 0.01$, and Item 37 at $p < 0.05$ within the scale of "Student cohesiveness". These gender differences in actual perceptions of the six aspects of "Student cohesiveness" are illustrated in Figure 7.2 on the next page.

As shown in Figure 7.2, the perception scores of female students on the six items of "Student cohesiveness" were all significantly higher than those of male students for the corresponding items. This implied that in the actual CE classroom psychosocial environments, female students were experiencing a higher degree of cohesiveness among class members than their male counterparts in terms of all the six aspects assessed in "Student cohesiveness" scale.

Table 7.3　Gender differences in students' actual perceptions of SC

	Questionnaire Item	Mean			T	Sig.
		MA	FA	MA-FA		
Pair 1 (Item 1)	*I make friendships among students in this class.*	3.67	4.09	-.42***	-5.512	.000
Pair 2 (Item 7)	*I know other students in this class.*	4.31	4.67	-.36***	-4.120	.000
Pair 3 (Item 13)	*I am friendly to members of this class.*	4.32	4.57	-.25**	-2.994	.005
Pair 4 (Item 19)	*Members of the class are my friends.*	3.85	4.27	-.42***	-5.200	.000
Pair 5 (Item 25)	*I work well with other class members.*	3.74	4.15	-.41***	-6.537	.000
Pair 6 (Item 37)	*Students in this class like me.*	3.72	3.87	-.16*	-2.295	.027

Note: $N=40$; *$p<0.05$; **$p<0.01$; ***$p<0.001$.

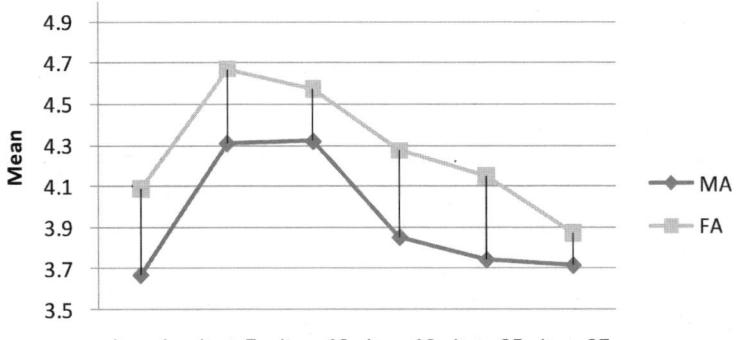

Figure 7.2　Gender differences in students' actual perceptions of SC

Chua *et al.* (2011) proposed in their studies that the gender differences in students' perceptions of "Student cohesiveness" in their actual Chinese language classroom environments could be explained by the bonding differences between male and female students in that female students were more likely to form their own circles of friends and share personal feelings and opinions among the members in their circles. Such differences in bonding between male and female students might also account for the significantly stronger group cohesiveness experienced by female students than their male counterparts in the CE classroom psychosocial environments in the Chinese context.

7.3.3 Gender differences in students' actual perceptions of TS

Results of paired samples *t*-tests in Table 7.4 below display that there were significant gender differences in perceptions of Item 8 and Item 38 at $p<0.001$, Item 2 at $p<0.01$, and Item 15, Item 26, Item 32, and Item 45 at $p<0.05$ within the scale of "Teacher support". No significant differences were found in perceptions of Item 21, Item 27, and Item 44 between male and female students.

Table 7.4 Gender differences in students' actual perceptions of TS

	Questionnaire Item	Mean			T	Sig.
		MA	FA	MA−FA		
Pair 1 (Item 2)	The teacher takes a personal interest in me.	3.16	2.85	.30**	3.659	.001
Pair 2 (Item 8)	The teacher makes an extra effort to help me.	2.86	2.47	.39***	4.623	.000
Pair 3 (Item 15)	The teacher asks me questions.	3.80	3.62	.17*	2.391	.022
Pair 4 (Item 21)	My ideas and suggestions are used during classroom discussions.	3.41	3.34	.07	.891	.378
Pair 5 (Item 26)	The teacher talks with me.	3.56	3.35	.21*	2.220	.032
Pair 6 (Item 27)	I ask the teacher questions.	3.17	3.02	.16	1.973	.056

Continued

	Questionnaire Item	Mean			T	Sig.
		MA	FA	MA-FA		
Pair 7 (Item 32)	The teacher is interested in my problems.	3.36	3.22	.14*	2.272	.029
Pair 8 (Item 38)	The teacher moves about the class to talk with me.	3.20	2.83	.37***	4.150	.000
Pair 9 (Item 44)	The teacher's questions help me to understand.	3.85	3.91	-.06	-.773	.444
Pair 10 (Item 45)	I am asked to explain how I solve problems.	3.25	3.05	.19*	2.188	.035

Note: * $p < 0.05$; ** $p < 0.01$; *** $p < 0.001$; Sample size is 40 pairs of within-class gender means.

Figure 7.3 presents a graph of the differences in actual perceptions between male and female students of the ten aspects of "Teacher support". To present a more parsimonious picture of gender differences in perceptions of the ten items, only the item scores with statistically significant differences were displayed in Figure 7.3. The item scores with no significant differences were represented as zero differences by averaging the relevant item mean scores in the pairs.

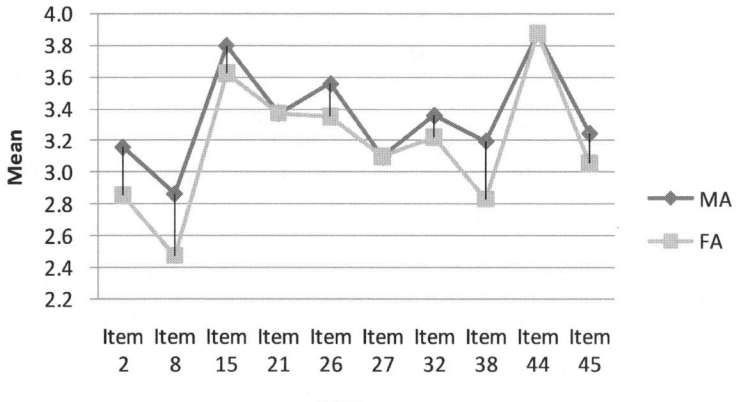

Figure 7.3 Gender differences in students' actual perceptions of TS

As shown in Figure 7.3, though "Teacher support" was generally perceived more positively by male students than their female counterparts as revealed previously, the zero differences in their perceptions of Item 21, Item 27, and Item 44 shown in Figure 7.3 imply that both male and female students actually received similar amounts of support from their instructors in regard of asking teacher questions, ideas and suggestions being used during class discussions, and understanding better with the help of teachers' questions.

Nevertheless, it is also shown in Figure 7.3 that male students did enjoy a greater extent of support that the instructor helped, befriended, trusted, and showed interests in them as measured in the other seven aspects in "Teacher support" scale. From personal observation of the researcher and discussions with instructors who participated in the study, it is found that such gender differences in perceptions of "Teacher support" could be explained by the low proportion (about 1 : 4) of male to female students in the CE classrooms, and therefore, it is natural that instructors, with self-consciousness or not to compensate such low proportion of male students, might tend to pay more attention to male students than their female counterparts in the same classrooms.

7.3.4 Gender differences in students' actual perceptions of TO

As shown by the results of paired samples t-tests in Table 7.5, differences between male and female students' perceptions of "Task orientation" (TO) were statistically significant for Item 22 at $p < 0.001$, Item 4 at $p < 0.01$, and Item 10 at $p < 0.05$. No significant differences were found for the other five items in the scale. Figure 7.4 depicts students' perceptions of "Task orientation" with significant and nonsignificant gender differences in the actual CE classroom psychosocial environments.

Table 7.5　Gender differences in students' actual perceptions of TO

	Questionnaire Item	Mean			T	Sig.
		MA	FA	MA-FA		
Pair 1 (Item 4)	Getting a certain amount of work done is important to me.	3.60	3.82	-.23**	-2.903	.006
Pair 2 (Item 10)	I do as much as I set out to do.	3.23	3.38	-.15*	-2.271	.029
Pair 3 (Item 16)	I know the goals for this class.	3.38	3.48	-.09	-.849	.401
Pair 4 (Item 22)	I am ready to start this class on time.	3.92	4.21	-.29***	-3.817	.000
Pair 5 (Item 28)	I know what I am trying to accomplish in this class.	3.39	3.51	-.12	-1.667	.104
Pair 6 (Item 34)	I pay attention during this class.	3.89	4.03	-.14	-1.890	.066
Pair 7 (Item 40)	I try to understand the work in this class.	3.90	3.97	-.06	-1.001	.323
Pair 8 (Item 46)	I know how much work I have to do.	3.64	3.75	-.11	-1.444	.157

Note: $N=40$; * $p<0.05$; ** $p<0.01$; *** $p<0.001$.

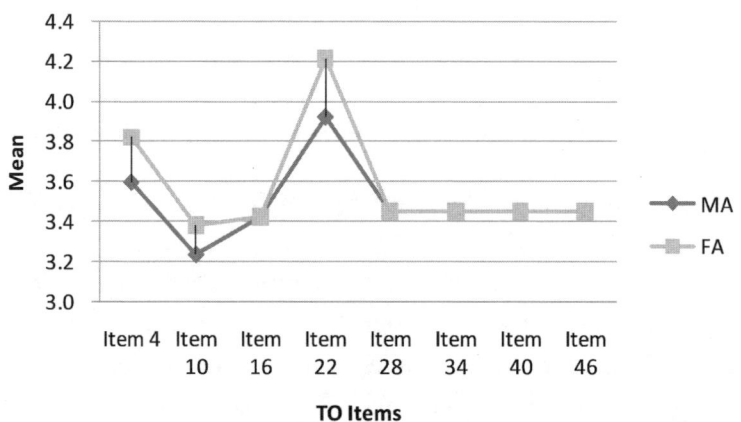

Figure 7.4　Gender differences in students' actual perceptions of TO

Chapter 7 Gender Differences in CE Classroom Psychosocial Environment Perceptions

As shown in Figure 7.4, female students experienced a more task-oriented classroom environment than male students, in which female students were more aware of the importance of getting a certain amount of work done, being more perseverant in study, and better prepared to start the class on time. As for the other five aspects of "Task orientation", both male and female students were consistent in their perceptions.

Furthermore, the significant gender differences in perceptions of "Task orientation" revealed in the present study also correspond to the traditional Chinese view on gender difference in study that female students are more industrious and observant than male students.

7.3.5 Gender differences in students' actual perceptions of CO

Results of paired samples t-tests of the items in "Cooperation" scales are listed in Table 7.6.

Table 7.6 Gender differences in students' actual perceptions of CO

	Questionnaire Item	Mean			T	Sig.
		MA	FA	MA-FP		
Pair 1 (Item 5)	I cooperate with other students when doing assignment work.	3.40	3.46	-.06	-.699	.488
Pair 2 (Item 11)	I share my books and resources with other students when doing assignments.	3.37	3.51	-.15*	-2.255	.030
Pair 3 (Item 17)	When I work in groups in this class, there is teamwork.	3.86	4.08	-.22**	-2.801	.008
Pair 4 (Item 23)	I work with other students on projects in this class.	3.64	3.83	-.20*	-2.439	.019
Pair 5 (Item 29)	I learn from other students in this class.	3.64	3.81	-.17**	-2.863	.007
Pair 6 (Item 31)	I help other class members who are having trouble with their work.	3.27	3.28	-.01	-.109	.914

Continued

	Questionnaire Item	Mean			T	Sig.
		MA	FA	MA−FP		
Pair 7 (Item 35)	I work with other students in this class.	3.71	3.88	−.17*	−2.188	.035
Pair 8 (Item 39)	Students discuss with me how to go about solving problems.	3.36	3.37	−.01	−.120	.905
Pair 9 (Item 41)	I cooperate with other students on class activities.	3.73	3.97	−.23*	−3.176	.003
Pair 10 (Item 43)	In this class, I get help from other students.	3.60	3.67	−.08	−.948	.349
Pair 11 (Item 47)	Students work with me to achieve class goals.	3.55	3.64	−.08	−1.004	.321

Note: $N=40$; * $p<0.05$; ** $p<0.01$.

It is shown in Table 7.6 that significant differences in perceptions between male and female students occurred on six items in "Cooperation" scale, with significance at $p<0.01$ for Item 17 and Item 29, and at $p<0.05$ for Item 11, Item 23, Item 35, and Item 41. There were no significant differences in perceptions of the other five items in the scale. These significant and nonsignificant gender differences in perceptions are graphed in Figure 7.5.

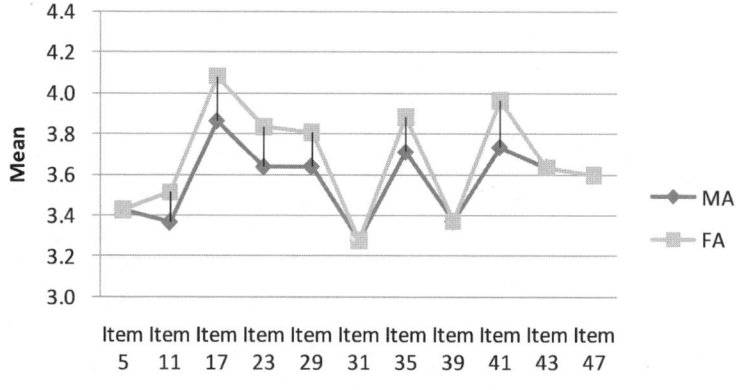

Figure 7.5 Gender differences in students' actual perceptions of CO

Figure 7.5 implied that female students experienced greater cooperation than their male counterparts in terms of sharing learning resources, working as a team, learning from classmates, and collaborating on class projects and activities. It was also depicted in Figure 7.5 that male and female students perceived similar level of cooperation among students in doing assignments, achieving class goals, helping each other with class work, and discussing with classmates about how to solve problems.

7.4 Gender differences in preferred classroom environment perceptions

7.4.1 Overall pattern of gender differences in preferred perceptions

Figure 7.6 on the next page represents the differences in expectations of CE classroom psychosocial environments held by male and female students. It is shown in Figure 7.6 that female students had higher expectations than their male counterparts for a more favorable CE classroom psychosocial environment by enhancing student cohesiveness, fostering greater involvement, providing clearer task orientation, and ensuring more cooperation and equity. As for the support of instructors in class, both male and female students had similar preferences or expectations for it. Overall, it could be summarized that female students would prefer a more favorable classroom psychosocial environment than their male counterparts.

The overall pattern of gender differences in perceptions of preferred classroom psychosocial environments among students discovered in the present study is consistent with the research findings reported in previous studies on gender differences in preferred chemistry laboratory environments in Singaporean secondary schools (Wong & Fraser, 1994), preferred Chinese language classroom environments in Singaporean secondary schools (Chua, Wong & Chen, 2011), and preferred science classroom environments in Indonesian secondary schools (Wuhyudi & Treagust, 2003). However, the discrepancies in perceptions of

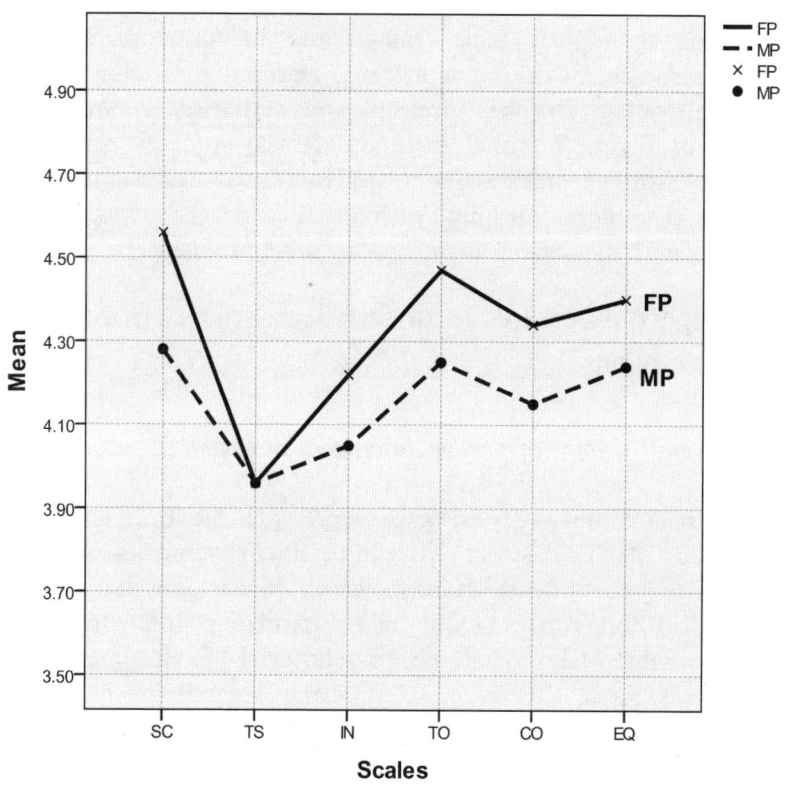

Figure 7.6 Gender differences in preferred CE classroom environment perceptions

preferred classroom psychosocial environments between male and female students revealed in the present study are in contrast to the result reported by Nair (2002) that first year university male and female students in Canadian and Australian institutions were generally in agreement about what their preferred classroom environments should be like, including classes of chemistry, physics, biology, computer science, mathematics and geography.

To further explore the differences in preferences or expectations of male and female students for an ideal CE classroom psychosocial environment with regard to the specific aspects within the environmental scales, a series of paired samples t-tests were carried out on the items of the preferred WIHIC scales with significant

7.4.2 Gender differences in students' preferred perceptions of SC

Results of paired samples t-tests in Table 7.7 show that differences in preferred perceptions between male and female students were statistically significant ($p<0.01$) for all the six items in "Student cohesiveness" scale. These significant differences in perceptions are graphed in Figure 7.7.

Table 7.7 Gender differences in students' preferred perceptions of SC

	Questionnaire Item	Mean			T	Sig.
		MP	FP	MP−FP		
Pair 1 (Item 1)	I would make friendships among students in this class.	4.12	4.56	−.44***	−6.738	.000
Pair 2 (Item 7)	I would know other students in this class.	4.29	4.58	−.29***	−4.717	.000
Pair 3 (Item 13)	I would be friendly to members of this class.	4.43	4.66	−.23**	−2.994	.005
Pair 4 (Item 19)	Members of the class would be my friends.	4.31	4.60	−.29***	−4.445	.000
Pair 5 (Item 25)	I would work well with other class members.	4.29	4.53	−.25**	−3.479	.001
Pair 6 (Item 37)	Students in this class would like me.	4.20	4.47	−.28***	−4.009	.000

Note: $N=40$ pairs of within-class gender means; * $p<0.05$; ** $p<0.01$; *** $p<0.001$.

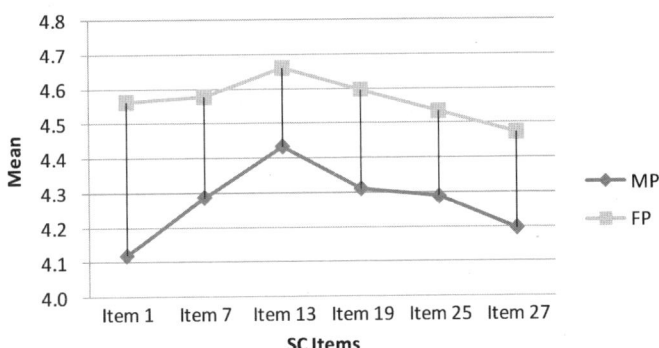

Figure 7.7 Gender differences in students' preferred perceptions of SC

Figure 7.7 shows that female students held greater expectations than male students for "Student cohesiveness" in terms of all the six aspects measured in the scale. In other words, the harmonious, friendly, and cohesive personal relationships among classmates were valued more by female students than their male counterparts. The discrepancies in preferences for "Student cohesiveness" between male and female students could also be explained by the bonding differences between males and females mentioned earlier in section 7.3.2.

7.4.3 Gender differences in students' preferred perceptions of IN

Results of paired samples t-tests in Table 7.8 show that there was significant difference in preferred perceptions of Item 2 in "Involvement" scale between male and female students. For the other two items, no significant differences in perceptions between male and female students were found. Figure 7.8 provides a graph of the similarities and differences in preferences for the three aspects of "Involvement".

Table 7.8 Gender differences in students' preferred perceptions of IN

	Questionnaire Item	Mean			T	Sig.
		MP	FP	MP-FP		
Pair 1 (Item 3)	I would discuss ideas in class.	4.07	4.21	-.14	-1.449	.155
Pair 2 (Item 9)	I would give my opinions during class discussions.	4.04	4.22	-.18*	-2.164	.037
Pair 3 (Item 33)	I would explain my ideas to other students.	4.11	4.23	-.12	-1.518	.137

Note: $N=40$.

As revealed previously in section 7.4.1, female students would generally prefer a greater level of "Involvement" than their male counterparts in an ideal CE classroom psychosocial environment; however, it is shown in Figure 7.8 that female and male students were particularly in agreement about their preferences for "Involvement" in terms of discussing and explaining ideas in class as measured in Item 3 and Item 33. Yet female students called for more active roles in giving ideas during class discussions.

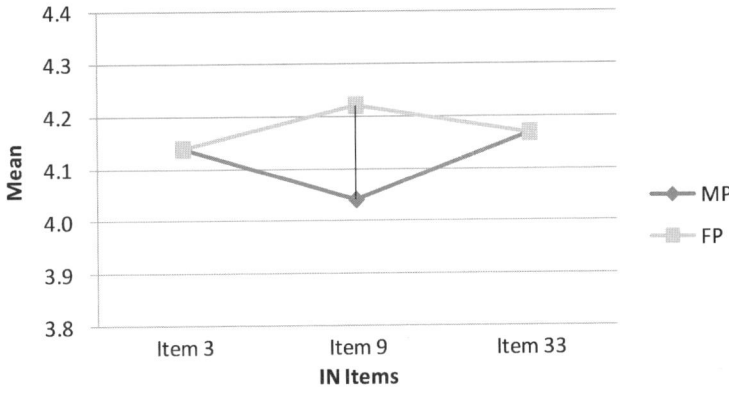

Figure 7.8 Gender differences in students' preferred perceptions of IN

7.4.4 Gender differences in students' preferred perceptions of TO

Results of paired samples t-tests listed in Table 7.9 show that there were significant gender differences in perceptions of "Task orientation" for Item 10 and Item 22 at $p<0.001$, Item 28 and Item 34 at $p<0.01$, and Item 4, Item 16, and Item 40 at $p<0.05$. No significant difference in perceptions of Item 46 was found. These gender differences in preferred perceptions of eight aspects of "Task orientation" are plotted in Figure 7.9.

Table 7.9 Gender differences in students' preferred perceptions of TO

		Mean			T	Sig.
	Questionnaire Item	MP	FP	MP−FP		
Pair 1 (Item 4)	Getting a certain amount of work done would be important to me.	4.05	4.22	−.18*	−2.067	.045
Pair 2 (Item 10)	I would do as much as I set out to do.	4.12	4.41	−.29***	−4.198	.000
Pair 3 (Item 16)	I would know the goals for this class.	4.31	4.49	−.18*	−2.386	.022

Continued

	Questionnaire Item	Mean			T	Sig.
		MP	FP	MP-FP		
Pair 4 (Item 22)	I would be ready to start this class on time.	4.36	4.60	-.24***	-4.396	.000
Pair 5 (Item 28)	I would know what I am trying to accomplish in this class.	4.26	4.52	-.25**	-3.482	.001
Pair 6 (Item 34)	I would pay attention during this class.	4.32	4.56	-.25**	-3.713	.001
Pair 7 (Item 40)	I would try to understand the work in this class.	4.40	4.53	-.13*	-2.223	.032
Pair 8 (Item 46)	I would know how much work I have to do.	4.32	4.45	-.13	-1.871	.069

Note: $N=40$; * $p<0.05$; ** $p<0.01$.

It is noted in Figure 7.9 that female students placed more stress on seven out of the eight aspects of "Task orientation" than their male counterparts. However, both male and female students were in agreement about the emphasis laid on the clear instruction of tasks as measured in Item 46, though in general female student tended to prefer a more task oriented classroom psychosocial environment than male students.

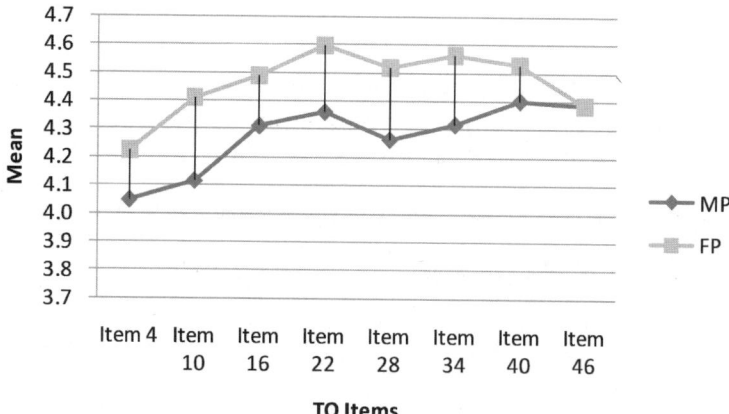

Figure 7.9 Gender differences in students' preferred perceptions of TO

7.4.5 Gender differences in students' preferred perceptions of CO

As shown by the results of paired samples t-tests in Table 7.10, gender differences in preferred perceptions of "Cooperation" were found to be significantly different for Item 17, Item 29, Item 39, and Item 31 at $p<0.01$, and Item 11, Item 23, Item 35, Item 43, and Item 47 at $p<0.05$. For the remaining two items, Item 5 and Item 31, there were no statistically significant differences in perceptions of them. Figure 7.10 provides a graph of these differences in perceptions.

Table 7.10 Gender differences in students' preferred perceptions of CO

	Questionnaire Item	Mean			T	Sig.
		MP	FP	MP−FP		
Pair 1 (Item 5)	I would cooperate with other students when doing assignment work.	4.10	4.19	−.09	−1.221	.230
Pair 2 (Item 11)	I would share my books and resources with other students when doing assignments.	4.06	4.23	−.17*	−2.505	.017
Pair 3 (Item 17)	When I work in groups in this class, there would be teamwork.	4.19	4.43	−.23**	−3.339	.002
Pair 4 (Item 23)	I would work with other students on projects in this class.	4.16	4.35	−.19*	−2.556	.015
Pair 5 (Item 29)	I would learn from other students in this class.	4.27	4.47	−.20**	−2.891	.006
Pair 6 (Item 31)	I would help other class members who are having trouble with their work.	4.21	4.32	−.11	−1.654	.106
Pair 7 (Item 35)	I would work with other students in this class.	4.21	4.40	−.19*	−2.511	.016
Pair 8 (Item 39)	Students would discuss with me how to go about solving problems.	4.09	4.26	−.17**	−3.079	.004
Pair 9 (Item 41)	I would cooperate with other students on class activities.	4.26	4.44	−.18**	−2.901	.006
Pair 10 (Item 43)	In this class, I would get help from other students.	4.14	4.30	−.17*	−2.375	.023
Pair 11 (Item 47)	Students would work with me to achieve class goals.	4.17	4.36	−.19*	−2.657	.011

Note: $N=40$; * $p<0.05$; ** $p<0.01$.

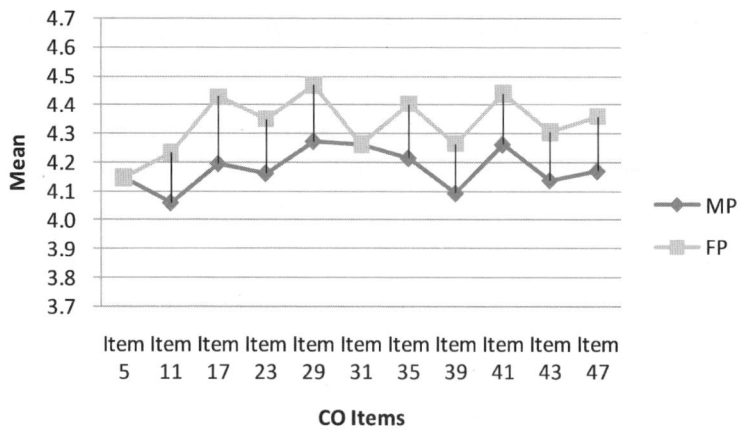

Figure 7.10 Gender differences in students' preferred perceptions of CO

It is observed in Figure 7.10 that greater cooperation was expected by female students with respect to nine out of the eleven aspects assessed in "Cooperation" scale. Both male and female students held similar expectations for the extent of cooperation among students in doing assignments and helping classmates who had trouble in their work as measured in Item 5 and Item 31.

7.4.6 Gender differences in students' preferred perceptions of EQ

Results of pair-wise comparisons in Table 7.11 on the next page show that there were three items in "Equity" scale for which the differences in preferred perceptions between male and female students were statistically significant. These items were Item 30 and Item 36 with significance at $p<0.01$, and Item 24 with significance at $p<0.05$. For the remaining seven items, no significant differences in preferred perceptions were found between male and female students. Differences in preferred perceptions between male and female students with and without statistical significance are illustrated in Figure 7.11.

Table 7.11 Gender differences in students' preferred perceptions of EQ

	Questionnaire Item	Mean			T	Sig.
		MP	FP	MP-FP		
Pair 1 (Item 6)	The teacher would give as much attention to my questions as to other students' questions.	4.23	4.38	-.15	-2.020	.050
Pair 2 (Item 12)	I would get the same amount of help from the teacher as do other students.	4.29	4.36	-.07	-.969	.339
Pair 3 (Item 14)	The teacher would consider my feelings.	4.19	4.33	-.14	-1.928	.061
Pair 4 (Item 18)	I would have the same amount of say in this class as other students.	4.23	4.37	-.14	-1.894	.066
Pair 5 (Item 20)	The teacher would help me when I have trouble with the work.	4.29	4.40	-.11	-1.692	.099
Pair 6 (Item 24)	I would be treated the same as other students in this class.	4.36	4.55	-.19*	-2.609	.013
Pair 7 (Item 30)	I would receive the same encouragement from the teacher as other students do.	4.20	4.44	-.24**	-3.497	.001
Pair 8 (Item 36)	I would get the same opportunity to contribute to class discussions as other students.	4.22	4.43	-.21**	-3.149	.003
Pair 9 (Item 42)	My work would receive as much praise as other students' work.	4.22	4.37	-.14	-1.921	.062
Pair 10 (Item 48)	I would get the same opportunity to answer questions as other students.	4.27	4.40	-.14	-1.929	.061

Note: $N=40$; * $p<0.05$; ** $p<0.01$.

As depicted in Figure 7.11, both male and female students had similar preferences for equal treatments by their instructors for seven out of the ten aspects of "Equity", though the overall pattern of preference was pointed out earlier in section 7.4 that in general female students would prefer more equity in class than their male counterparts. However, female students did expect a greater level

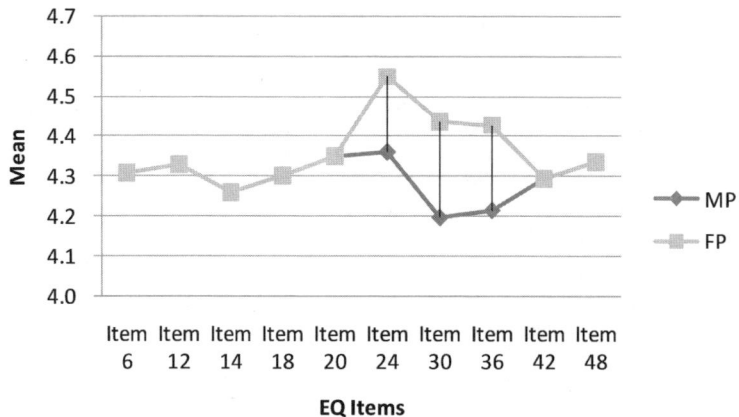

Figure 7.11 Gender differences in students' preferred perceptions of EQ

of equity than male students in terms of being treated the same as other students, receiving the same encouragement from the teacher, and getting the same opportunities to contribute to class discussions.

7.5 Summary

In this chapter, significant gender differences in both students' actual and preferred classroom psychosocial environment perceptions were found based on the MANOVA for repeated measures and post-hoc tests with Bonferroni correction on the WIHIC scales, and paired samples t-tests on the items of each WIHIC scale.

In general, at the level of WIHIC scales, it is found that female students perceived their existing CE classroom psychosocial environments more favorably than male students on WIHIC scales of "Students cohesiveness", "Task orientation", and "Cooperation". Male students perceived more "Teacher support" than their female counterparts. Both male and female students were experiencing the same level of "Involvement" and "Equity". Female students would prefer a more favorable CE classroom psychosocial environment than their male counterparts on all the WIHIC scales except for

"Teacher support" which was agreed by male and female students on preferences. Therefore, it can be overall summarized that female students had more positive views of the actual and preferred CE classroom psychosocial environments.

In particular, at the level of items within WIHIC scales, gender differences were further examined for the scales that were found to be perceived and expected differently by male and female students. It has been ascertained that gender differences in both students' actual and preferred perceptions of the items within WIHIC scales varied in magnitude. In addition, it is also found that agreement in both their actual and preferred perceptions of CE classroom psychosocial environments also existed in the items within certain WIHIC scales that were found to be perceived differently by male and female students. In summary, more subtle differences between male and female students' perceptions of actual and preferred CE classroom psychosocial environments were presented and interpreted in this part so as to offer more in-depth insights into the nature of CE classroom psychosocial environments.

Chapter 8
Associations Between Classroom Environment Perceptions and English Learning Motivation

8.1 Introduction

This chapter attempts to determine whether the nature of the CE classroom psychosocial environment has impacts on the English learning motivation of students. It begins with describing the profile of motivation types of English learning for first-year and second-year English majors in the School of International Studies (SIS) at Sun Yat-sen University (SYSU). Then the associations between students' actual perceptions of Comprehensive English (CE) classroom psychosocial environments and their motivation types are investigated utilizing a Canonical Correlation analysis (CCA) to find out how the two sets of variables are related with each other through shared variance.

8.2 Overall status of motivation types of English majors

8.2.1 Conceptualization of motivation types of English majors

The seven types of motivation assessed in the modified motivation types of Chinese college undergraduates (MTCCU) in the present study have been conceptualized by Gao *et al.* (2004, 2007) into three categories (i.e. instrumental, cultural, and situational motivation) in accordance with the classic models in motivational theories, which are presented in Figure 8.1.

Motivation types of "Immediate achievement" (IA), "Individual development" (ID) and "Information medium" (IM) can be placed under the instrumental orientation in

Gardner's (1985) model, since the three types of motivation share the common feature of instrumentality of learning English, referring to the employment of English language as an instrument to obtain certain goals, but they vary in the purposes achieved by learning English. Motivation of "Immediate achievement" aims at relatively short-term purpose of obtaining satisfactory results in exams while "Individual development" targets at a long-term goal of increasing one's own ability and social status in future development. Motivation of "Information medium" takes a view on English language learning as a long-lasting and effective way of communicating information and learning other academic subjects.

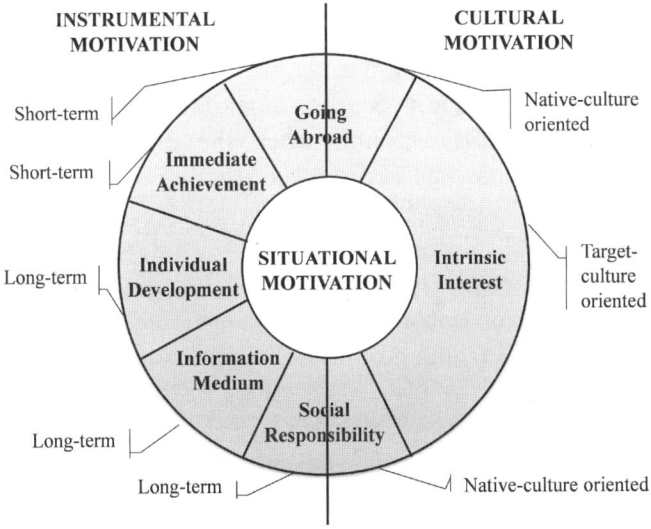

Figure 8.1 Conceptual classification of motivation types

Source: Adapted from Gao et al., 2004: 13.

Motivation of "Intrinsic interest" (Ⅱ), which reflects the appreciation and fondness of English learners for the target language and culture, is identified into the category of cultural motivation by Gao et al. (2007). "Intrinsic interest" is further specified as target-culture oriented motivation, considering the interests and concerns of learners in the target language and culture.

In contrast, "Going abroad" (GA) and "Social responsibility" (SR) are partially labeled as native-culture oriented motivation when they reflect the desires of English learners to present and promote their native culture through English language. Furthermore, the two motivation types show the feature of instrumentality when the English language is served as a short-term instrument in "Going abroad" to get better education or job opportunities abroad and as a long-term instrument in "Social responsibility" to fulfill social expectations as one's responsibility based on Confucian tradition particularly originated in the Chinese context. Therefore, "Going abroad" and "Social responsibility" are also partially grouped into the category of instrumental motivation. However, motivation of "Going abroad" is also characterized with the integrativeness in Gardner's (2005: 7) sense referring to "an individual's openness to taking on characteristics of another cultural/linguistic group" when the English learners go abroad with the purposes of experiencing English-speaking cultures or immigration.

Motivation of "Learning situation" (LS), referring to learning English because of the aspects of learning environments such as the quality of teaching, teaching materials, teachers, and affiliation with the learning group, is classified into the category of situational motivation by Gao et al. (2007) since it matches the level of learning situation in Dörnyei's (1994) three-level model of L2 motivation. Motivation of "Learning situation" covers the three sets of motivational components of the learning situation level synthesized by Dörnyei (1994), namely, course-specific motivational components covering teaching materials, teacher-specific motivational components including the quality of teaching, teacher's personality and teaching style, and group-specific motivational components concerning the affiliation and cohesion of learning groups.

In addition, the types of motivation measured in the MTCCU can also be broadly classified into the two categories according to the SDT theory of motivation, namely, intrinsic motivation and extrinsic motivation. Motivation of "Intrinsic interest" corresponds with intrinsic motivation, which is defined by Ryan and Deci (2000a) as the doing of an activity for interest, enjoyment, and inherent satisfactions, while "Immediate achievement", "Individual development", "Information Medium", "Social responsibility", "Going abroad", and "Learning situation" fall into the category of extrinsic motivation, referring to "doing something because it leads to a separable outcome" according to Ryan and Deci (2000a: 55–56). Furthermore, these types of extrinsic motivation vary in their degrees of self-determination or internalization of external regulations.

8.2.2 Motivation types of English majors in SIS, SYSU

To examine the overall status of English learning motivation types of English majors in the SIS at SYSU, descriptive statistics were performed on the data collected by the modified MTCCU including average mean score, standard deviation (SD), minimum (Min.), and maximum (Max.) for each type of motivation listed in Table 8.1.

Table 8.1 Descriptive statistics for motivation types

	N	No. of items	Mean	SD	Min.	Max.
II	943	6	3.42	0.79	1.00	5.00
IA	945	5	3.22	0.78	1.00	5.00
LS	945	5	3.12	0.81	1.00	5.00
GA	943	3	3.14	0.81	1.00	5.00
SR	943	3	3.33	0.80	1.00	5.00
ID	943	5	4.05	0.62	1.80	5.00
IM	943	2	3.56	0.82	1.00	5.00

Note: "Strongly disagree" =1; "Disagree" =2; "Uncertain" =3; "Agree" =4; "strongly agree" =5.

Figure 8.2 on the next page provides a graph of distributions of the seven motivation types assessed in the MTCCU based on the mean scores displayed in Table 8.1. It is shown in Figure 8.2 that the first-year and second-year English majors involved in the study were driven to learn English by all the seven motivation types with varied levels.

The most prominent motivation type for students was "Individual development". The second highest mean score occurred for "Information medium" motivation. Furthermore, the mean scores of "Individual development" and "Information medium", which fell within the range of 3.50–5.00, indicated a high level of motivation. This suggests that students were primarily motivated to learn English by using English language as an instrument to increase social status in future development and obtain information for communication or learning other subjects. In fact, "Individual development" and "Information medium" have already been found to be the prominent and stable English learning motivation types for Chinese college students in their first two years of both non-English majors by Gao *et al.* (2008) and English majors by Zhou and Gao (2009). The consistent research findings of the two prominent motivation types for students in Chinese universities might indicate the instrumental nature of English learning in the EFL context.

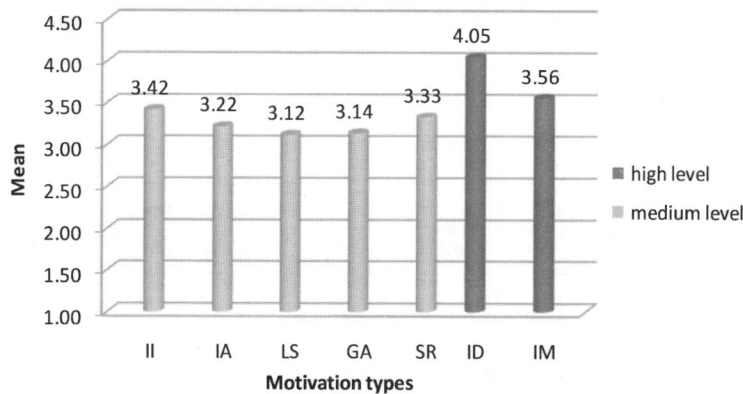

Figure 8.2 Distributions of students' English learning motivation types

A medium level of motivation of students was indicated by the mean scores of the other five motivation types, ranking from the highest mean score of 3.42 for "Intrinsic interest", mean score of 3.33 for "Social responsibility", mean score of 3.22 for "Immediate achievement", mean score of 3.14 for "Going abroad", and to the lowest mean score of 3.12 for "Learning situation". This implies that students were moderately motivated to learn English by the "cultural motivation" of their fondness of English language and culture as well as the presentation and promotion of Chinese language and culture, by the "instrumental motivation" of satisfying a specific requirement or qualification by targeting at immediate external achievements, and by the "situational motivation" of the quality of teaching, teaching materials, teachers, and affiliation with the learning groups. Furthermore, as shown in Figure 8.2, among the five types of motivation, students' motivation of "Intrinsic interest" was stronger than the other four types, while "Learning situation" motivation was the least prominent for the first-year and second-year English majors in the SIS at SYSU.

Therefore, the motivation of English learning for first-year and second-year English majors in the SIS at SYSU can be broadly characterized by the prominent impact of long-term instrumental motivation of "Individual development" and "Information medium", followed by the moderate influence of cultural motivation of both target-culture oriented motivation of "Intrinsic interest" and native-culture oriented motivation of "Social responsibility" and "Going abroad", together with the long-term instrumental motivation partially presented in "Social responsibility" and the short-term instrumental motivation of "Immediate achievement", and "Going abroad", and ended by the relatively less moderate affect of situational motivation of "Learning situation".

Viewed from another perspective, it was also revealed that first-year and second-year English majors in the SIS at SYSU were more strongly motivated to learn English by the extrinsic motivation regulated by the external values of increasing social status in the future development and obtaining information effectively than the intrinsic motivation of the intellectual and aesthetic interests in English language and culture.

8.3 Associations between classroom environment perceptions and motivation types

Relationships between students' perceptions of the actual CE classroom psychosocial environments assessed by the adapted WIHIC and motivation types measured by the modified MTCCU were examined through a Canonical Correlation analysis (CCA) run by SPSS 19.0. Two pairs of positive and substantial canonical correlation emerged in the CCA with significance at $p<0.001$ using the Wilks' Lambda criterion. The canonical correlation coefficient (R_c) was 0.37 for the first pair of canonical variables (X_a1-Y_a1) and 0.23 for the second pair of canonical variables (X_a2-Y_a2).

Table 8.2 reports the major CCA statistics for the two sets of variables, including structure coefficients (r_s), standardized canonical coefficients (Coef.), proportion of variance of the two sets of canonical variables explained by its own and opposite canonical variables.

According to Sherry and Henson (2005), a structure coefficient (r_s) is the bivariate correlation between an observed variable and a canonical variable, and thus, the square of the structure coefficient (r_s^2) indicates the proportion of variance an observed variable linearly shares with the canonical variable. Standardized canonical coefficients (Coef.), explained by Sherry and Henson (2005), represent the standardized weights of the observed variables in the linear equations to combine into the canonical variables. A structure coefficient (r_s), also termed as a canonical loading by Guo (2006) refers to the total effect of observed variables on the canonical variable, while a standardized canonical coefficient represents the direct effect of observed variables on the canonical variable. In the present study, only those observed variables with absolute value of structure coefficients (r_s) or canonical loadings higher than 0.40 and standardized canonical coefficients (Coef.) higher than 0.30 were taken into account as to be represented by the canonical variables.

Chapter 8 Associations Between Classroom Environment Perceptions and English Learning Motivation

Table 8.2 Canonical correlation statistics for actual perceptions and motivation types

Perceptions	Canonical variables		Motivation types	Canonical variables	
	$X_a 1$	$X_a 2$		$Y_a 1$	$Y_a 2$
SC	−0.67	−0.14	II	−0.75	0.13
	−0.20	−0.40		−0.38	0.15
TS	−0.71	0.50	IA	0.19	0.41
	−0.12	1.08		0.17	0.48
IN	−0.77	0.19	LS	−0.22	0.44
	−0.34	−0.12		−0.10	0.26
TO	−0.92	−0.08	GA	−0.34	0.34
	−0.66	−0.40		0.14	0.27
CO	−0.70	0.39	SR	−0.77	0.27
	0.10	0.85		−0.43	0.25
EQ	−0.72	−0.07	ID	−0.74	−0.33
	0.02	0.86		−0.43	−0.90
			IM	−0.56	0.41
				−0.13	0.54
% observed perception variables	56.5	7.8	% observed motivation type variables	31.3	11.9
% cumulative representation	56.5	64.3	% cumulative representation	31.3	43.2
% observed motivation type variables explained	7.6	0.4	% observed perception variables explained	4.2	0.6
Cumulative % of explanation	7.6	8.0	Cumulative % of explanation	4.2	4.8

Note: Coefficients in the shaded areas are structure coefficients (r_s) or canonical loadings; coefficients in the line under the shaded areas are standardized canonical coefficients (Coef.).

As regard to the variable set of perceptions, canonical variable X_a1 mainly represents perceptions of "Involvement" ($r_s = -0.77$; Coef. $= -0.34$) and "Task orientation" ($r_s = -0.92$; Coef. $= -0.66$). The structure coefficients of "Student cohesiveness" ($r_s = -0.67$), "Teacher support" ($r_s = -0.71$), "Cooperation" ($r_s = -0.70$), and "Equity" ($r_s = -0.72$) are also greater than 0.40, which indicates that these variables could contributed substantially to canonical variable X_a1, yet their standardized canonical coefficients (Coef.) are less than 0.30, which suggests that the variance of these variables were weakly incorporated in the linear equation to combine canonical variable X_a1. So these observed variables were not considered into the canonical correlation path model. Furthermore, it is observed from the square of the structure coefficients (r_s^2) and standardized canonical coefficients (Coef.) that "Task orientation" ($r_s^2 = 0.85$; Coef. $= -0.66$) was the primary contributor to canonical variable X_a1, with a secondary contribution made by "Involvement" ($r_s^2 = 0.59$; Coef. $= -0.34$). Canonical variable X_a2 mainly stands for "Teacher support" ($r_s = 0.50$; Coef. $= 1.08$). As displayed in Table 8.2, canonical variables X_a1 and X_a2 together accounted for 64.3% of the variance in the variable set of perceptions in total and they could explain 8.0% of the variance in the variable set of motivation types.

Regarding the variable set of motivation types, canonical variable Y_a1 mainly stands for motivations of "Intrinsic interest" ($r_s = -0.75$; Coef. $= -0.38$), "Social responsibility" ($r_s = -0.77$; Coef. $= -0.43$), and "Individual development" ($r_s = -0.74$; Coef. $= -0.43$). The structure coefficient of "Information Medium" motivation ($r_s = -0.56$) was also higher than 0.40, but its standardized canonical coefficient (Coef. $= -0.13$) was too less than 0.30 to be accepted in the canonical correlation path model. The similar squared structure coefficients (r_s^2) and standardized canonical coefficients (Coef.) show that "Intrinsic interest" ($r_s^2 = 0.56$), "Social responsibility" ($r_s^2 = 0.59$), and "Individual development" ($r_s^2 = 0.55$) made similar contributions to canonical variable Y_a1. Canonical variable Y_a2 consists of motivation types of

"Information medium" ($r_s = 0.41$; Coef. $= 0.54$) and "Immediate achievement" ($r_s = 0.41$; Coef. $= 0.48$). The structure coefficient of "Learning situation" motivation ($r_s = 0.44$) was also higher than 0.40, but its standardized canonical coefficient (Coef. $= 0.26$) was less than 0.30. As a result, it is not included in the canonical correlation path model. The squared structure coefficients ($r_s^2 = 0.17$) of both "Information medium" and "Immediate achievement" together with their similar standardized canonical coefficients show that these two types of motivation contributed similarly to canonical variable Y_a2. As shown in Table 8.2, the two canonical variables of Y_a1 and Y_a2 represent 43.2% of the variance in the observed motivation type variables in total, and explain 4.8% of the variance in the observed perception variables. The canonical correlation path model is presented in Figure 8.3.

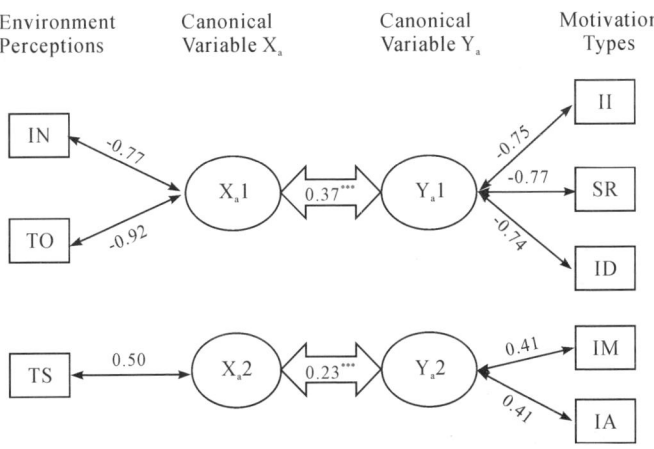

Figure 8.3 The canonical correlation path model for actual perceptions and motivation types

The canonical correlation path model in Figure 8.3 reveals the associations between the actual CE classroom environment dimensions and students' motivation types of English learning. The bi-directional arrows were used in Figure 8.3 to indicate the reciprocal influence between environmental perceptions and motivation types, considering the nature of CCA as a correlational analysis.

The interpretation of the first pair of canonical variables (X_a1-Y_a1) in the CCA model was that students who experienced higher levels of "Task orientation" and "Involvement" in CE classes were more likely to develop stronger English learning motivation, in particular, of "Intrinsic interest", "Social responsibly", and "Individual development". The association between the nature of CE classroom psychosocial environments and motivation of English learning emerged in the first significant canonical correlation in the present research supported the findings reported in the study of Chua (2009) that academically motivated students were those students who were task-oriented. In addition, viewed from the reverse direction, the first pair of canonical variables (X_a1-Y_a1) also reveals that the more strongly students were motivated to learn English by their fondness of the English language and culture, their sense of social responsibility, and their expectation of individual development, the more positively they tended to perceive their participation in class activities to complete learning tasks planned in the existing CE classrooms.

The second significant canonical correlation (X_a2-Y_a2) in the CCA model informed that when students perceived that they received more personal and academic support from their instructors, they were more likely to foster stronger English learning motivation of "Information Medium" and "Immediate Achievement". In other words, the perception of "Teacher support" positively and substantially affects student's motivation of English learning as an instrument to gain satisfactory results in exams and to take in various sources of information. On the other hand, it was also indicated in the second pair of canonical variables (X_a2-Y_a2) that students who were motivated to learn English by a greater need for satisfactory test scores and information of various sources were likely to perceive the support of teachers more positively in the CE classrooms. One of the possible reasons for this positive link between perception and motivation might be the role of teacher in class as a transmitter of knowledge and information. Therefore, if students want to get satisfactory scores in exams and obtain more information, they would be naturally more initiative in seeking help and trust from instructors in class and they would also value the support of their instructors more. Moreover, as indicated by bi-directional arrows in the CCA path model, students' environmental perceptions and motivation identified in the two pairs of canonical variables would be mutually influenced and enhanced during the recursive and continuous interaction.

In addition, a close examination of the results of CCA revealed that situational motivation of "Learning situation", which refers to the influence of learning environments including the quality of teaching, teaching materials, teachers, and affiliation with the learning groups, did not enter the canonical correlation path model. As shown in Table 8.2, its structure coefficient ($r_s = -0.22$) and standardized canonical coefficient (Coef. $= -0.10$) in the first canonical correlation were both too small to be accepted in to the model, while in the second canonical correlation, the structure coefficient ($r_s = 0.44$) showed that its correlation with canonical variable Y_a2 or its total effect on Y_a2 was greater than 0.40, however, its standardized canonical coefficient (Coef. $= 0.26$) indicates that its weight in the linear equations to combine into canonical variable Y_a2 or its direct effect on canonical variable Y_a2 was less than 0.30. As a result, it is not included in the canonical correlation path model as being prominently associated with the nature of CE classroom psychosocial environments.

8.4 Summary

This chapter started with the examination and report of the status quo and characteristics of English learning motivation of English majors in their first and second years in the SIS at SYSU. It has been found that students' motivation of English learning involved all the seven types of motivation measured in the modified MTCUU. The long-term instrumental motivation of "Individual development" and "Information medium" were found to be the prominent driving forces for students to learn English. Besides, students were moderately driven to learn English by the cultural motivation, the instrumental motivation, and the situational motivation reflected in "Intrinsic interest", "Social responsibility", "Going abroad", "Immediate achievement", and "Learning situation".

Associations were investigated and established between students' perceptions of the actual CE classroom psychosocial environments and their English learning motivation types. The results of the Canonical Correlation Analysis yielded the statistically significant associations between classroom environment perceptions and English learning motivation types through two pairs of canonical correlation. Perceptions of "Involvement" and "Task orientation" were found to be the predictor of motivation types of "Intrinsic interest", "Social responsibility", and "Individual development". Perception of "Teacher support" was found to have positive associations with motivation types of "Immediate achievement" and "Information medium".

In particular, students tended to develop stronger fondness of the English language and culture, greater sense of social responsibility, and higher expectation of individual development in the CE classrooms where they felt more active participation in class activities to complete learning tasks planned. Moreover, the more favorably students perceived the personal and academic support of the instructors in the CE classrooms, the more strongly they were motivated to learn English as an instrument to get satisfactory test scores for external requirement and to obtain information of various sources.

In addition, the canonical correlation revealed in CCA also indicates that environment perceptions and motivation were in a reciprocal relationship to each other and they were mutually influenced and enhanced during the recursive and continuous interaction. Examining how the environment perceptions were related to the English learning motivation, we could gain some better insights into the psychosocial nature of the EFL classroom environments and the learning mechanism of students.

Chapter 9
Conclusions and Implications

9.1 Summary of major research findings

As stated in section 1.2 in Chapter 1, this book is aimed at revealing the psychosocial characteristics of EFL classroom environments in Chinese colleges and universities. In line with the research objectives proposed in section 1.2 in Chapter 1, three major research questions were raised in section 3.2 in Chapter 3. The three major research questions are:

(1) What are the construct validity and internal reliability of the modified WIHIC to assess the psychosocial environments of English classrooms in Chinese colleges and universities?

(2) What are the characteristics of English classroom psychosocial environments at the tertiary level in the Chinese EFL context?

(3) What associations exist between students' perceptions of the psychosocial aspects of English classroom environments and their motivation of learning the English language?

Two sub-studies have been carried out to answer the three research questions. The first sub-study comprises Chapter 4, Chapter 5, Chapter 6, and Chapter 7. Chapter 4 has answered the first research question by providing sufficient evidence of construct validity and internal reliability for the modified WIHIC which was adapted to the Chinese EFL context. Chapter 5, Chapter 6, and Chapter 7 have solved the second research question by presenting the status quo of the English classroom psychosocial environments as perceived and preferred by both students and instructors, exploring the discrepancies in perceptions and preferences of the

English classroom psychosocial environments between students and instructors, and delving into the gender differences in perceptions and preferences of the English classroom psychosocial environments among students. The second sub-study in Chapter 8 has answered the third research question by investigating and demonstrating the associations between the psychosocial dimensions of English classroom environments and the English learning motivation types of college students in the Chinese EFL context. The major findings of the present study are summarized in the sections below.

9.1.1 Validation of research instruments

As the initial part of the main study, the modified WIHIC was validated with 945 college students in 40 intact classes in the Chinese EFL context in terms of the construct validity, the internal consistency reliability, and the ability to differentiate the perceptions of students from different classrooms. In regard to the construct validity, results of principal components factor analysis with varimax rotation on the student actual form and the student preferred form of the modified WIHIC with the individual student mean as the unit of analysis showed that most of the items fell into their *a prior* six scales in both the two forms, with the exception that 8 out of the 48 items in the student actual form and their corresponding items in the student preferred form loaded into different scales from their *a priori* scales. On the whole, the modified WIHIC displayed strong factorial validity in both the student actual form and the student preferred form. With respect to the internal consistency reliability, the Cronbach's alpha coefficient was used as the index. The values of Cronbach's alpha coefficients for the scales in both the student actual form and the student preferred form were similar to the statistics of internal consistency reliability reported for the WIHIC by Aldridge *et al.* (1999) and for the CLCEI, the customized version of the WIHIC, by Chua *et al.* (2006). Moreover, the Cronbach's alpha coefficients for the scales in both the instructor actual form and the instructor preferred form also demonstrated satisfactory internal consistency reliability.

Chapter 9 Conclusions and Implications

In addition, each scale of the student actual form was found to be able to differentiate significantly ($p < 0.05$) the perceptions of students from different classes. Therefore, the student and instructor actual and preferred forms of the modified WIHIC were validated to be effective in measuring the perceptions of classroom psychosocial environments in college English classrooms in the Chinese EFL context.

The slightly modified MTCCU was also validated through statistical analyses of the construct validity and the internal consistency reliability based on the data collected from 945 English majors in their first two years in the SIS at SYSU. The results of these statistical analyses were consistent with those reported for the original MTCCU by Gao et al. (2003) with a stratified sampling of 2,278 undergraduates from 30 Chinese universities in 29 provinces, autonomous regions and municipalities. As expected, the modified MTCCU was found to exhibit strong construct validity and internal consistency reliability to assess the learning motivation of English majors in their first years in the SIS at SYSU.

9.1.2 *The status quo of CE classroom psychosocial environments*

The typical CE classroom psychosocial environments in the SIS at SYSU were represented by depicting the features of students' and instructors' perceptions of their actual and preferred classroom psychosocial environments. The overall profile of the perceptions of the six WIHIC environmental scales was examined followed by the investigation of perception features in terms of favorability of the six environmental scales perceived and preferred by students and instructors, and variation in both students' and instructors' perceptions and preferences of each environmental scale.

For the actual CE classroom psychosocial environments as perceived by students, there was a high level of perception of students for scales "Student cohesiveness" ($M=4.20$, $SD=0.56$), "Equity" ($M=3.82$, $SD=0.65$), "Task orientation" ($M=3.73$, $SD=0.59$), and "Cooperation" ($M=3.64$, $SD=0.60$), and a medium level of perception for scales of "Involvement" ($M=3.42$,

SD =0.74) and "Teacher support" (M =3.19, SD =0.67). The six scales were found to be perceived with substantial differences by students through the analysis of one-way repeated ANOVA. Results of Bonferroni post-hoc tests showed that "Student cohesiveness" was perceived most favorably, followed by "Task orientation", "Equity", "Cooperation", "Involvement", and to "Teacher support" which was perceived relatively least favorably. An inspection on the values of SD for the six scales revealed that students were most consistent with each other in their actual perceptions of "Student cohesiveness" while their perceptions of "Involvement" varied greatest.

For the actual CE classroom psychosocial environments as perceived by instructors, their perceptions of all the six WIHIC scales reached a high level of perception. Results of one-way ANOVA for repeated measures and Bonferroni post-hoc tests indicated that among the six scales, "Student cohesiveness", "Teacher support", and "Equity" were perceived similarly by instructors while "Cooperation" was perceived relatively least favorably. The values of SD for the six scales revealed that in the actual CE classrooms instructors agreed more on their perceptions of "Task orientation" than the other scales as suggested by the smallest value of SD, while they differed more on their perceptions of "Involvement" than the other scales as indicated by the largest value of SD.

For the preferred CE classroom psychosocial environments, both students and instructors preferred a high level of perception for all the six WIHIC scales. As indicated by the results of one-way ANOVA for repeated measures and Bonferroni post-hoc tests on the six scales, students attached more importance to "Student cohesiveness" than the other five scales while they placed the least emphasis on "Teacher support". The values of SDs for the six scales showed that students were most in agreement with each other on their stress on the cohesive ties among themselves measured in "Student cohesiveness" and they differed most in their preferences of the active participation in class activities assessed in "Involvement". As for instructors, "Student cohesiveness",

"Involvement", and "Task orientation" were valued more than the other three scales for the preferred CE classroom environments, while "Teacher support" and "Equity" were stressed less in comparison with other scales. Moreover, the lowest SD value for "Task orientation" scale revealed that instructors were most in agreement with each other on their expectations of task-oriented students, while the highest SD value for "Equity" scale indicated that the greatest variation existed among instructors on their emphasis on the practice of equal treatment to students.

In summary, results of the investigation generally indicated the remarkable feature that both students and instructors were actually experiencing a positive CE classroom environment and they were in favor of a more favorable CE classroom environment. An interesting feature of CE classroom psychosocial environments observed was the similarities between students and instructors in their actual and preferred perceptions of "Student cohesiveness" and "Teacher support" in terms of favorability. It was noticed that "Student cohesiveness" was perceived by both students and instructors as one of the most favorable scales, while "Teacher support" as one of the least favorable scales in both the actual and preferred classroom environments.

9.1.3 *Discrepancies in perceptions between students and instructors*

As one of the main research objectives of this study, students' and instructors' actual and preferred perceptions of the CE classroom environments were compared through one-way repeated MANOVA for repeated measures and post-hoc tests with Bonferroni correction. Two general patterns of discrepancies in perceptions of students and instructors emerged. First, both students and instructors would prefer a more favorable CE classroom environment in comparison with what they were experiencing at present. Second, instructors perceived both the actual and preferred CE classroom environments more positively than did their students. The two general patterns of the CE classroom psychosocial environments are in support of the research findings reported in previous studies.

More subtle differences in perceptions of students and instructors were inspected both at the level of WIHIC scales and at the level of the items within each scale. Comparisons between actual and preferred perceptions for both students and instructors indicated that they would like to see improvements in all the six WIHIC scales with different magnitude. For students, they would expect the greatest improvement for "Teacher support" and the smallest for "Student cohesiveness", while for instructors, they would like to see the greatest change for "Cooperation" and the smallest for "Teacher support".

A closer examination on the differences in the actual and preferred perceptions between students and instructors of each aspect within the six scales were conducted by performing paired samples t-tests to compare all the items with each scale. Results of comparisons showed that students would expect improvements for all the items within the six environmental scales in different degrees with the exception in the perceptions of Item 7 in "Student cohesiveness" scale. A noteworthy feature spotted was that students would prefer a less degree of familiarity among classmates which was assessed by Item 7 than what was perceived at present. One of the possible reasons accounted for such lower-than-actual expectation on familiarity for the ideal classroom environments might come from the overmuch intimacy in students' daily lives on campus. Results of paired samples t-tests indicated that students would like to see changes for most of the items within the six environmental scales in different degrees, but there existed congruency, which indicated no need for further improvements, in their actual and preferred perceptions of some items in scales of "Student cohesiveness", "Teacher support", and "Equity".

Comparisons of the actual perceptions of CE classroom psychosocial environments between students and instructors indicated that instructors' perceptions were at the same level with those of students on three scales, namely, "Student cohesiveness", "Cooperation", and "Equity", and that instructors' perceptions were more positive than those of their students on the other three scales, namely, "Teacher support", "Involvement", and "Task orientation". The largest gap of perceptions between students and instructors occurred for "Teacher support". Results of paired samples t-tests on the items within the three scales with significant differences in perceptions showed that instructors had more positive perceptions of all the aspects in "Teacher support" and "Involvement" than their students. However, five out of eight aspects in the scale of "Task orientation" were found to be perceived similarly by students and instructor, though in general instructors experienced a more task-oriented classroom than their students.

Comparisons of the preferred perceptions of CE classroom psychosocial environments between students and instructors showed that instructors had preferences for a more favorable classroom environment in terms of all the six environmental scales than their students. Results of paired samples t-tests on the items within the six scales indicated that instructors had greater expectations for every aspect within the six scales except for the similar expectations between students and instructors on four out of ten aspects within scale "Equity".

In summary, the present study has conducted an exhaustive analysis and interpretation to reveal the nature of CE classroom psychosocial environments by illustrating how the same CE classroom environment was perceived and preferred differently by students and instructors in the Chinese EFL context.

9.1.4 Gender differences in perceptions among students

Gender of students was investigated as another determinant of perceptions of CE classroom environments. Two overall patterns of gender differences in students' perceptions emerged from the results of one-way repeated measures MANOVA and post-hoc tests with Bonferroni correction on the WIHIC scales. First, female students were found to generally perceive the existing CE classroom environments more positively than their male counterparts.

Second, female students would like to have a more favorable CE classroom environment than their male counterparts. The two overall patterns of gender differences in perceptions confirmed the research findings reported in previous studies.

More subtle differences in perceptions between male and female students were also examined at both the level of WIHIC scales and the level of the items within each scale. Comparisons of the actual perceptions between male and female students indicated that male and female students differed in their actual perceptions of four WIHIC scales. Female students' perceptions were more favorable than those of male students on three scales, namely, "Student cohesiveness", "Task orientation", and "Cooperation". However, different from previous research, male students' perceptions of "Teacher support" were found to be more positive than those of female students. Results of paired samples t-tests for comparing all the items within the four scales indicated that female students experienced a more cohesive relationship among students in all the aspects assessed in the scale of "Student cohesiveness". As for the other three scales, it was found that there was still congruency in perceptions between male and female students for some aspects measured in each of the three scales.

Comparisons of the preferred perceptions between male and female students indicated that female students would prefer a more favorable CE classroom environment than their male counterparts in terms of five out of the six environmental scales, except for their similar expectations on "Teacher support". Further analysis of pair-wise comparisons of all the items within the five scales showed that female students expected a more cohesive relationship among students in terms of all the aspects assessed in "Student cohesiveness". As for the other four scales, there were still some similar expectations on certain aspects within each scale.

All in all, the research findings of gender difference in perceptions of classroom environments discovered in the present study have confirmed that students' perceptions of their classroom environments are related to the gender of students.

9.1.5 Associations between classroom environment perceptions and English learning motivation

The status quo of the English majors' learning motivation in the first two years in the SIS at SYSU was depicted before the investigation of its associations with classroom psychosocial environment factors. All the seven types of motivation measured in the modified MTCCU were identified for the students involved in the study with different magnitude. The descriptive statistics indicated that the motivation of English learning for first-year and second-year English majors in the SIS at SYSU could be broadly characterized by the prominent impact of long-term instrumental motivation of "Individual development" and "Information medium", followed by the moderate influence of cultural motivation and instrumental motivation of "Intrinsic interest", "Social responsibility", "Going abroad", and "Immediate achievement", as well as situational motivation of "Learning situation".

The Canonical Correlation Analysis (CCA) was employed to examine the associations between classroom psychosocial environment factors and students' motivation to learn English language. Results of CCA indicated that students' perceptions of the actual CE classroom environments were positively correlated to their English learning motivation through two pairs of canonical variables.

The first canonical correlation showed that students' perceptions of "Involvement" and "Task Orientation" and their cultural and instrumental motivations of "Intrinsic Interest", "Social Responsibility", and "Individual Development" were interrelated positively. In other words, students who experienced more active involvement in task accomplishment in classes tended to demonstrate stronger motivation of learning English to appreciate the English language and culture, to fulfill the social expectations, and to increase one's ability and social status in future development. In turn, the changes of these three types of motivation would also take effects on students' perceptions of the two environmental factors.

The second canonical correlation indicated that there was a positive relationship between students' perceptions of "Teacher support" and their instrumental motivation of "Information medium" and "Immediate achievement". It was found that a more favorable perception of the academic and personal support from instructors would stimulate students' motivation of learning English to obtain information and to gain satisfactory results in exams for a specific requirement or qualification. On the other hand, an increase of students' motivation of "Information Medium" and "Immediate Achievement" was more likely to return a positive change for students' perceptions of "Teacher support".

By examining how the classroom environment factors affect the English learning motivation of students, we could gain some better insights into the psychosocial nature of the EFL classroom environments and the learning mechanism of students. In addition, it also indicated and confirmed the importance and function of classroom psychosocial environments in influencing student affective learning outcomes of motivation.

9.2 Pedagogical implications

The research findings in the present study provide some implications and suggestions of pedagogical practice for tertiary educators of English in the Chinese EFL context. These implications are primarily based on the assumptions verified in previous person-environment fit studies that the congruency or the reduction in the discrepancy between the actual and preferred perceptions of classroom environments can lead to better affective and cognitive achievements of students.

Firstly, the present study contributes a valid and reliable instrument, the customized WIHIC, for educators in Chinese colleges and universities to explore the nature of English classroom psychosocial environments.

Secondly, the status quo of the classroom psychosocial

environments revealed in the study can help educators to gain a fuller understanding of the English language classroom environments at the tertiary level. The study also informs educators that although students and instructors in general perceive their CE classroom environments positively, there are still gaps between their actual and preferred CE classroom environments in terms of all the six WIHIC environmental scales. Specific differences in their actual and ideal perceptions of all the aspects within the six scales elaborated in the study provide valuable guidance for educators to implement systematic changes as to improve the classroom environments effectively and eventually lead to more effective English language learning outcomes. In fact, Fraser, Malone, and Neale (1989) have proposed a five-step procedure for environmental improvement utilizing a classroom environment instrument to assess the actual and preferred perceptions of students of their mathematics classroom environment. This procedure involves the cyclical repetition of the five steps of assessment, feedback, reflection and discussion, intervention, and reassessment. Chinese educators are also suggested to follow this approach to create a better English language classroom environment for college and university students.

Thirdly, it is of importance for instructors to be aware that their students were actually experiencing a substantially different classroom environment from their own on three environmental scales of "Teacher support", "Involvement", and "Task orientation". Among these scales, their perceptions differ most in the scale of "Teacher support". Detailed discrepancies between their perceptions of all the aspects within the three scales reported in the study will provide tertiary instructors with indications to reconsider the way in which they teach, to search for the possible reasons, and to take appropriate and effective measures to eliminate these gaps in perceptions of the same teaching and learning practices in class.

Fourthly, the present study informs educators that male and female students differ in their perceptions of the actual existing classroom environments and their preferences for the ideal classroom environments. The subtle differences in their actual and preferred perceptions of the aspects within the environmental scales reported in the study will help educators gain a better understanding of the different feelings and expectations of the classroom environments for male and female students. Being aware of these gaps in perceptions, instructors are suggested to take gender needs and preferences into consideration when they endeavor to create a more supportive environment for teaching and learning for both male and female students.

Finally, the associations between the nature of classroom psychosocial environments and English learning motivation of students revealed in the present study are practically important since it can shed light on the particular dimensions of English language classroom environments that need to be improved in order to enhance student affective learning achievement of motivation.

9.3　Limitations and suggestions for future research

The present research has some limitations to recognize, and furthermore, in view of these limitations, suggestions are proposed for some possible future studies. A limitation of the study might be that the research findings obtained based on the case study should be generalized with caution. Since the present study was designed to reveal the nature of English classroom psychosocial environments in the Chinese EFL context based on the case study of English majors in their first two years in the SIS at SYSU, the research findings might not be roughly generalized to represent all the English classrooms in Chinese colleges and universities, but the research findings do shed light on the psychosocial characteristics of English classroom environments in China's higher education. Therefore, more comprehensive studies based on larger stratified samples selected from Chinese colleges and universities are encouraged to confirm and supplement the research findings reported in this book.

In addition, due to the space limitation of the book, the present study mainly focused the discussions and analyses of the

Chapter 9 Conclusions and Implications

determinants of classroom environments on the differences in perceptions between students and instructors as well as between male and female students, which are among the most extensively studied determinants in previous studies on classroom environments. In view of this, future studies are suggested to reveal the nature of English language classroom environments from more determinants such as the demographic background of students and instructors, grade levels of students, etc.

Furthermore, the present study takes the initiative step to examine and establish the associations between factors of English classroom psychosocial environments and student' motivation to learn English. Further research is recommended to explore whether there is a cause and effect relationship between dimensions of the environmental perceptions and motivation. Studies with controlled interventions are also suggested to reveal the process that classroom environmental perceptions take effects on students' motivation to learn English.

References

Adelman, H. S. & Taylor, L. (2005). Classroom climate [M] // Lee, S. W., Lowe, P. A. & Robinson, E. (Eds.), *Encyclopedia of School Psychology*. Thousand Oaks, CA: Sage, 88-90.

Aldridge, J. M. & Fraser, B. J. (2000). A cross-cultural study of classroom learning environments in Australia and Taiwan Province [J]. *Learning Environments Research*, 3, 101-134.

Aldridge, J. M., Fraser, B. J. & Huang, T. C. I. (1999). Investigating classroom environments in Taiwan Province and Australia with multiple research methods [J]. *Journal of Educational Research*, 93, 48-62.

Aldridge, J. M., Fraser, B. J. & Laugksch, R. C. (2011). Relationships between the school-level and classroom-level environment in secondary schools in South Africa [J]. *South African Journal of Education*, 31, 127-144.

Aldridge, J. M., Laugksch, R. C., Seopa, M. A., et al. (2006). Development and validation of an instrument to monitor the implementation of outcomes-based learning environments in science classrooms in South Africa [J]. *International Journal of Science Education*, 28, 45-70.

Amidon, E. J. & Flanders, N. A. (1963). *The Role of the Teacher in the Classroom: A Manual for Understanding and Improving Teachers' Classroom Behavior* [M]. Minneapolis, Minn.: Paul S. Amidon & Associates.

Amidon, E. J. & Simon, A. (1965). Chapter IV: Teacher-pupil interaction [J]. *Review of Educational Research*, 35, 130-139.

Chandra, V. & Fisher, D. L. (2009). Students' perceptions of a blended web-based learning environment [J]. *Learning Environments Research*, 12, 31-44.

Chávez, R. C. (1984). The use of high-inference measures to study classroom climates: A review [J]. *Review of Educational Research*, 54, 237-261.

Chávez, R. C. (1988). Theoretical issues relevant to bilingual multicultural classroom climate research [J]. *Journal of Educational Issues of Language Minority Students*, 3, 5-14.

Chionh, Y. H. & Fraser, B. J. (2009). Classroom environment, achievement, attitudes and self esteem in geography and mathematics in Singapore [J]. *International Research in Geographical and Environmental Education*, 18, 29-44.

Chua, S. L., Wong, A. F. L. & Chen, D. (2006). Validation of the "Chinese language classroom learning environment inventor" for investigating the nature of Chinese language classrooms [J]. *Issues in Educational Research*, 16, 139-151.

Chua, S. L., Wong, A. F. L. & Chen, D. (2009). Associations between Chinese language classroom environments and students' motivation to learn the language [J]. *Australian Journal of Educational & Developmental Psychology*, 9, 53-64.

Chua, S. L., Wong, A. F. L. & Chen, D. (2011). The nature of Chinese language classroom learning environments in Singapore secondary schools [J]. *Learning Environments Research*, 14, 75-90.

Clément, R., Dörnyei, Z. & Noels, K. A. (1994). Motivation, self-confidence, and group cohesion in the foreign language classroom [J]. *Language Learning*, 44, 417-448.

Clément, R. & Kruidenier, B. G. (1983). Orientations in second language acquisition: I. The effects of ethnicity, milieu and target language on their emergence [J]. *Language Learning*, 33, 272-291.

Cornell, F. G., Lindvall, C. M. & Saupe, J. L. (1952). *An exploratory measurement of individualities of schools and classrooms* [M]. Urbana: Bureau of Education Research, University of Illinois.

Csizér, K. & Dörnyei, Z. (2005). The Internal structure of language learning motivation and its relationship with language choice and learning effort [J]. *The Modern Language Journal*, 89, 19-36.

Deci, E. L. & Ryan, R. M. (1985). *Intrinsic motivation and self-determination in human behavior* [M]. New York: Plenum.

Deci, E. L. & Ryan, R. M. (2008). Self-determination theory: A macrotheory of human motivation, development, and health [J]. *Canadian Psychology*, 49, 182-198.

Den Brok, P., Fisher, D., Rickards, T. & Bull, E. (2006). Californian science students' perceptions of their classroom learning environments [J]. *Educational Research and Evaluation*, 12, 3-25.

De Young, A. J. (1977). Classroom climate and class success: A case study at the university level [J]. *The Journal of Educational Research*, 70, 252-257.

Dorman, J. P. (2001). Associations between classroom environment and academic efficacy [J]. *Learning Environments Research*, 4, 243-257.

Dorman, J. P. (2003). Cross national validation of the What Is Happening In this Class? (WIHIC) questionnaire using confirmatory factor analysis [J]. *Learning Environments Research*, 6, 231-245.

Dorman, J. P. (2008). Use of multitrait-multimethod modeling to validate actual and preferred forms of the What Is Happening In this Class? (WIHIC) questionnaire [J]. *Learning Environments Research*, 11, 179-193.

Dorman, J. P. & Fraser, B. J. (2009). Psychosocial environment and affective outcomes in technology-rich classrooms: Testing a causal model [J]. *Social Psychology of Education*, 12, 77-99.

Dörnyei, Z. (1990a). Conceptualizing motivation in foreign-language learning [J]. *Language Learning*, 40, 45-78.

Dörnyei, Z. (1990b). Analysis of motivation components in foreign language learning [C] // Paper presented at the 9th World Congress of Applied Linguistics, Thessaloniki, Greece.

Dörnyei, Z. (1994). Motivation and motivating in the foreign language classroom [J]. *The Modern Language Journal*, 78, 273-284.

Dörnyei, Z. (2001/2005). *Teaching and Researching Motivation* [M]. England/Beijing: Pearson Education Limited/Foreign

References

Language Teaching and Research Press.

Dörnyei, Z. & Clément, R. (2001). Motivational characteristics of learning different target languages: Results of a nationwide survey [M]// Dörnyei, Z. & Schmidt, R. (Eds.), *Motivation and Second Language Acquisition*. Honolulu: University of Hawaii, 399-432.

Dowdell, T., Tomson, L. M. & Davies, M. (2011). Measuring sports class learning climates: The development of the Sports Class Environment Scale [J]. *Learning Environments Research*, 14, 123-133.

Eccles, J. S., Wigfield, A. & Schiefele, A. (1998). Motivation to succeed [M]// Damon, W. & Eisenberg, N. (Eds.), *Handbook of Child Psychology* (5th ed.), Vol. 3: Social, emotional, and personality development. New York: John Wiley & Sons, 1017-1095.

Fan, C. L. (范春林) & Dong, Q. (董奇) (2005). Ketang huanjing yanjiu de xianzhuang yiyi ji qushi (课堂环境研究的现状、意义及趋势, "The actuality, value and trend of research on classroom environment") [J]. *Bijiao jiaoyu yanjiu* (比较教育研究, "Comparative Education Review"), 8, 61-66.

Fisher, D. J. & Fraser, B. J. (1983a). Use of classroom environment scale in investigating effects of psychosocial milieu on science students' outcomes [C]// Paper presented at the annual meeting of the National Association for Research in Science Teaching, Dallas, TX.

Fisher, D. J. & Fraser, B. J. (1983b). A comparison of actual and preferred classroom environments as perceived by science teachers and students [J]. *Journal of Research in Science Teaching*, 20, 55-61.

Fisher, D. L., Fraser, B. J. & Bassett, J. (1995). Using a classroom environment instrument in an early childhood classroom [J]. *Australian Journal of Early Childhood*, 20, 10-15.

Fisher, D., Henderson, D. & Fraser, B. (1995). Interpersonal behavior in senior high school biology classes [J]. *Research in Science Education*, 25, 125-133.

Fraser, B. J. (1981). Australian research on classroom environment: State of the art [J]. *Australian Journal of Education*, 25, 238-268.

Fraser, B. J. (1982). Differences between student and teacher perceptions of actual and preferred classroom learning environment [J]. *Educational Evaluation and Policy Analysis*, 4, 511-519.

Fraser, B. J. (1984). Differences between preferred and actual classroom environment as perceived by primary students and teachers [J]. *British Journal of Educational Psychology*, 54, 336-339.

Fraser, B. J. (1986). Validity and use of an instrument for assessing classroom psychosocial environment in higher education [J]. *Higher Education*, 15, 37-57.

Fraser, B. J. (1990). *Individualised classroom environment questionnaire* [M]. Melbourne, Australia: Australian Council for Educational Research.

Fraser, B. J. (1994). Research on classroom and school climate [M] // Gabel, D. (Ed.), *Handbook of research on science teaching and learning*. New York: Macmillan, 493-541.

Fraser, B. J. (1998a). Classroom environment instruments: Development, validity, and applications [J]. *Learning Environments Research*, 1, 7-33.

Fraser, B. J. (1998b). Science learning environments: Assessments, effects and determinants [M] // Fraser, B. J. & Tobin, K. G. (Eds.), *International handbook of science education*. Dordrecht: Kluwer Academic Publishers, 527-564.

Fraser, B. J. (2002). Learning environment research: Yesterday, today and tomorrow [M] // Goh, S. C. & Khine, M. S. (Eds.), *Studies in educational learning environments: An international perspective*. Singapore: World Scientific Publishing, 1-25.

Fraser, B. J. (2007). Classroom learning environments [M] // Abell, S. K. & Lederman, N. G. (Eds.), *Handbook of research on science education*. Mahwah, New Jersey: Lawrence Erlbaum Associates, 103-124.

Fraser, B. J., Anderson, G. J. & Walberg, H. J. (1982). *Assessment of Learning Environments: Manual for Learning Environment Inventory (LEI) and My Class Inventory (MCI)* (3rd version) [M]. Chicago: University of Illinois Chicago.

Fraser, B. J., Aldridge, J. M. & Soerjaningsih, W. (2010). Instructor-student interpersonal interaction and student outcomes at the university level in Indonesia [J]. *The Open Education Journal*, 3, 21-33.

Fraser, B. J., Malone, J. A. & Neale, J. M. (1989). Assessing and improving the psychosocial environment of mathematics classrooms [J]. *Journal for Research in Mathematics Education*, 20, 191-201.

Fraser, B. J. & O'Brien, P. (1985). Student and teacher perceptions of the environment of elementary school classrooms [J]. *The Elementary School Journal*, 85, 567-580.

Fraser, B. J. & Fisher, D. L. (1982). Predicting students' outcomes from their perceptions of classroom psychosocial environment [J]. *American Educational Research Journal*, 19, 498-518.

Fraser, B. J. & Fisher, D. L. (1983a). Student achievement as a function of person-environment fit: A regression surface analysis [J]. *British Journal of Educational Psychology*, 53, 89-99.

Fraser, B. J. & Fisher, D. L. (1983b). Use of actual and preferred classroom environment scales in person-environment fit research [J]. *Journal of Educational Psychology*, 75, 303-313.

Fraser, B. J., Fisher, D. L. & McRobbie, C. J. (1996). Development, validation, and use of personal and class forms of a new classroom environment instrument [C] // Paper presented at the annual meeting of the American Educational Research Association, New York, NY.

Fraser, B. J., Giddings, G. J. & McRobbie, C. J. (1995). Evolution and validation of a personal form of an instrument for assessing science laboratory classroom environments [J]. *Journal of Research in Science Teaching*, 32, 399-422.

Fraser, B. J. & Lee, S. S. U. (2009). Science laboratory classroom environments in Korean high schools [J]. *Learning Environments*

Research. 12, 67-84.

Fraser, B. J. & McRobbie, C. J. (1995). Science laboratory classroom environments at schools and universities: A cross-national study [J]. *Educational Research and Evaluation*, 1, 289-317.

Fraser, B. J. & Rentoul, A. J. (1980). Person-environment fit in open classrooms [J]. *The Journal of Educational Research*, 73, 159-167.

Fraser, B. J. & Rentoul, A. J. (1982). Relationships between school-level and classroom-level environment [J]. *Alberta Journal of Educational Research*, 28, 212-225.

Fraser, B. J. & Treagust, D. F. (1986). Validity and use of an instrument for assessing classroom psychosocial environment in higher education [J]. *Higher Education*, 15, 37-57.

Fraser, B. J. & Wubbles, T. (1995). Classroom learning environments [M] // Fraser, B. J. & Walberg, H. J. (Eds.), *Improving Science Education: International perspectives*. Chicago: The National Society for the Study of Education.

Freiberg, H. J. (Ed.) (1999). *School climate: Measuring, improving, and sustaining healthy learning environments* [M]. London: Falmer Press.

Gao, Y. H. (高一虹), Cheng, Y. (程英), Zhao, Y. (赵媛), et al. (2003). Yingyu xuexi dongji leixing yu dongji qiangdu de guanxi — Dui daxuesheng benkesheng de dingliang kaocha (英语学习动机类型与动机强度的关系——对大学生本科生的定量考察, "The relationship between types of English learning motivation and motivational intensity — A quantitative investigation on Chinese college undergraduates") [J]. *Waiyu yanjiu* (外语研究, "Foreign Languages Research"), (1), 60-64.

Gao, Y. H. (高一虹), Liu, L. (刘璐), Xiu, L. M. (修立梅), et al. (2008). Daxuesehng jichu jieduan yingyu xuexi dongji genzong — Zonghe daxue yingyu zhuanye yangben baogao (大学生基础阶段英语学习动机跟踪——综合大学英语专业样本报告, "Chinese students English learning motivation in the first two college years — A longitudinal study on English majors in a comprehensive university") [J]. *Tianjin waiguoyu xueyuan xuebao* (天津外国语学院学报, "Journal of Tianjin Foreign Studies University"), 15, 67-73.

Gao, Y. H. (高一虹), Zhao, Y. (赵媛), Cheng, Y. (程英), et al. (2003). Zhongguo daxue benkesheng yingyu xuexi dongji leixing (中国大学本科生英语学习动机类型, "Motivation types of Chinese college undergraduates") [J]. *Xiandai waiyu* (现代外语, "Modern Foreign Languages"), 1, 28-38.

Gao, Y. H., Zhao, Y., Cheng, Y., et al. (2004). Motivation Types of Chinese University Undergraduates [J]. *Asian Journal of English Language Teaching*, 14, 45-64.

Gao, Y. H., Zhao, Y., Cheng, Y., et al. (2007). Relationship between English learning motivation types and self-identity changes among Chinese students [J]. *TESOL Quarterly*, 41, 133-155.

Gardner, R. C. (1985). *Social Psychology and Second Language Learning: The Role of Attitudes and Motivation* [M]. London: Edward Arnold.

Gardner, R. C. (1988). The socio-educational model of second-language learning: Assumptions, findings and issues [J]. *Language Learning*, 38, 101-126.

Gardner, R. C. (1991). Second-language learning in adults correlates of proficiency [J]. *Applied Language Learning*, 2, 1-28.

Gardner, R. C. (2005, May). Integrative motivation and second language acquisition [C] // Paper presented at the Canadian Association of Applied Linguistics/Canadian Linguistics Association Joint Plenary Talk at the University of Western Ontario, London, Canada.

Gardner, R. C. (2010). *Motivation and Second Language Acquisition: the Socio-educational Model* [M]. New York: Peter Lang Publishing, Inc.

Gardner, R. C., Day, J. B. & MacIntyre, P. D. (1992). Integrative motivation, induced anxiety, and language learning in a controlled environment [J]. *Studies in Second Language Acquisition*, 14, 197-242.

Gardner, R. C. & Lambert, W. E. (1959). Motivational variables in second-language acquisition [J]. *Canadian Journal of Psychology*, 13, 266-272.

Gardner, R. C. & Lambert, W. E. (1972). *Attitudes and Motivation in Second Language Learning* [M]. Rowley, MA: Newbury House.

Gardner, R. C. & MacIntyre, P. D. (1993). On the measurement of affective variables in second language learning [J]. *Language Learning*, 43, 157-194.

Gardner, R. C. Masgoret, A.-M., Tennant, J., et al. (2004). Integrative motivation: Changes during a year-long intermediate-level course [J]. *Language Learning*, 54, 1-34.

Gardner, R. C. & Smythe, P. C. (1981). On the Development of the Attitude/Motivation Test Battery [J]. *Canadian Modern Language Review*, 37, 510-525.

Gardner, R. C. Tremblay, P. F. & Masgoret, A.-M. (1997). Towards a full model of second language learning: An empirical investigation [J]. *Modern Language Journal*, 81, 344-362.

Getzels, J. W. & Thelen, H. A. (1960). The classroom group as a unique social system [M] // Henry, N. B. (Ed.), *The Dynamics of Instructional Groups: Sociopsychological Aspects of Teaching and Learning* (Fifty-Ninth Yearbook of the National Society for the Study of Education, Part II). Chicago: University of Chicago Press, 53-82.

Goh, S. C. & Fraser, B. J. (1998). Teacher interpersonal behavior, classroom environment and student outcomes in primary mathematics in Singapore [J]. *Learning Environments Research*, 1, 199-229.

Goh, S. C. & Fraser, B. J. (2000). Teacher interpersonal behavior, and elementary students' outcomes [J]. *Journal of Research in Childhood Education*, 14, 216-231.

Guo, J. D. (郭继东) (2009). Yanjiusheng yingyu xuexi dongji yu chengji、xingbie zhi guanxi yanjiu (研究生英语学习动机与成绩、性别之关系研究, "Achievement and gender related study on graduate students English learning motivation") [J]. *Waiyujie* (外语界, "Foreign Language World"), 5, 42-49.

References

Guo, Z. G. (郭志刚) (2006). *Shehui tongji fenxi fangfa—SPSS ruanjian yingyong* (社会统计分析方法——SPSS 软件应用, "The Social Statistics Analysis—Application of SPSS software") [M]. Beijing: China Renmin University Press.

Haertel, G. D., Walberg, H. J. & Haertel, E. H. (1981). Socio-psychological environments and learning: A quantitative synthesis [J]. *British Educational Research Journal*, 7, 27-36.

Hao, M. (郝玫) & Hao, R. P. (郝若平) (2001). Yingyu chengji yu chengji dongji、zhuangtai jiaolü de xiangguan yanjiu (英语成绩与成就动机、状态焦虑的相关研究, "Research on the relationship between English achievement and achievement motivation as well as anxiety state: A case study") [J]. *Waiyu jiaoxue yu yanjiu* (外语教学与研究, "Foreign Language Teaching and Research"), 2, 111-115.

Harris, J. & Murtagh, L. (1999). *Teaching and Learning Irish in Primary School* [M]. Dublin: Institiúid Teangeolaíochta Éireann.

Hofstein, A. & Lazarowitz, R. (1986). A comparison of the actual and preferred classroom learning environment in biology and chemistry as perceived by high school students [J]. *Journal of Research in Science Teaching*, 23, 189-199.

Hua, H. F. (华惠芳) (1998). Shilun yingyu xuexi dongji yu celue de yanjiu (试论英语学习动机与策略的研究, "A study on learning motivation and strategy"). *Waiyu jie* (外语界, "Foreign Language World"), 3, 44-47.

Huang, S. L. (2006). Validation of an instrument for assessing psychosocial environments at colleges and universities in Taiwan [M] // Fisher, D. L. & Khine, M. S. (Eds.), *Contemporary Approaches to Research on Learning Environments: Worldviews*. Singapore: World Scientific Publishing, 479-496.

Jin, L. & Cortazzi, M. (2003). English language teaching in China: A bridge to the future [M] // Ho, W. K. & Wong, R. Y. L. (Eds.), *English Language Teaching in East Asia Today*. Singapore: Times Academic Press, 131-145.

Khine, M. S. & Fisher, D. L. (2001, December). Classroom environment and teacher's cultural background in secondary science classes in Asian context [C] // Paper presented at the annual conference of the Australian Association of Research in Education, Perth, Australia.

Khoo, H. S. & Fraser, B. J. (2008). Using classroom psychosocial environment in the evaluation of adult computer application courses in Singapore [J]. *Technology, Pedagogy and Education*, 17, 67-81.

Kim, H. B., Fisher, D. L. & Fraser, B. J. (1999). Assessment and investigation of constructivist science learning environments in Korea [J]. *Research in Science and Technological Education*, 17, 239-249.

Koul, R. B. & Fisher, D. L. (2005). Cultural background and students' perceptions of science classroom learning environment and teacher interpersonal behavior in Jammu, India [J]. *Learning Environments Research*, 8, 195-211.

Kraemer, R. (1993). Social Psychological Factors Related to the Study of Arabic Among Israeli High School [J]. *Studies in Second Language Acquisition*, 15, 83-105.

Lang, Q. C., Wong, A. F. L. & Fraser, B. J. (2005). Gifted students' attitudes toward chemistry in laboratory classrooms in Singapore [J]. *Journal of Classroom Interaction*, 40, 18-28.

Lapointe, J. M., Legault, F. & Batiste, S. J. (2005). Teacher interpersonal behavior and adolescents' motivation in mathematics: A comparison of learning disabled, average, and talented students [J]. *International Journal of Educational Research*, 43, 39-54.

Leary, T. (1957). *Interpersonal Diagnosis of Personality* [M]. New York: Ronald.

Lee, S. S. U. & Fraser, B. J. (2001, March). High school science classroom learning environments in Korea [C] // Paper presented at the annual meeting of the National Association for Research in Science Teaching, St. Louis, MO.

Lee, C.-K. J., Lee, L.-M. F. & Wong, H.-W. (2003). Development of a classroom environment scale in Hong Kong [J]. *Educational Research and Evaluation: An International Journal on Theory and Practice*, 9, 317-344.

Lewin, K. (1935). *A Dynamic Theory of Personality* [M]. New

York: McGraw-Hill.

Lewin, K. (1936). *Principles of Topological Psychology* [M]. New York: McGraw-Hill.

Li, S. J. (李淑静), Gao, Y. H. (高一虹) & Qian, M. (钱岷) (2003a). Yanjiusheng yingyu xuexi dongji kaocha (研究生英语学习动机考察, "Motivation types in English learning among Chinese graduate students") [J]. *Jiefangjun waiguoyu xueyuan xuebao* (解放军外国语学院学报, "Journal of PLA University of Foreign Languages"), 26, 63-68.

Li, S. J. (李淑静), Gao, Y. H. (高一虹) & Qian, M. (钱岷) (2003b). Yanjiusheng yingyu xuexi dongji leixing yu ziwo rentong bianhua de guanxi (研究生英语学习动机类型与自我认同变化的关系, "Relationship between English learning motivations and self-identity changes among Chinese graduate students") [J]. *Waiguo yuyan wenxue* (外国语言文学, "Foreign Languages in Fujian"), 2, 14-19.

Li, N. (李楠) & Wu, Y. A. (吴一安) (2007). Renwu tezheng yu xuexi dongji yanjiu (任务特征与学习动机研究, "Task features and language learning motivation") [J]. *Waiyu jiaoxue* (外语教学, "Foreign Langauge Educaiton"), 2, 43-47.

Liu, W. Y. (刘文宇) & Cha, J. A. (查吉安) (2010). Wangluo zizhu xuexi huanjing xia yingyu de xuexi dongji yu celue yanjiu (网络自主学习环境下英语的学习动机与策略研究, "A study of web-based English learning motivations and strategies") [J]. *Waiyu yanjiu* (外语研究, "Foreign Languages Research"), 3, 46-51.

Liu, L. (刘璐) & Gao, Y. H. (高一虹) (2008). Yingyu xuexi dongji yu ziwo rentong bianhua—Zonghe daxue yingzhuan ernianji genzong diaocha (英语学习动机与自我认同变化——综合大学英专二年级跟踪调查, "English learning motivation and self-identity changes — A longitudinal study on second-year English majors in a comprehensive university") [J]. *Zhongguo waiyu* (中国外语, "Foreign Languages in China"), 5, 40-45.

Liu, L. (刘璐) & Gao, Y. H. (高一虹) (2010). Yingyu xuexi dongji yu ziwo rentong bianhua genzong—Zonghe daxue yingyu zhuanye sannianji yangben baogao (英语学习动机与自我认同

变化跟踪——综合大学英语专业三年级样本报告,"Empirical studies of FLE English learning motivation and self-identity changes—A longitudinal study on third-year English majors in a comprehensive university")[J]. *Waiyu yu waiyu jiaoxue*(外语与外语教学, Foreign Language and Their Teaching),1,18-21.

Liu, L. Y.(刘丽艳)& Liu, Y. B.(刘永兵)(2010). Zhongxue yingyu ketang huanjing liangbiao de bianzhi yu chubu yingyong(中学英语课堂环境量表的编制与初步应用,"The making of the English classroom environment inventory and its application")[J]. *Waiyu jiaoxue lilun yu shijian*(外语教学理论与实践, Foreign Language Learning Theory and Practice),4, 71-78.

Lu, G. S.(陆根书)& Yang, Z. F.(杨兆芳)(2008). Xuexi huanjing yu xuesheng fazhan yanjiu pingshu(学习环境与学生发展研究述评,"Learning environment and students development")[J]. *Bijiao jiaoyu yanjiu*(比较教育研究,"Comparative Education Review"),7, 1-6.

Ma, G. H.(马广惠)(2005). Xuexi dongji he nuli chengdu dui waiyu xuexi chengji de yingxiang(学习动机和努力程度对外语学习成绩的影响,"The effects of motivation and effort on foreign language achievement")[J]. *Jiefangjun waiguoyu xueyuan xuebao*(解放军外国语学院学报,"Journal of PLA University of Foreign Languages"),4, 37-41.

Macleod, C. & Fraser, B. J.(2010). Development, validation and application of a modified Arabic translation of the What Is Happening In this Class?(WIHIC)questionnaire[J]. *Learning Environments Research*, 13, 105-125.

Majeed, A., Fraser, B. J. & Aldridge, J. M.(2002). Learning environment and its associations with student satisfaction among mathematics students in Brunei Darussalam[J]. *Learning Environments Research*, 52, 203-226.

Margianti, E. S., Fraser, B. J. & Aldridge, J. M.(2001). Classroom environment and students' outcomes among university computing students in Indonesia[C]// Paper presented at the annual meeting of the American Educational

Research Association, Seattle, WA.

Masgoret, A.-M. & Gardner, R. C. (2003). Attitudes, motivation, and second language learning: A meta-analysis of studies conducted by Gardner and associates [J]. *Language Learning*, 53, 123-163.

McRobbie, C. J. & Fraser, B. J. (1993). Associations between student outcomes and psychosocial science environment [J]. *The Journal of Educational Research*, 87, 78-85.

Medley, D. M. & Mitzel, H. E. (1958). A technique for measuring classroom behavior [J]. *Journal of Educational Psychology*, 49, 86-92.

Meux, M. O. (1967). Studies of learning in the school setting [J]. *Review of Educational Research*, 37, 539-562.

Moos, R. H. (1973). Conceptualization of human environments [J]. *American Psychologist*, 28 (8), 652-665.

Moos, R. H. (1974). *The Social Climate Scales: An Overview* [M]. Palo Alto, CA: Consulting Psychologists Press.

Moos, R. H. (1979). *Evaluating Educational Environments* [M]. San Francisco, CA: Jossey-Bass.

Moos, R. H. & Trickett, E. J. (1987). *Classroom Environment Scale Manual* (2nd ed.) [M]. Palo Alto, CA: Consulting Psychologists Press.

Murray, H. A. (1938). *Explorations in Personality* [M]. New York: Oxford University Press.

Murtagh, L. (2007). Out-of-school use of Irish, motivation and proficiency in immersion and subject-only post-primary programmes [J]. *International Journal of Bilingual Education and Bilingualism*, 10, 428-453.

Musella, D. (1970). Improving teacher evaluation [J]. *Journal of Teacher Education*, 21, 15-21.

Nair C. S. (2002). Changing learning environments for quality tertiary classes [M] // Goody, A. & Ingram, D. D. (Eds), *Spheres of Influence: Ventures and Visions in Educational Development*. Perth: University of Western Australia, 1-12.

Nielsen, H. D. & Moos. R. H. (1978). Exploration and adjustment in high school classrooms: A study of person-environment fit

[J]. *The Journal of Educational Research*, 72, 52-57.

Noels, K. A. (2001a). New orientations in language learning motivation: Towards a model of intrinsic, extrinsic, and integrative orientations and motivation [M] // Dörnyei, Z. & Schmidt, R. (Eds.), *Motivation and Second Language Acquisition*. Honolulu: University of Hawaii, 43-68.

Noels, K. A. (2001b). Learning Spanish as a second language: Learner's orientations and perceptions of their orientations and perceptions of their teachers' communication style [J]. *Language Learning*, 51, 107-144.

Noels, K. A., Clément, R. & Pelletier, L. G. (1999). Perceptions of teachers' communicative style and students' intrinsic and extrinsic motivation [J]. *The Modern Language Journal*, 83, 23-34.

Noels, K. A., Pelletier, L. G., Clément, R., et al. (2003). Why are you learning a second language? Motivational orientations and self-determination theory [J]. *Language Learning*, 53, 33-64.

Opolot-Okurut, C. (2010). Classroom learning environment and motivation towards mathematics among secondary school students in Uganda [J]. *Learning Environments Research*, 13, 267-277.

Oxford, R., & Burry-Stock, J. A. (1995). Assessing the use of language learning strategies worldwide with the ESL/EFL version of the strategy inventory for language learning (SILL) [J]. *System*, 23, 1-23.

Oxford, R., Park-Oh, Y., Ito S., et al. (1993). Learning a language by satellite television: What influences student achievement? [J]. *System*, 21, 31-48.

Pace, C. R. (1963). *CUES: College and University Environment Scales* [M]. Princeton, N. J.: Educational Testing Service.

Pace, C. R. & Stern, G. G. (1958). An approach to the measurement of psychological characteristics of college environments [J]. *Journal of Educational Psychology*, 49, 269-277.

Qin, X. Q. (秦晓晴) (2002). Daxuesheng waiyu xuexi guiyin

qingxiang jiqi dui guiyin xianxiang de lijie (大学生外语学习归因倾向及其对归因现象的理解, "Causal attribution and its conceptions by EFL learners at the tertiary level: A case study") [J]. *Xiandai waiyu* (现代外语, "Modern Foreign Languages"), 71-78.

Qin, X. Q. (秦晓晴) (2007). *Zhongguo daxuesheng waiyu xuexi dongji yanjiu* (中国大学生外语学习动机研究, "English learning motivation of Chinese college undergraduates") [M]. Beijing: Higher education press.

Qin, X. Q. (秦晓晴) (2009). *Waiyu jiaoxue wenjuan diaochafa* (外语教学问卷调查法, "Questionnaire in foreign language teaching") [M]. Beijing: Foreign Language Teaching and Research Press.

Qu, Z. Y. (屈智勇) (2002). Guowai ketang huanjing yanjiu de fazhan gaikuang (国外课堂环境研究的发展概况, "A brief introduction to the development of foreign studies on classroom environment") [J]. *Waiguo jiaoyu yanjiu* (外国教育研究, "Studies in Foreign Education"), 7, 21-25.

Quek, C. L., Wong, A. F. L. & Fraser, B. J. (2005). Teacher-student interaction and gifted students' attitudes toward chemistry in laboratory classrooms in Singapore [J]. *Journal of Classroom Interaction*, 40, 18-28.

Randhawa, B. S. & Fu, L. L. W. (1973). Assessment and effect of some classroom environment variables [J]. *Review of Educational Research*, 43, 303-321.

Rich, H. L. & Bush, A. J. (1978). The effect of congruent teacher-student characteristics on instructional outcomes [J]. *American Educational Research Journal*, 15, 451-457.

Rita, R. D. & Martin-Dunlop, C. S. (2011). Perceptions of the learning environment and associations with cognitive achievement among gifted biology students [J]. *Learning Environments Research*, 14, 25-38.

Rivera, T. C. & Ganaden, M. F. (2001). The development and validation of a classroom environment scale for Filipinos [J]. *International Online Journal of Science and Mathematics Education in Southeast Asia*. Retrieved March 7, 2010, from http: //upd. edu. ph/~ismed/online/articles/dev/refer. htm.

Rosenshine, B. (1970). Enthusiastic Teaching: A Research Review [J]. *The School Review*, 78, 499-514.

Ryan, R. M. & Deci, E. L. (2000a). Intrinsic and extrinsic motivations: Classic definitions and new directions [J]. *Contemporary Educational Psychology*, 25, 54-67.

Ryan, R. M. & Deci, E. L. (2000b). Self-determination theory and the facilitation of intrinsic motivation, social development, and well-being [J]. *American Psychologist*, 55, 68-78.

Santiboon, T., Chumpolkulwong, S., Yabosdee, P., et al. (2012). Assessing science students' perceptions in learning activities achievements in physics laboratory classrooms in Udon Thani Rajabhat University [J]. *International Journal of Innovation, Management and Technology*, 3, 171-180.

Schmidt, R., Boraie, D. & Kassabgy, O. (1996). Foreign language motivation: Internal structure and external connections [M]// Oxford, R. (Ed.), *Language Learning Motivation: Pathways to the New Century*. Honolulu: University of Hawaii, 9-70.

Sherry, A. & Henson, R. K. (2005). Conducting and interpreting canonical correlation analysis in personality research: A user-friendly primer [J]. *Journal of Personality Assessment*, 84, 37-48.

Shi, Y. Z. (石永珍) (2000). Daxuesheng yingyu xuexi dongji diaocha baogao (大学生英语学习动机调查报告, "A Report on the English Learning Motivation of undergraduates") [J]. *Guowai waiyu jiaoxue* (国外外语教学, "Foreign Language Teaching"), 4, 8-11.

Sinclair, B. B. & Fraser, B. J. (2002). Changing classroom environments in urban middle schools [J]. *Learning Environments Research*, 5, 301-328.

Stern, G. G. (1970). *People in context: Measuring Person-Environment Congruence in Dducation and Industry* [M]. New York: Wiley.

Sun, H. Y. (孙汉银) (2010). Ketang huanjing yanjiu fanshi de huigu yu fenxi (课堂环境研究范式的回顾与分析, "A review and analysis of the research paradigm on classroom environment") [J].

Jiaoyu kexue(教育科学,"Education Science"),3, 32-37.

Sun, Y. M. (孙云梅) (2007). *The Study on Chinese learners' Sociopsychological Environment in the Foreign Language Classrooms* [D]. Wuhan: Huazhong University of Science and Technology.

Sun, Y. M. (孙云梅) (2009). Daxue yingyu kouyu ketang huanjing diaocha — Yixiang jiyu xuexizhe xinli ganzhi de shizheng yanjiu (大学英语口语课堂环境调查——一项基于学习者心理感知的实证研究, "A study on oral English classroom environment of university undergraduates— An empirical study based on learners psychosocial perception") [J]. *Gaodeng jiaoyu yanjiu* (高等教育研究, "Journal of Higher Education"), 5, 71-77.

Sun, Y. M. (孙云梅) (2010). Daxue zonghe yingyu ketang huanjing diaocha yu yanjiu (大学综合英语课堂环境调查与研究, "A study of college comprehensive English classroom environment") [J]. *Waiyu jiaoxue yu yanjiu* (外语教学与研究, "Foreign Language Teaching and Research"), 6, 438-444.

Sun, Y. M. (孙云梅) & Lin, W. (林巍) (2008). Fei yingyu zhuanye yanjiusheng kouyu ketang xide huanjing diaocha — Yixiang jiyu xuexizhe xinli ganzhi de shizheng yanjiu (非英语专业研究生口语课堂习得环境调查——一项基于学习者心理感知的实证研究, "Oral classroom environment of non-English major postgraduates: A study based on learners psychosocial perception") [J]. *Jiefangjun waiguoyu xueyuan xuebao* (解放军外国语学院学报, "Journal of PLA University of Foreign Languages"), 6, 32-36.

Taylor, P. C., Fraser, B. J. & Fisher, D. L. (1997). Monitoring constructivist classroom learning environments [J]. *International Journal of Educational Research*, 27, 293-302.

Teh, G. & Fraser, B. J. (1995). Associations between student outcomes and geography classroom environment [J]. *Interpersonal Research in Geographical and Environmental Education*, 4, 3-18.

Telli, S., den Brok, P. & Cakiroglu, J. (2007). Students' perceptions of science teachers' interpersonal behavior in secondary schools: Development of a Turkish version of the Questionnaire on Teacher Interaction [J]. *Learning Environments*

Research, 10, 115-129.

Thomas, G. P. & Mee, D. A. K. (2005). Changing the learning environment to enhance students' metacognition in Hong Kong primary school classrooms [J]. *Learning Environments Research*, 8, 221-243.

Tian, H. S. (田慧生) (1992). Lun jiaoxue huanjing (论教学环境, "On classroom environment") [J]. *Xibei shida xuebao* (西北师大学报, "Journal of the Northwest Normal University"), 6, 58-63.

Tian, H. S. (田慧生) (1995). Luelun jiaoxue huanjing yanjiu de lishi xianzhuang jiqi fazhan qushi (略论教学环境研究的历史、现状及其发展趋势, "The history, the present and the trend of research on classroom environment") [J]. *Waiguo jiaoxue yanjiu* (外国教育研究, "Studies in Foreign Education"), 6, 14-19.

Tremblay, P. F. & Gardner, R. C. (1995). Expanding the motivation construct in language learning [J]. *The Modern Language Journal*, 79, 505-518.

Trickett, E. & Moos, R. H. (1973). The social environment of junior high and high school classrooms [J]. *Journal of Educational Psychology*, 65, 93-102.

Vahala, M. E. & Winston, R. B. Jr. (1994). College classroom environments: Disciplinary and institutional-type differences and effects on academic achievement in introductory course [J]. *Innovative Higher Education*, 19, 90-122.

Wahyudi & Treagust, D. F. (2006). Science education in Indonesia: A classroom learning environment perspective [M] // Fisher, D. & Khine, L. (Eds.), M. S. *Contemporary Approaches to Research on Learning Environments: Worldviews*. Singapore: World Scientific Publishing, 211-246.

Walberg, H. J. (1966). *Classroom Climate Inventory* [M]. Cambridge, Mass.: Harvard University.

Walberg, H. J. (1968a). Teacher personality and classroom climate [J]. *Psychology in the Schools*, 5, 163-169.

Walberg, H. J. (1968b). Structural and affective aspects of classroom climate [J]. *Psychology in the Schools*, 5, 247-253.

Walberg, H. J. (1969). Social environment as a mediator of

classroom learning [J]. *Journal of Educational Psychology*, 60, 443-448.

Walberg, H. J. & Anderson, G. J. (1968a). Classroom climate and individual learning [J]. *Journal of Educational Psychology*, 59 (6), 414-419.

Walberg, H. J. & Anderson, G. J. (1968b). The achievement-creativity dimension and classroom climate [J]. *The Journal of Creative Behavior*, 2, 281-291.

Wang, X. L. (王湘玲) & Liu, X. L. (刘晓玲) (2002). Yingxiang ligongke xuesheng yingyu yuedu xiaolü de xuesheng yinsu diaocha (影响理工科学生英语阅读效率的学生因素调查, "Research on the student factors which influence English reading efficiency of science students") [J]. *Waiyu jiaoxue* (外语教学, "Foreign Language Education"), 1, 49-54.

Warden, C. A. & Lin, H. J. (2000). Existence of integrative motivation in an Asian EFL setting [J]. *Foreign Language Annals*, 33, 535-545.

Waxman, H. C. & Huang, S-Y. L. (1998). Classroom learning environments in urban elementary, middle, and high schools [J]. *Learning Environments Research*, 1, 95-113.

Wei, M., den Brok, P. & Zhou, Y. L. (2009). Teacher interpersonal behavior and student achievement in English as a Foreign Language classrooms in China [J]. *Learning Environments Research*, 12, 157-174.

Wen, Q. F. (文秋芳) (2001). Yingyu xuexizhe dongji、guannian、celue de bianhua guilü yu tedian (英语学习者动机、观念、策略的变化规律与特点, "Development patterns inmotivation, beliefs and strategies of English learners in China") [J]. *Waiyu jiaoxue yu yanjiu* (外语教学与研究, "Foreign Language Teaching and Research"), 2, 105-110.

Wen, Q. F. & Johnson, R. K. (1997). L2 learner variables and English achievement: A study of tertiary-level English majors in China [J]. *Applied Linguistics*, 18, 27-48.

Wen, Q. F. (文秋芳) & Wang, H. X. (王海啸) (1996). Xuexizhe yinsu yu daxue yingyu siji kaoshi chengji de guanxi (学习者因素与大学英语四级考试成绩的关系, "The relationship of learner variables to scores on college English test — Band 4") [J]. *Waiyu jiaoxue yu yanjiu* (外语教学与研究, "Foreign Language Teaching and Research"), 4, 33-80.

Wilson, B. G. (1996). Introduction: What is a constructivist learning environment? [M]// Wilson, B. G. (Ed.), *Constructivist learning environments: Case studies in instructional design*. Englewood Cliffs, N. J: Educational Technology Publications, 3-8.

Withall, J. (1949). The development of a technique for the measurement of social-emotional climate in classrooms [J]. *Journal of Experimental Education*, 17, 347-361.

Wong, A. L. F. & Fraser, B. J. (1994). Science laboratory classroom environments and student attitudes in chemistry classes in Singapore [C]// Paper presented at the Annual Meeting of the American Educational Research Association, New Orleans, LA.

Wong, A. L. F. & Fraser, B. J. (1996). Environment-attitude associations in the chemistry laboratory classroom [J]. *Research in Science and Technological Education*, 14, 91-102.

Wong, N. Y. (1993). The psychosocial environment in the Hong Kong mathematics classroom [J]. *Journal of Mathematical Behavior*, 12, 303-309.

Wong, N. Y. (1995). The Discrepancies between preferred and actual mathematics classroom environment as perceived by students and teachers in Hong Kong [J]. *Psychologia*, 38, 124-131.

Wong, N. Y. & Watkins, D. (1996). Self-monitoring as a mediator of person-environment fit: An investigation of Hong Kong mathematics classroom environments [J]. *British Journal of Educational Psychology*, 66, 223-229.

Wu, Y. A. (吴一安), Liu, R. Q. (刘润清) & Jeffrey, P. (1993). Zhongguo yingyu benke xuesheng sushi diaocha baogao (中国英语本科学生素质调查报告, "Learner factors and language learning achievement: A survey") [J]. *Waiyu jiaoxue yu yanjiu* (外语教学与研究, "Foreign Language Teaching and Research"), 1, 36-46.

Wubbles, T. (2006). Preface [M]// Fisher, D. L. & Khine, M. S. (Eds.), *Contemporary Approaches to Research on Learning environments: Worldviews.* Singapore: World Scientific Publishing, v-vi.

Wubbels, T., Créton, H. A. & Hooymayers, H. P. (1985). Discipline problems of beginning teachers [C] // Paper presented at the AERA annual meeting in Chicago, Illinois.

Wubbles, T. & Levy, J. (1991). A comparison of interpersonal behavior of Dutch and American teachers [J]. *International Journal of Intercultural Relations*, 15, 1-18.

Wubbles, T. & Levy, J. (1993). *Do You Know What You Look like? Interpersonal Relationships in Education* [M]. London: Falmer Press.

Xin, Z. Q. (辛自强), Lin, C. D. (林崇德) & Yu, G. L. (俞国良) (2000). Jiaoshi hudong wenjuan zhongwenban de chubu xiuding ji yingyong (教师互动问卷中文版的初步修订及应用, "Preliminary revision and application of the questionnaire on teacher in interaction") [J]. *Xinli kexue* (心理科学, "Psychological Science"), 4, 404-407.

Xu, H. C. (许宏晨) & Gao, Y. H. (高一虹) (2011). Yingyu xuexi dongji yu ziwo rentong bianhua—dui wusuo gaoxiao genzong yanjiu de jiegou fangcheng moxing fenxi (英语学习动机与自我认同变化——对五所高校跟踪研究的结构方程模型分析, "The development of English learning motivation and learners' self-identities: A structural equation modeling Analysis of longitudinal data from five universities") [J]. *Waiyu jiaoxue lilun yu shijian* (外语教学理论与实践, "Foreigh Langnage learning Theory and Proctice"), 3, 63-70.

Yang, X. H. (杨小虎) & Ding, R. L. (丁仁仑) (2004). Daxuesheng yingyu tingli xuexi dongji weidu jiegou leixing jiqi yu tingli xuexi xingwei de guanxi (大学生英语听力学习动机维度结构类型及其与听力学习行为的关系, "Dimensions of college students motivation for English listening and their relationships to listening activity") [J]. *Xiandai waiyu* (现代外语, "Modern Foreign Languages"), 3, 311-330.

Yashima, T. (2002). Willingness to communicate in a second language: The Japanese EFL context [J]. *The Modern Language Journal*, 86, 54-66.

Yuan, Y. F.(袁永芳)(2003). Daxuesheng yingyu yuedu dongji yanjiu(大学生英语阅读动机研究,"A study of Chinese college English learners motivation in reading")[J]. *Waiyu jiaoxue*(外语教学,"Foreign Language Education"), 2, 91-94.

Zhang, W. P.(张文鹏)(1998). Waiyu xuexi dongli yu celue yuyong zhi guanxi(外语学习动力与策略运用之关系,"Student motivation and strategy use in foreign language learning")[J]. *Waiyu yu waiyu jiaoxue*(外语与外语教学,"Foreign Languages and Their Teaching"), 3, 25-27.

Zhang, Y.(张引)(1989). Xifang ketang qifen yanjiu pingshu(西方课堂气氛研究评述,"A review of research on classroom environment in the western countries")[J]. *Waiguo jiaoxue yanjiu*(外国教育研究,"Studies in Foreign Education"), 1, 1-7.

Zhou, Y.(周燕) & Gao, Y. H.(高一虹)(2009). Daxue jichu jieduan yingyu xuexi dongji de fazhan: Dui wusuo gaoxiao de genzong yanjiu(大学基础阶段英语学习动机的发展——对五所高校的跟踪研究,"The development of Chinese undergraduates motivation for English learning in their first and second years: Findings from a longitudinal study in five universities"). *Waiyu jiaoxue yu yanjiu*(外语教学与研究,"Foreign Language Teaching and Research"), 41, 113-118.

Zhou, Y.(周燕), Gao, Y. H.(高一虹) & Zang, Q.(臧青)(2011). Daxue gaonianji jieduan yingyu xuexi dongji de fazhan: Dui wusuo gaoxiao xuesheng de genzong diaoyan(大学高年级阶段英语学习动机的发展——对五所高校学生的跟踪调研,"The development of Chinese undergraduates motivation for English learning in their junior and senior years: Findings from a longitudinal study in five universities"). *Waiyu jiaoxue yu yanjiu*(外语教学与研究,"Foreign Language Teaching and Research"), 43, 251-260.

Zeng, P. C.(曾葡初).(2005). *Yingyu jiaoxue huanjinglun*(英语教学环境论,"On Environment Concepts of English Language Teaching and Learning")[M]. Beijing: People's Education Press.

Appendices

Appendix A What Is Happening in This Class? (A Modified Form)

Student Actual Form

This questionnaire contains statements about practices which could take place in your **actual** *Comprehensive English class*. There are no "right" or "wrong" answers. Your opinion is what is wanted. Think how well each statement describes *what your* **actual** *class* is like.

Draw a circle around

1	if the practice takes place	**Almost never**
2	if the practice takes place	**Seldom**
3	if the practice takes place	**Sometimes**
4	if the practice takes place	**Often**
5	if the practice takes place	**Almost always**

Do not worry if some statements in this questionnaire are fairly similar.

Personal Information

A. Which sex are you? (Select one with a circle.) 0=Male 1=Female
B. What is your current class standing? (Select one with a circle.) 0=Freshman 1=Sophomore
C. Which class are you in? _____
D. What was your age at your last birthday? _____
E. How long have you been learning English? _____
F. Which province are you from? _____

You are rating your **actual** Comprehensive English class. Draw **a circle** (画圈) around the number.

Statement	Almost never	Seldom	Sometimes	Often	Almost always
1. I make friendships among students in this class.	1	2	3	4	5
2. The teacher takes a personal interest in me.	1	2	3	4	5
3. I discuss ideas in class.	1	2	3	4	5
4. Getting a certain amount of work done is important to me.	1	2	3	4	5
5. I cooperate with other students when doing assignment work.	1	2	3	4	5
6. The teacher gives as much attention to my questions as to other students' questions.	1	2	3	4	5
7. I know other students in this class.	1	2	3	4	5
8. The teacher makes an extra effort to help me.	1	2	3	4	5
9. I give my opinions during class discussions.	1	2	3	4	5
10. I do as much as I set out to do.	1	2	3	4	5
11. I share my books and resources with other students when doing assignments.	1	2	3	4	5
12. I get the same amount of help from the teacher as do other students.	1	2	3	4	5
13. I am friendly to members of this class.	1	2	3	4	5

Continued

Statement	Almost never	Seldom	Some-times	Often	Almost always
14. The teacher considers my feelings.	1	2	3	4	5
15. The teacher asks me questions.	1	2	3	4	5
16. I know the goals for this class.	1	2	3	4	5
17. When I work in groups in this class, there is teamwork.	1	2	3	4	5
18. I have the same amount of say in this class as other students.	1	2	3	4	5
19. Members of the class are my friends.	1	2	3	4	5
20. The teacher helps me when I have trouble with the work.	1	2	3	4	5
21. My ideas and suggestions are used during classroom discussions.	1	2	3	4	5
22. I am ready to start this class on time.	1	2	3	4	5
23. I work with other students on projects in this class.	1	2	3	4	5
24. I am treated the same as other students in this class.	1	2	3	4	5
25. I work well with other class members.	1	2	3	4	5
26. The teacher talks with me.	1	2	3	4	5
27. I ask the teacher questions.	1	2	3	4	5
28. I know what I am trying to accomplish in this class.	1	2	3	4	5

Continued

Statement	Almost never	Seldom	Sometimes	Often	Almost always
29. I learn from other students in this class.	1	2	3	4	5
30. I receive the same encouragement from the teacher as other students do.	1	2	3	4	5
31. I help other class members who are having trouble with their work.	1	2	3	4	5
32. The teacher is interested in my problems.	1	2	3	4	5
33. I explain my ideas to other students.	1	2	3	4	5
34. I pay attention during this class.	1	2	3	4	5
35. I work with other students in this class.	1	2	3	4	5
36. I get the same opportunity to contribute to class discussions as other students.	1	2	3	4	5
37. Students in this class like me.	1	2	3	4	5
38. The teacher moves about the class to talk with me.	1	2	3	4	5
39. Students discuss with me how to go about solving problems.	1	2	3	4	5
40. I try to understand the work in this class.	1	2	3	4	5
41. I cooperate with other students on class activities.	1	2	3	4	5
42. My work receives as much praise as other students' work.	1	2	3	4	5

Continued

Statement	Almost never	Seldom	Sometimes	Often	Almost always
43. In this class, I get help from other students.	1	2	3	4	5
44. The teacher's questions help me to understand.	1	2	3	4	5
45. I am asked to explain how I solve problems.	1	2	3	4	5
46. I know how much work I have to do.	1	2	3	4	5
47. Students work with me to achieve class goals.	1	2	3	4	5
48. I get the same opportunity to answer questions as other students.	1	2	3	4	5

Appendix B What Is Happening In this Class? (A Modified Form)

Student Preferred Form

This questionnaire contains statements about practices which could take place in your **ideal** *Comprehensive English class*. There are no "right" or "wrong" answers. Your opinion is what is wanted. Think how well each statement describes *what your* **ideal** *class* is like.

Draw a circle around

1	if the practice takes place	**Almost never**
2	if the practice takes place	**Seldom**
3	if the practice takes place	**Sometimes**
4	if the practice takes place	**Often**
5	if the practice takes place	**Almost always**

Do not worry if some statements in this questionnaire are fairly similar.

You are rating your **ideal** *Comprehensive English class. Draw* **a circle** *around the number.*

Statement	Almost never	Seldom	Some-times	Often	Almost always
1. I would make friendships among students in this class.	1	2	3	4	5
2. The teacher would take a personal interest in me.	1	2	3	4	5
3. I would discuss ideas in class.	1	2	3	4	5
4. Getting a certain amount of work done would be important to me.	1	2	3	4	5

Continued

Statement	Almost never	Seldom	Sometimes	Often	Almost always
5. I would cooperate with other students when doing assignment work.	1	2	3	4	5
6. The teacher would give as much attention to my questions as to other students' questions.	1	2	3	4	5
7. I would know other students in this class.	1	2	3	4	5
8. The teacher would make an extra effort to help me.	1	2	3	4	5
9. I would give my opinions during class discussions.	1	2	3	4	5
10. I would do as much as I set out to do.	1	2	3	4	5
11. I would share my books and resources with other students when doing assignments.	1	2	3	4	5
12. I would get the same amount of help from the teacher as do other students.	1	2	3	4	5
13. I would be friendly to members of this class.	1	2	3	4	5
14. The teacher would consider my feelings.	1	2	3	4	5
15. The teacher would ask me questions.	1	2	3	4	5
16. I would know the goals for this class.	1	2	3	4	5
17. When I work in groups in this class, there would be teamwork.	1	2	3	4	5

Continued

Statement	Almost never	Seldom	Sometimes	Often	Almost always
18. I would have the same amount of say in this class as other students.	1	2	3	4	5
19. Members of the class would be my friends.	1	2	3	4	5
20. The teacher would help me when I have trouble with the work.	1	2	3	4	5
21. My ideas and suggestions would be used during classroom discussions.	1	2	3	4	5
22. I would be ready to start this class on time.	1	2	3	4	5
23. I would work with other students on projects in this class.	1	2	3	4	5
24. I would be treated the same as other students in this class.	1	2	3	4	5
25. I would work well with other class members.	1	2	3	4	5
26. The teacher would talk with me.	1	2	3	4	5
27. I would ask the teacher questions.	1	2	3	4	5
28. I would know what I am trying to accomplish in this class.	1	2	3	4	5
29. I would learn from other students in this class.	1	2	3	4	5
30. I would receive the same encouragement from the teacher as other students do.	1	2	3	4	5

Continued

Statement	Almost never	Seldom	Sometimes	Often	Almost always
31. I would help other class members who are having trouble with their work.	1	2	3	4	5
32. The teacher would be interested in my problems.	1	2	3	4	5
33. I would explain my ideas to other students.	1	2	3	4	5
34. I would pay attention during this class.	1	2	3	4	5
35. I would work with other students in this class.	1	2	3	4	5
36. I would get the same opportunity to contribute to class discussions as other students.	1	2	3	4	5
37. Students in this class would like me.	1	2	3	4	5
38. The teacher would move about the class to talk with me.	1	2	3	4	5
39. Students would discuss with me how to go about solving problems.	1	2	3	4	5
40. I would try to understand the work in this class.	1	2	3	4	5
41. I would cooperate with other students on class activities.	1	2	3	4	5
42. My work would receive as much praise as other students' work.	1	2	3	4	5
43. In this class, I would get help from other students.	1	2	3	4	5

Continued

Statement	Almost never	Seldom	Sometimes	Often	Almost always
44. The teacher's questions would help me to understand.	1	2	3	4	5
45. I would be asked to explain how I solve problems.	1	2	3	4	5
46. I would know how much work I have to do.	1	2	3	4	5
47. Students would work with me to achieve class goals.	1	2	3	4	5
48. I would get the same opportunity to answer questions as other students.	1	2	3	4	5

Appendix C Motivation Types of Chinese College Undergraduates (A modified form)

Read each statement below, and tick a number that indicates your opinion of the statement.

	Strongly Disagree	Disagree	Un-certain	Agree	Strongly Agree
1. I fell in love with English at the first sight, without particular reasons.	1	2	3	4	5
2. I began to study English because my parents/school required me to learn it.	1	2	3	4	5
3. Before entering university, my purpose of learning English was mainly to obtain high scores in the university entrance examination.	1	2	3	4	5
4. Before entering university, my effort of English learning depended to a large extent on test scores.	1	2	3	4	5
5. Before entering university, my effort of English learning depended to a large extent on whether I liked my English teacher or not.	1	2	3	4	5
6. After entering university, my effort of English learning has depended to a large extent on test scores.	1	2	3	4	5
7. After entering university, my effort of English learning has depended to a large extent on whether I like my English teacher or not.	1	2	3	4	5
8. After entering university, my effort of English learning has depended to a large extent on the quality of English classes.	1	2	3	4	5
9. After entering university, my effort of English learning has depended to a large extent on the quality of English textbooks.	1	2	3	4	5

Continued

	Strongly Disagree	Disagree	Un-certain	Agree	Strongly Agree
10. After entering university, my effort of English learning has depended to a large extent on whether I like the fellow students in the English class.	1	2	3	4	5
11. An important purpose for my English learning is to obtain a university degree.	1	2	3	4	5
12. Learning English is important for me, because English is a very useful tool in contemporary society.	1	2	3	4	5
13. Learning English can give me a sense of achievement.	1	2	3	4	5
14. I learn English in order to facilitate the learning of other academic subjects.	1	2	3	4	5
15. Only with good English skills can I find a good job in the future.	1	2	3	4	5
16. I learn English so as to catch up with economic and technological development in the world.	1	2	3	4	5
17. I learn English because I am interested in English speaking people and their cultures.	1	2	3	4	5
18. I have special interests in language learning.	1	2	3	4	5
19. Out of my love of English songs/movies, I have developed a great interest in the language.	1	2	3	4	5
20. I learn English just because I like this language.	1	2	3	4	5
21. I learn English in order to let the world know more about China.	1	2	3	4	5

Continued

	Strongly Disagree	Disagree	Un-certain	Agree	Strongly Agree
22. Out of my love of English literature, I have developed a great interest in the language.	1	2	3	4	5
23. Only when I have a good command of English can I well contribute to China's prosperity.	1	2	3	4	5
24. Only when I have a good command of English can I live up to the expectations of my parents.	1	2	3	4	5
25. I learn English in order to find better education and job opportunities abroad.	1	2	3	4	5
26. I learn English so that I can go abroad to experience English-speaking cultures.	1	2	3	4	5
27. The ultimate purpose of my English learning is to become an immigrant in English-speaking countries.	1	2	3	4	5
28. Acquiring good English skills is a stepping-stone to one's success in life.	1	2	3	4	5
29. Fluent oral English is a symbol of good education and accomplishment.	1	2	3	4	5

Appendix D WIHIC (A Modified Version)

Instructor Actual Form

This questionnaire contains statements about practices which could take place in your **actual** *Comprehensive English class*. There are no "right" or "wrong" answers. Your opinion is what is wanted. Think how well each statement describes *what your* **actual** *class* is like.

Draw a circle around

1	if the practice takes place	**Almost never**
2	if the practice takes place	**Seldom**
3	if the practice takes place	**Sometimes**
4	if the practice takes place	**Often**
5	if the practice takes place	**Almost always**

Do not worry if some statements in this questionnaire are fairly similar.

Personal Information
A. Which sex are you? (Select one with a circle.) 0 = Male 1 = Female
B. What is your students' current class standing? (Select one with a circle.)
   0 = Freshman   1 = Sophomore
C. Which class are you teaching? _____
D. What was your age at your last birthday? _____
E. How long have you worked as an English teacher? _____ years

You are rating your **actual** *Comprehensive English class. Draw* **a circle** (画圈) *around the number.*

Appendices

Statement	Almost never	Seldom	Some-times	Often	Almost always
1. Students make friendships among one another in this class.	1	2	3	4	5
2. I take a personal interest in students.	1	2	3	4	5
3. Students discuss ideas in class.	1	2	3	4	5
4. Getting a certain amount of work done is important to students.	1	2	3	4	5
5. Students cooperate with others when doing assignment work.	1	2	3	4	5
6. I give the same attention to the questions asked by each student.	1	2	3	4	5
7. Students know other members in this class.	1	2	3	4	5
8. I make an extra effort to help students.	1	2	3	4	5
9. Students give their opinions during class discussions.	1	2	3	4	5
10. Students do as much as they set out to do.	1	2	3	4	
11. Students share their books and resources with others when doing assignments.	1	2	3	4	5
12. I give the same amount of help to all the students in this class.	1	2	3	4	5
13. Students are friendly to other members in this class.	1	2	3	4	5
14. I consider students' feelings.	1	2	3	4	5

Continued

Statement	Almost never	Seldom	Some-times	Often	Almost always
15. I call on individual student to answer questions.	1	2	3	4	5
16. Students know the goals for this class.	1	2	3	4	5
17. When students work in groups in this class, there is teamwork.	1	2	3	4	5
18. All students have the same amount of say in this class.	1	2	3	4	5
19. Members of the class are friends.	1	2	3	4	5
20. I help students when they have trouble with their work.	1	2	3	4	5
21. Students' ideas and suggestions are used during classroom discussions.	1	2	3	4	5
22. Students are ready to start this class on time.	1	2	3	4	5
23. Students work with other members on projects in this class.	1	2	3	4	5
24. All students are treated the same in this class.	1	2	3	4	5
25. Students work well with other class members.	1	2	3	4	5
26. I talk with students.	1	2	3	4	5
27. Students ask me questions.	1	2	3	4	5
28. Students know what they are trying to accomplish in this class.	1	2	3	4	5

Continued

Statement	Almost never	Seldom	Sometimes	Often	Almost always
29. Students learn from other members in this class.	1	2	3	4	5
30. All students receive the same encouragement from me.	1	2	3	4	5
31. Students help other class members who are having trouble with their work.	1	2	3	4	5
32. I am interested in students' problems.	1	2	3	4	5
33. Students explain their ideas to other members.	1	2	3	4	5
34. Students pay attention during this class.	1	2	3	4	5
35. Students work with other members in this class.	1	2	3	4	5
36. Students get the same opportunity to contribute to class discussions.	1	2	3	4	5
37. Students in this class like other members of this class.	1	2	3	4	5
38. I move about the class to talk with students.	1	2	3	4	5
39. Students discuss with others how to go about solving problems.	1	2	3	4	5
40. Students try to understand the work in this class.	1	2	3	4	5
41. Students cooperate with other members on class activities.	1	2	3	4	5

Continued

Statement	Almost never	Seldom	Sometimes	Often	Almost always
42. Student's work receives as much praise as other class members from me.	1	2	3	4	5
43. In this class, students get help from other members.	1	2	3	4	5
44. My questions help students to understand.	1	2	3	4	5
45. Students are asked to explain how they solve problems.	1	2	3	4	5
46. Students know how much work they have to do.	1	2	3	4	5
47. Students work with others to achieve class goals.	1	2	3	4	5
48. All students get the same opportunity to answer questions.	1	2	3	4	5

Appendix E WIHIC (A Modified Version)

Instructor Preferred Form

This questionnaire contains statements about practices which could take place in your **ideal** *Comprehensive English class*. There are no "right" or "wrong" answers. Your opinion is what is wanted. Think how well each statement describes *what your* **ideal** *class* is like.

Draw a circle around

1	if the practice takes place	**Almost never**
2	if the practice takes place	**Seldom**
3	if the practice takes place	**Sometimes**
4	if the practice takes place	**Often**
5	if the practice takes place	**Almost always**

Do not worry if some statements in this questionnaire are fairly similar.

You are rating your **ideal** *Comprehensive English class. Draw* **a circle** *around the number.*

Statement	Almost never	Seldom	Sometimes	Often	Almost always
1. Students would make friendships among one another in this class.	1	2	3	4	5
2. I would take a personal interest in students.	1	2	3	4	5
3. Students would discuss ideas in class.	1	2	3	4	5
4. Getting a certain amount of work done would be important to students.	1	2	3	4	5

Continued

Statement	Almost never	Seldom	Some-times	Often	Almost always
5. Students would cooperate with others when doing assignment work.	1	2	3	4	5
6. I would give the same attention to the questions asked by each student	1	2	3	4	5
7. Students would know other members in this class.	1	2	3	4	5
8. I would make an extra effort to help students.	1	2	3	4	5
9. Students would give their opinions during class discussions.	1	2	3	4	5
10. Students would do as much as they set out to do.	1	2	3	4	5
11. Students would share their books and resources with others when doing assignments.	1	2	3	4	5
12. I would give the same amount of help to all the students in this class.	1	2	3	4	5
13. Students would be friendly to other members in this class.	1	2	3	4	5
14. I would consider students' feelings.	1	2	3	4	5
15. I would call on individual student to answer questions.	1	2	3	4	5
16. Students would know the goals for this class.	1	2	3	4	5
17. When students work in groups in this class, there would be teamwork.	1	2	3	4	5

Continued

Statement	Almost never	Seldom	Some-times	Often	Almost always
18. All students would have the same amount of say in this class.	1	2	3	4	5
19. Members of the class would be friends.	1	2	3	4	5
20. I would help students when they have trouble with their work.	1	2	3	4	5
21. Students' ideas and suggestions would be used during classroom discussions.	1	2	3	4	5
22. Students would be ready to start this class on time.	1	2	3	4	5
23. Students would work with other members on projects in this class.	1	2	3	4	5
24. All students would be treated the same in this class.	1	2	3	4	5
25. Students would work well with other class members.	1	2	3	4	5
26. I would talk with students.	1	2	3	4	5
27. Students would ask me questions.	1	2	3	4	5
28. Students would know what they are trying to accomplish in this class.	1	2	3	4	5
29. Students would learn from other members in this class.	1	2	3	4	5
30. All students would receive the same encouragement from me.	1	2	3	4	5

Continued

Statement	Almost never	Seldom	Some-times	Often	Almost always
31. Students would help other class members who are having trouble with their work.	1	2	3	4	5
32. I would be interested in students' problems.	1	2	3	4	5
33. Students would explain their ideas to other members.	1	2	3	4	5
34. Students would pay attention during this class.	1	2	3	4	5
35. Students would work with other members in this class.	1	2	3	4	5
36. Students would get the same opportunity to contribute to class discussions.	1	2	3	4	5
35. Students would work with other members in this class.	1	2	3	4	5
36. Students would get the same opportunity to contribute to class discussions.	1	2	3	4	5
37. Students in this class would like other members of this class.	1	2	3	4	5
38. I would move about the class to talk with students.	1	2	3	4	5
39. Students would discuss with others how to go about solving problems.	1	2	3	4	5
40. Students would try to understand the work in this class.	1	2	3	4	5
41. Students would cooperate with other members on class activities.	1	2	3	4	5

Continued

Statement	Almost never	Seldom	Sometimes	Often	Almost always
42. Student's work receives as much praise as other class members from me.	1	2	3	4	5
43. In this class, students would get help from other members.	1	2	3	4	5
44. My questions would help students to understand.	1	2	3	4	5
45. Students would be asked to explain how they solve problems.	1	2	3	4	5
46. Students would know how much work they have to do.	1	2	3	4	5
47. Students would work with others to achieve class goals.	1	2	3	4	5
48. All students would get the same opportunity to answer questions.	1	2	3	4	5